MW01031159

ARTEMIS

Artemis is a literary, iconographic and archaeological study of the ancient Greek goddess of the hunt, who presided over the transitions and mediations between the wild and the civilized, youth and maturity, life and death. Beginning with a study of the early origins of Artemis and her cult in the Bronze and Archaic Ages, Budin explores the goddess' persona and her role in the lives of her worshippers.

This volume examines her birth and childhood, her place in the divine family, her virginity and her associations with those places where the wilds become the 'cities of just men'. The focus then turns to Artemis' role in the lives of children and women, particularly how she helps them navigate the transition to adulthood and, perhaps too often, death. Budin goes on to reconsider some of the more harrowing aspects of Artemis' mythology, such as plague and bloodshed, while also examining some of her kinder, oft overlooked associations. Finally, the role of Artemis in the Renaissance and modern society is addressed, from the ongoing fascination with the 'breasts' on the statue of Artemis of Ephesos to the Artemisian aspects of Katniss Everdeen, from the *Hunger Games* trilogy.

Written in an accessible style, *Artemis* is a crucial resource not only for students of Greek myth, religion, and cult, but also for those seeking to understand the lives and roles of girls and women in ancient Greece, as this goddess presided over all their significant milestones, from maiden to wife to mother.

Stephanie Lynn Budin is an ancient historian who focuses on ancient Greece and the Near East. Her published works include *Images of Woman and Child from the Bronze Age* (2011), *The Ancient Greeks: An Introduction* (2009), *The Myth of Sacred Prostitution in Antiquity* (2008) and *The Origin of Aphrodite* (2003), as well as numerous articles on ancient religion and iconography.

Gods and Heroes of the Ancient World

Series editor Susan Deacy
Roehampton University

Routledge is pleased to present an exciting new series, Gods and Heroes of the Ancient World. These figures from antiquity are embedded in our culture, many functioning as the source of creative inspiration for poets, novelists, artists, composers and filmmakers. Concerned with their multifaceted aspects within the world of ancient paganism and how and why these figures continue to fascinate, the books provide a route into understanding Greek and Roman polytheism in the 21st century.

These concise and comprehensive guides provide a thorough understanding of each figure, offering the latest in critical research from the leading scholars in the field in an accessible and approachable form, making them ideal for undergraduates in Classics and related disciplines.

Each volume includes illustrations, time charts, family trees and maps where appropriate.

Also available:

Herakles
Emma Stafford

Medea
Emma Griffiths

Aphrodite
Monica S. Cyrino

Dionysos
Richard Seaford

Apollo
Fritz Graf

Oedipus
Lowell Edmunds

Perseus
Daniel Ogden

Forthcoming:

Athena
Susan Deacy

Diana
Fay Glinister

Zeus
Ken Dowden

Gilgamesh
Louise Pryke

Prometheus
Carol Dougherty

Ishtar
Louise Pryke

Susan Deacy is Lecturer in Greek History and Literature at Roehampton University. Her main research interests are Greek religion, and gender and sexuality. Publications include the co-edited volumes *Rape in Antiquity* (1997), and *Athena in the Classical World* (2001), and the monograph *A Traitor to Her Sex? Athena the Trickster* (forthcoming).

 # ARTEMIS

Stephanie Lynn Budin

Routledge
Taylor & Francis Group

LONDON AND NEW YORK

First published 2016
by Routledge
2 Park Square, Milton Park, Abingdon, Oxon OX14 4RN

and by Routledge
711 Third Avenue, New York, NY 10017

First issued in paperback 2018

Routledge is an imprint of the Taylor & Francis Group, an informa business

British Library Cataloguing-in-Publication Data
A catalogue record for this book is available from the British Library

Library of Congress Cataloging-in-Publication Data
Budin, Stephanie Lynn.
Artemis / Stephanie Budin.
pages cm.— (Gods and heroes of the ancient world)
Includes index.
1. Artemis (Greek deity) I. Title.
BL820.D5B83 2015
292.2'114—dc23
2014048381

ISBN 13: 978-0-367-00100-1 (pbk)
ISBN 13: 978-0-415-72541-5 (hbk)

Typeset in Utopia
by Swales & Willis Ltd, Exeter, Devon, UK

To Jean MacIntosh Turfa

φίλιστη πότνια θηρῶν

CONTENTS

SERIES FOREWORD

It is proper for a person who is beginning any serious discourse and task to begin first with the gods.

(Demosthenes, *Epistula* 1.1)

WHY GODS AND HEROES?

The gods and heroes of classical antiquity are part of our culture. Many function as sources of creative inspiration for poets, novelists, artists, composers, film makers and designers. Greek tragedy's enduring appeal has ensured an ongoing familiarity with its protagonists' experiences and sufferings, while the choice of Minerva as the logo of one of the newest British universities, the University of Lincoln, demonstrates the ancient gods' continued emblematic potential. Even the world of management has used them as representatives of different styles: Zeus and the "club" culture for example, and Apollo and the "role" culture (see C. Handy, *The Gods of Management: Who they are, how they work and why they fail*, London, 1978).

This series is concerned with how and why these figures continue to fascinate and intrigue. But it has another aim too, namely to explore their strangeness. The familiarity of the gods and heroes risks obscuring a vital difference between modern meanings and ancient functions and purpose. With certain exceptions, people today do not worship them, yet to the Greeks and Romans they were real beings in a system comprising literally hundreds of divine powers. These range from the major gods, each of whom was worshipped in many guises via their epithets or "surnames," to the heroes – deceased individuals associated with local communities – to other figures such as daemons and nymphs. The landscape was dotted with sanctuaries, while natural features such as mountains, trees and rivers were thought to be inhabited by religious beings. Studying ancient paganism involves finding strategies to comprehend a world where everything was, in the often quoted words of Thales, "full of gods."

In order to get to grips with this world, it is necessary to set aside our preconceptions of the divine, shaped as they are in large part by Christianised notions of a transcendent, omnipotent God who is morally good. The Greeks and Romans worshipped numerous beings, both male and female, who looked, behaved and suffered like humans, but who, as immortals, were not bound by the human condition. Far from being omnipotent, each had limited powers: even the sovereign, Zeus/Jupiter, shared control of the universe with his brothers Poseidon/Neptune (the sea) and Hades/Pluto (the underworld). Lacking a creed or anything like an organised church, ancient paganism was open to continual reinterpretation, with the result that we should not expect to find figures with a uniform essence. It is common to begin accounts of the pantheon with a list of the major gods and their function(s) (Hephaistos/Vulcan: craft, Aphrodite/Venus: love, and Artemis/Diana: the hunt and so on), but few are this straightforward. Aphrodite, for example, is much more than the goddess of love, vital though that function is. Her epithets include *hetaira* ("courtesan") and *porne* ("prostitute"), but also attest roles as varied as patron of the citizen body (*pandemos*: "of all the people") and protectress of seafaring (*Euploia, Pontia, Limenia*).

Recognising this diversity, the series consists not of biographies of each god or hero (though such have been attempted in the past), but of investigations into their multi-faceted aspects within the complex world of ancient paganism. Its approach has been shaped partly in response to two distinctive patterns in previous research. Until the middle of the twentieth century, scholarship largely took the form of studies of individual gods and heroes. Many works presented a detailed appraisal of such issues as each figure's origins, myth and cult; these include L.R. Farnell's examination of major deities in his *Cults of the Greek States* (five volumes, Oxford, 1896–1909) and A.B. Cook's huge three-volume *Zeus* (Cambridge, 1914–1940). Others applied theoretical developments to the study of gods and heroes, notably (and in the closest existing works to a uniform series), K. Kerényi in his investigations of gods as Jungian archetypes, including *Prometheus: Archetypal image of human existence* (English trans. London 1963) and *Dionysos: Archetypal image of indestructible life* (English trans. London 1976).

In contrast, under the influence of French structuralism, the later part of the century saw a deliberate shift away from research into particular gods and heroes towards an investigation of the system of which they were part. Fuelled by a conviction that the study of isolated gods could not do justice to the dynamics of ancient religion, the pantheon came to be represented as a logical and coherent network in which the various powers were systematically opposed to one another. In a classic study by J.-P. Vernant for example, the Greek concept of space was shown to be consecrated through the opposition between Hestia (goddess of the hearth – fixed space) and Hermes (messenger and traveller god – moveable space: Vernant, *Myth and Thought among the Greeks* London, 1983, 127–75). The gods as individual entities were far from neglected however, as may be exemplified by the works by Vernant, and his colleague M. Detienne, on particular deities, including Artemis, Dionysos and Apollo: see, most recently, Detienne's *Apollon, le couteau en main: une approche expérimentale du polythéisme grec* (Paris, 1998).

In a sense, this series is seeking a middle ground. While approaching its subjects as unique (if diverse) individuals, it pays attention to their significance as powers within the collectivity of religious beings. *Gods and Heroes of the Ancient World* sheds new light on many of the most important religious beings of classical antiquity; it also provides a route into understanding Greek and Roman polytheism in the twenty-first century.

The series is intended to interest the general reader as well as being geared to the needs of students in a wide range of fields from Greek and Roman religion and mythology, classical literature and anthropology, to Renaissance literature and cultural studies. Each book presents an authoritative, accessible and refreshing account of its subject via three main sections. The introduction brings out what it is about the god or hero that merits particular attention. This is followed by a central section which introduces key themes and ideas, including (to varying degrees) origins, myth, cult, and representations in literature and art. Recognising that the heritage of myth is a crucial factor in its continued appeal, the reception of each figure since antiquity forms the subject of the third part of the book. The books include illustrations of each god/hero and, where appropriate, time charts, family trees and maps. An annotated bibliography synthesises past research and indicates useful follow-up reading.

For convenience, the masculine terms "gods" and "heroes" have been selected for the series title, although (and with an apology for the male-dominated language), the choice partly reflects ancient usage in that the Greek *theos* ("god") is used of goddesses too. For convenience and consistency, Greek spellings are used for ancient names, except for famous Latinised exceptions, and BC/AD has been selected rather than BCE/CE.

I am indebted to Catherine Bousfield, the editorial assistant until 2004, who (literally) dreamt up the series and whose thoroughness and motivation brought it close to its launch. The hard work and efficiency of her successor, Matthew Gibbons, has overseen its progress to publication, and the former classics publisher of Routledge, Richard Stoneman, has provided support and expertise throughout. The anonymous readers for each proposal gave frank and helpful advice, while the authors' commitments to advancing scholarship while producing accessible accounts of their designated subjects has made it a pleasure to work with them.

Susan Deacy, Roehampton University, June 2005

LIST OF FIGURES

ABBREVIATIONS

The following conventional abbreviations are used to cite certain standard works. Ancient authors and their works are given in full in the text. Works by modern scholars are referred to by author-date in notes with full publication details in the Bibliography.

AO — *The Sanctuary of Artemis Orthia at Sparta*. R.M. Dawkins (ed.) Macmillan and Co, Ltd. London. 1929

BCH — *Bulletin de Correspondance Hellénique*

CMS — *Corpus der Minoischen und Mykenischen Siegel*. I. Pini (ed.). Gebr. Mann Verlag. Berlin

FrGrHist — Jacoby, F. (1923–58) *Die Fragmente der Griechischen Historiker*, Leiden. This collection of fragments of Greek historical writing has recently been made a great deal more accessible to students via the online project *Brill's New Jacoby* (ed. I. Worthington, Leiden 2006–), available via university libraries which have an institutional site licence. Each fragment is provided with an English translation as well as the Greek text, a commentary and Bibliography

GA — *Greek Anthology*

IG — *Inscriptiones Graecae*

LIMC — *Lexicon Iconographicum Mythologiae Classicae*, Zurich and Munich 1981–99

LSCG — Sokolowski, F. (1969) *Lois sacrées des cités grecques*, Paris

SEG — *Supplementum Epigraphicum Graecum*, Leiden 1923–

INTRODUCING ARTEMIS

Artemis was one of the most important deities in the ancient Greek pantheon, with cults that stretched from Bactria (modern-day Afghanistan) in the east to Iberia in the west. Her range of honors and functions in daily Greek life were just as impressive. Most commonly known as the goddess of the hunt and wilderness, Artemis was also responsible for helping women in childbirth (when she was not killing them), turning children into adults, marking boundaries between political territories and between periods of war and peace, bringing and curing plague, bringing light, and manumitting slaves, especially female slaves. At some time in the early centuries of our era an Orphic poet gave a fine summary of Artemis in a hymn:

> *Of Artemis (frankincense powder incense)*
> Hear me, O Queen, many-named daughter of Zeus
> Titanic, sounding, glorious, archer, reverend,
> All-shining, torch-bearing Goddess, Diktynna,[1] Lokheia,[2]
> Aid to those in childbirth and untouched by childbirth,
> Lysizonê,[3] frenzy-loving huntress, who drives away cares,
> Swift, arrow-pouring, wilds-loving, night-roaming,
> Fame-bringing, gracious deliverer, tomboy,
> Ortheia,[4] giver of swift birth, divine kourotrophos of mortals,
> Immortal, earthy, beast-killing, of blessed good fortune,
> You who dwell in the mountain dells, deer-shooter, reverend,
> Lady, all-royal, fair sprout forever,
> Sylvan puppy, Kydonian[5] of changing form,
> Come, dear Goddess, Savior! To all initiates
> Gracious, bringer of fine fruits from the land
> And lovely peace and fair-tressed health.
> You lead to the mountain peaks illnesses and pain.

The range presented in the literature is matched by the variety seen in the goddess's votive dedications. Consider, for example, the items offered to Artemis at the Scala Graeca sanctuary of ancient Syracuse in Sicily. Here we find terracotta votives of Artemis carrying a boat, and thus as protector of sailors; Artemis as Potnia Therôn ("Mistress of Animals") resting her hands on the heads of lions and panthers; Artemis snuggling young deer against her chest as the goddess who loves the young of wild animals; while the goddess holding adult deer by the tail or hind legs reveals

Artemis Elaphebolos—"Deer-Shooter." Artemis with her bow is the huntress, while Artemis with plants or palm trees is a more protective goddess of nature and fertility. Dedications of horse figures may refer to a cult of Artemis Hippikê, the goddess who, according to Pindar (*Pyth.* 2) helped Hieron of Syracuse tame his horses and thus win a Pythian chariot race.[6] At other sanctuaries, Artemis the goddess of women is more prominent, as at Brauron in Attika, where were found statuettes of standing and crouching children; terracotta figurines of seated, mortal kourotrophoi; and Classical votive reliefs showing families with babies coming to sacrifice at her altar.[7]

Artemis' importance in cult is belied by her comparatively rare appearances in literature. She has a single scene in Homer's *Iliad*—a quite embarrassing one, really, where she literally gets bitch-slapped by her step-mother Hera. Although alluded to in the *Odyssey*, she makes no personal appearance. Hesiod is thorough enough to mention her once, and she appears in only one of the extant Athenian tragedies—*Hippolytos.* The goddess is more prominent in the more "personal" genres of literature: lyric poetry and dedicatory epigrams. But even in the former she is not as popular as Aphrodite, perhaps because a virgin huntress does not fit in as well as a seductress at the drinking parties at which lyric songs were sung.

This lack of literary presence is an important consideration in the study of Greek religion. Because so many students approach Greek religion through a class in Classical mythology, the importance of Greek deities tends to be correlated with their prominence in the written sources. Athena is clearly a powerful, important deity, as is Zeus. Hestia, by contrast, appears to be irrelevant, and Hera is just some jealous bitch. It is only by considering the non-literary evidence that one gets an appreciation of such deities' true importance in Greek religion. For example, as the goddess of the hearth, Hestia is the core of the household, the core of the polis, the goddess who admits new members to both, who extends her reach to bind daughter colonies to mother cities, and in whose domain all burnt sacrifices and most libations must take place. Her Homeric hymn (29) does not exaggerate:

> Hestia, who in the high halls of all the immortal
> Deities and of earth-dwelling men too
> Has an everlasting seat and foremost honor;
> She has a fair prize and right. For without you
> Mortals cannot revel—where does one not begin the libations
> Of sweet wine, first and last, to Hestia?

The study of Artemis allows one a golden (perhaps silver?) opportunity to look at Greek religion from a multiplicity of sources, and so come to appreciate the importance of a goddess who has only a marginal presence in the standard mythological stories.

In addition to her geographic reach, Artemis also had one of the longest enduring cults in the ancient Mediterranean. She is attested iconographically in Bronze Age Crete and Greece and in the Linear B documents from Pylos, and her cult at Ephesos in Anatolia endured long and well enough to give the early Christians apoplexy.

Although demonstrating a broad range of aspects and functions, Artemis has at the core of her persona the role of goddess of transitions. As noted above, it is she who helps children to metamorphose into adults. But her role goes far beyond this. As the goddess of the hunt, she is the deity who mediates between the savage world of wild animals and the tool-using (and just as savage) world of humans. As a goddess of the wilds, her cult marks transitions between the wild and the civilized, and between political domains. She helps girls to become women and, more importantly, mothers, just as she is present to help slaves become free. In most of her functions, to one extent of another, Artemis is the goddess who presides over changes of states of being.

Because of her range in time, space, and functions, Artemis had a very high potential for syncretizing with other goddesses. As such, Artemis provides an ideal case study for the examination of syncretism in ancient religion. This fact is going to come up repeatedly in this book, so it is worthwhile here to give the reader a basic introduction to the concept of syncretism.

SYNCRETISM

At its simplest, "syncretism" is the process by which deities merge identities. This typically occurs when peoples with different pantheons come into contact with each other and, consciously or unconsciously, try to get their religious systems to mesh.

The word has come to have a rather wide span of related meanings over the past two centuries, ranging from a general notion of "relationship" to an equation of deities equivalent to henotheism. The various nuances or subdivisions of the notion of syncretism were established by P. Lévêque in his 1975 article "Essai de typologie des syncrétismes," ("Essay on the Typology of Syncretisms") and reconsidered by A. Motte and V. Pirenne-Delforge in their 1994 article "Du 'bon usage' de la notion de syncrétisme" ("On the 'Proper Use' of the Notion of Syncretism"). In this latter work "syncretism" is separated out from the related notions of "influence" and "borrowing." Then, in proper Platonic fashion, it is studied in its various manifestations. An *interpretatio*-type syncretism, for example, is "that tendency . . . to baptize foreign divinities by the name of one's own deities."[8] Thus the Greeks recognize the Phoenician goddess Aštart as simply a foreign version of their own goddess Aphrodite, just as Etruscan Fufluns is Dionysos, and Gaulish Epona is Athena. The "amalgam" type of syncretism occurs when a mixing of two or more deities, possibly from different pantheons, creates a new divinity.[9] Thus, in Hellenistic Egypt, the Greeks combined the Egyptian deities Apis (a bull) and Osiris (God of the Dead) to create the new deity Serapis. By contrast, with "syncrétisme-hénothéisme" (henotheism) several deities of the same gender in one or more pantheons are seen as being the same god or goddess.[10] Thus, Greek Aphrodite = Phoenician Aštart = Egyptian Hathor.

P. Pakkanen, in her 1996 work *Interpreting Early Hellenistic Religion*, took the study of syncretism a step farther, arguing that syncretism is in fact a process, rather than merely a state of being. Thus, the various terms as defined above are actually steps within the overarching process of syncretism. Local societies with their own pantheons and cults come into contact with new peoples and new religious ideologies and deities. First, an *interpretatio*, or parallelism, process takes place, whereby one group (or both) identifies one or more of the "foreign" deities with members of their own pantheon. Long-term parallelism may eventually cause amalgamation to occur, so that a new deity, or a new conception of the old deities, comes into existence. This may either occur naturally, as the iconographic merging of Demeter and Isis in the Hellenistic period, or artificially, as the creation of that Helleno-Egyptian Serapis mentioned above. With this new deity in place, the process may then repeat.[11]

In the study of Artemis, these processes of syncretism need to be understood in at least two categories. In the earlier Greek history there were the local syncretisms, when the Olympian goddess Artemis came into contact and merged with similar Greek or pre-Greek goddesses. As we shall see in Chapter 1, such a syncretism took place in Sparta with an indigenous goddess called Worthasia, such that the original goddess came to be eclipsed by the Greek goddess henceforth known as Artemis Ortheia ("Ortheia" derives from the original name Worthasia).

In Chapter 5, we shall see that Artemis merged identities with the age-old goddess of childbirth Eileithyia. How these goddesses syncretized wholly depended on where they were in ancient Greece. In Crete and the Peloponnese, Artemis and Eileithyia remained individual deities (not surprising considering Eileithyia's long-standing cult in Crete since the Bronze Age). In Attika, however, the goddesses began to merge identities; both might be worshipped individually, but Artemis also came to be known as Artemis-Eileithyia, and she took on Eileithyia's role as goddess of childbirth. Farther north, in Boiotia, Eileithyia had no independent identity; she only existed as an aspect of Artemis. A similar process seems to have occurred between Artemis and a local goddess of central Greece called Iphimedê/Iphianassa/Iphigeneia, as discussed in Chapter 6. Here, the original goddess continued to exist, but was demoted to "heroine" status and recognized in the literature as a priestess of the goddess who displaced her.

In the second category, Artemis syncretizes with foreign deities. Some occurred earlier in Greek history, as the syncretism between Artemis and Anatolian Hekatê, as discussed in Chapter 6. As with Eileithyia, these two goddesses were worshipped both independently and linked to each other. Other syncretisms occurred later, with goddesses farther afield, and whose syncretized identities had little impact on Greek religion at home. It is also important to note that deities did not necessarily have to be similar in character or attributes to be syncretized. Often merely a single detail was sufficient for the Greeks (and others) to identify their deities with those of others, and it was frequently the case that individual deities could be syncretized with more than one foreign divinity.

Such oddities come across well in the case of the Mesopotamian goddess Nanaya, who was syncretized with Artemis in the Hellenistic period and whose combined cult endured into the Roman period. In Mesopotamia Nanaya was a goddess of sex. In the Sumerian BALBALE hymns of the second millennium, the goddess is often addressed as "sister" (a common term for a "beloved," but in no way referring to incest!). Her most titillating hymn—in dialogue format—is, due to its fragmentary nature, perhaps appropriately, quite a tease:

> Worthy of An, ..., ... unsurpassed in ladyship, a throne ...... a man in the house, a throne ...... a woman in the shrine, a gold ornament ...... on the dress, a ...... pin ...... the niĝlam garment.

Let me ...... on your ...... – Nanaya, its ...... is good. Let me (?) ...... on your breast – Nanaya, its ...... flour is sweet. Let me put ...... on your navel -- Nanaya, ... Come with me, my lady, come with me, come with me from the entrance to the shrine. May ...... for you. Come my beloved sister, let my heart rejoice.

Your hand is womanly, your foot is womanly. Your conversing with a man is womanly. Your looking at a man is womanly. Your ...... a hand towards a man is womanly. Your ...... a foot is womanly. Your ...... forearm makes my heart rejoice. Your ...... a foot brings me pleasure. As you rest against the wall, your patient heart pleases. As you bend over, your hips are particularly pleasing.

My resting against the wall is one lamb. My bending over is one and a half giĝ. Do not dig a canal, let me be your canal. Do not plough a field, let me be your field. Farmer, do not search for a wet place, my precious sweet, let this be your wet place. ......, let this be your furrow. ......, let this be your desire! Caring for ......, I come .... I come ...... with bread and wine.

You come to me with bread and wine. Come, my beloved sister, let me ...... this heart. Nanaya, let me kiss you.[12]

So far, this deity has remarkably little in common with virgin huntress Artemis. Nevertheless, in the first millennium developments occur in Nanaya's cult and persona that bring her more "in line" with Artemis. For example, in the list of monthly festivals in the city of Uruk, Nanaya was revered with a feast on the first of the month of Dumuzi. The texts record that a quiver was placed in the hands of one of the statues before being paraded around the temple.[13] Likewise, already in the late second millennium Nanaya came to be seen as the consort of the scribal god Nabû, and together they were the chief deities of the city of Borsippa. In later years, the Greeks identified Nabû as Apollo, just as they equated Nanaya with Artemis, and we read in Strabo (16.1.7) that Artemis and Apollo were the primary deities of the city in his day. Artemis-Nanaya was also worshipped in Dura-Europos. In her study of Nanaya, Joan Goodnick Westenholz noted some of the difficulties in understanding how these goddesses came to be identified with each other, but also highlighted their closely shared iconographies:

[T]his was during a period of syncretism so that when Strabo identifies Nanaya as Artemis and we find representations of Nanaya with bow and arrows or with moon crescents, it is difficult to discern if the appellation or the depiction is secondary—whether she was depicted with bow and arrows because she was called Artemis, or whether she was called Artemis because she was depicted with bow and arrows. In Susa, on the coins of the Parthian period issued in 110 B.C., she is depicted as a sun/moon goddess with her head surrounded by rays . . . Her dress is adorned with crescents in the offering scene on the pithos from Assur, while her head is crowned with a crescent and a sun . . . Nanaya appears on several tesserae from Palmyra and was also represented there with bow and arrows.[14]

In addition to their syncretism with each other, it is clear that both goddesses were influenced by the Roman Age conflation of Artemis with Diana, such that all three goddesses came to take on lunar (and even solar) imagery.

The late syncretism of Artemis with Nanaya is an extreme case—it had no influence on how Artemis was perceived or worshipped in Greece—but it is not wholly atypical of the "Age of Syncretism" that prevailed in the Hellenistic and Roman eras. Perhaps more typical and relevant for the study of Greek Artemis was her syncretism with the goddess of Ephesos, whose cult spread from the coasts of Anatolia to *la côte d'azure* in southern France (more on this in the next chapter).

The notion of syncretism, then, has a rich variety of meanings. At its simplest level, there is the *interpretatio* syncretism, whereby two or more deities are seen as the same. The degree of initial distance and the degree of identification can vary, with the example of Artemis and Worthasia being an example of extreme closeness and merging. Often, syncretisms emerged between deities of different pantheons. If the merging of identities were sufficient to create a new deity, amalgam is said to take place. In this instance, it is possible for one or more of the original, pre-amalgamated deities to continue in existence and cult beside the new deity. If, however, the merging of identities causes one of the "creator" deities to cease to exist, then we might say that an "eclipse" type of syncretism has occurred, as with Iphigeneia. When there is no limit on *interpretatio* syncretisms within a cosmopolitan social system, henotheism begins to emerge. Here, an ever-growing and complex system of parallelisms can lead to the notion that, in fact, *all* gods are one, or all goddesses. Here we might call to mind a passage from Apuleius' *Metamorphoses* (aka *The Golden Ass*) wherein the goddess Isis says to Lucius (11.5):

> I am the parent of nature, mistress of all elements, first-born of the ages, supreme authority, queen of the dead, first in heaven, the singular manifestation of gods and goddesses . . . whose sole divinity is multiform, of varied rites, worshipped by many names throughout the whole world. Amongst the first-born Phrygians I am Pessinuntia, divine mother; here the autochthonous Athenians call me Cecropian Minerva, there the wave-tossed Cyprians call me Paphian Venus; arrow-bearing Cretans call me Diana Dictynna. The trilingual Sicilians call me Stygian Proserpina, the Eleusinians the ancient goddess Ceres, others Juno, others Bellona, these Hecate, those Rhamnusia; and the Ethiopians, first lit by the rays of the sun, and the Egyptians strong in ancient doctrines, honor me with my own rites, and call me by my true name: Queen Isis.

SOURCES AND METHODOLOGY

The reader will notice that this book contains a lot of primary sources. This is deliberate. From a very personal perspective, I have always found it terribly annoying to have statements made in books with the evidence buried in an endnote somewhere that references a primary source that I then had to go look up myself. I have tried to avoid the need for you to do this by having the source right on the page next to the assertion. For any university students beginning on the road to ancient studies, I hope this helps to show how the process of ancient studies is done, how one goes from the primary sources to the conclusions. For those of you who are more advanced, I wanted to be very explicit in how I went about this process myself, because, as you will see, many of the conclusions I came to are not what are regarded as standard understandings of Artemis. Or, to put it another way, Artemis led me on a wild, nocturnal hunt in the writing of this book, and now I am going to make you share in the experience.

There is an embarrassment of riches when it comes to studying Artemis, in spite of her relative paucity in the literary accounts. In addition to her brief appearances in Homer, Hesiod, and the Athenian playwrights, she appears in some of the lyric poetry, has two Homeric Hymns as well as an exceptionally long hymn by Kallimakhos and the Orphic Hymn given above. The cults of Artemis appear in Herodotos and Xenophon as well as in the works of Plutarch, Pausanias, and Strabo, and she is mentioned in various contexts by Plato. There are many, many dedicatory epigrams to the goddess, and her cults feature prominently in the epigraphic inscriptions from throughout Greece. Many of her sanctuaries have been thoroughly excavated *and* published, providing evidence on where she was worshipped, when, and even to a certain extent how. The site reports also detail the votives offered to the goddess (as with Scala Graeca above), giving further evidence as to how the people envisioned both the goddess and their relationship to her. Artemis appears in visual arts of Greece—vase painting, sculpture, reliefs—and these are also sources of data about the goddess and her cults.

This study focuses mainly on Artemis from the Archaic and Classical periods (800–323 BCE). As such, I have always privileged data coming from those eras in preference to the later—if copious—data from authors such as Plutarch and Pausanias. Their works are used, of course. However, if a statement about something that occurred in the fifth century made by, say, Plutarch is contradicted by a statement made by Herodotos, then Herodotos' account is considered to be the more trustworthy. Furthermore, if a statement made by one of the later authors has no correlating data in earlier Greek history, then these data are considered slightly suspect, possibly only reflecting a later aspect of Artemis' cults, possibly once she was already conflated with Roman Diana. This is going to have some serious consequences for some of the conclusions reached in this book, so it is important to understand my methodology up front.

OVERVIEW

Artemis was a highly versatile goddess worshipped over a large swathe of the ancient world, from Iberia to Afghanistan to Egypt. Although a goddess of the wilds, her various roles made her very present in the lives of the ancient Greeks, literally from birth through the attainment of adulthood and beyond. More than anything, she was the goddess of transitions, marking those places both physical and conceptual between different states of being—wild and civilized, human and animal, child and adult, maiden and mother, slave and free. Often she helped her worshippers to cross those boundaries, sometimes she forced them, and those who tried to resist quickly learned much about the anger of the goddess.

NOTES

1 A cult epithet used in Crete.
2 Of childbirth.
3 Belt-loosener: pertaining both to first intercourse and childbirth.

4 A cult epithet used in Sparta and Messenê.

5 Of Kydonia in Crete.

6 Fischer-Hansen 2009: 211–212.

7 Hadzisteliou Price 1978: 121.

8 Motte and Pirenne-Delforge 1994: 21.

9 Ibid.: 19.

10 Ibid.: 20.

11 Pakkanen 1996: 87–88, 92.

12 Translation from http://etcsl.orinst.ox.ac.uk/cgi-bin/etcsl.cgi?text=t.4.07.8#.

13 Westenholz 1997: 77.

14 Ibid.: 79–80.

I

AN EARLY HISTORY OF ARTEMIS

Several deities in the Greek pantheon have origins that are relatively straightforward to trace. Zeus, for example, is a derivative of the Indo-European Sky Father (his name is etymologically related to *dyaus pitar* = "sky father") who appears to have adopted some aspects, especially iconographic, of the Near Eastern storm gods, such as Semitic Hadad or Hittite Telipinu. Aphrodite, for her part, is originally a Cypriot adoption and adaptation of the Mesopotamian goddesses of sex, Inanna/Ištar and Išḫara.

Other deities are more difficult to trace in this respect, and Artemis definitely falls into this more obscure category. It is perhaps more fruitful, then, to speak not so much of Artemis' *origins* as it is to speak of her *antecedents*—iconographic and textual entities who show aspects of the Greek goddess's persona, who foreshadow her in Bronze Age times, and who may have contributed to her formation in the Iron Age. The tentative nature of such a search is necessary because although there are numerous entities in the Aegean, and even Near Eastern, Bronze Age who show aspects of Artemis' character, it is not yet possible to show *continuity* between these Bronze Age divinities and the goddess of the Classical period. One might hope that future excavations and research will shed greater light on these matters.

LINEAR B[1]

What is probably the clearest evidence for Artemis in the Aegean Bronze Age is two, possibly three, appearances of her name in the Linear B corpus. Linear B is the name given to a syllabic writing system employed by the Mycenaean Greeks in the fourteenth and thirteenth centuries BCE. This system, adopted and adapted from the Minoan Linear A (hence the name), was used in the Mycenaean palaces at Thebes, Orchomenos, Athens, Eleusis, Mycenae, Pylos, Tiryns, Knossos, and Khania primarily to keep track of the economic affairs of the palatial elite, such as who owned what land, how much, and what animals and offerings were offered to what deities, when, and where. The corpus basically consists of lists traced into sheets and leaves of clay to serve as temporary records, later to be remoistened to keep track of the following year's data. The main reason we have any at all now is that the clay was accidentally fired in the mass conflagrations that destroyed most of the palaces at the end of the Bronze Age in the thirteenth to twelfth centuries BCE.

Two documents from the site of Pylos in south-western Greece (homeland of Nestor in the Homeric epics) appear to list the name of Artemis. The first is document PY Un 219, where PY stands for Pylos, and the Un means that the text refers to provisions. The text reads:

e-ke-ra-ne, tu-wo 2 O 1[
pa-de-we, O 1 pa-de-we , O 1
ka-ru-ke, PE 2 KA 1 O 6
te-qi-jo-ne, O 1 a-ke-ti-ri-ja-i , KA 1
a-ti-mi-te, O 1 da-ko-ro-i , (E) 1
di-pte-ra-po-ro, RA 1 O 3 ko-(ro)[ ] (1)
(wa)-na-ka-te, TE 1 po-ti-ni-ja[
e-[ ] U 1 e-ma-a$_2$, U 1 pe-[
a-ka-wo-ne, MA 1 pa-ra-[ ]2
ra-wa-ke-ta, MA 1 KO 1 [ ]ME 1 O 1 WI 1
KE 1 [ ] *vacat*
vacat x 2

Translated, this comes out to:

To e-ke-ra-(wo), perfume, 2 units and 1 unit of oregano
To pa-de-u, 1 unit of oregano, to pa-de-u, 1 unit of oregano
To the herald, 2 units of seed, 1 unit of KA, 6 units of oregano
To te-qu-ri-jo, 1 unit of oregano, to the tailors, 1 unit of KA
To Artemis (*a-ti-mi-te*) 1 unit of oregano, to the sweepers of the temple 1 unit of E
To the animal skin carriers 1 unit of RA, 3 units of oregano, to the ko-ro . . .
To the king 1 unit of TE, to the Lady . . .
To . . . , to Hermes 1 unit of U, to pe- . . .
To a-ka-wo 1 unit of fennel, to pa-ra . . . 2 units
To the lawagetas 1 unit of fennel, 1 unit of coriander, 1 of ME, 1 of oregano, 1 of WI

The second text, also coming from Pylos, is PY Es 650, where the designation Es means that the text refers to grain and land-holding. The text has:

ki-ri-ti-jo-jo, ko-pe-re-u e-ke , to-so-de pe-mo GRA 6
a-re-ku-tu-ru-wo, e-ke (,) to-so-de pe-mo GRA 7
se-no e-ke to-so-de pe-mo, GRA 1
o-po-ro-me-no e-ke to-so-de (,) pe-mo , GRA 4
a$_3$-ki-wa-ro, **a-te-mi-to**, do-e-ro e-ke to-so-de pe-mo GRA 1
we-da-ne-wo, do-e-ro e-ke to-so-de pe-mo GRA T 4
wo-ro-ti-ja-o e-ke to-so-de pe-mo GRA T 4
wo-ro-ti-ja-o e-ke to-so-de pe-mo GRA 2
ka-ra-i e-ke, to-so-de pe-mo GRA T 3
a-ne-o e-ke to-so-de pe-mo GRA 1 T 5

The word *e-ke* means "has," *to-so-de* means "so much," *pe-mo* means "seed," and GRA is an ideogram referring to seed. As such, the document gives the list of a number of personal names and how much seed each person has. In line five we see "a₃-ki-wa-ro, slave (*do-e-ro*) of Artemis (*a-te-mi-to*), so much seed—1 unit."

There continues to be debate about whether the words a-ti-mi-te (dative) and a-te-mi-to (genitive) do in fact mean Artemis. Text PY Un 219 lists both deities and mortal functionaries, each receiving comparable gifts (oregano), while PY Es 650 lists no deities at all. Furthermore, the names are not spelled the same, with a-ti- in the former text, a-te- in the latter. In spite of these objections, it is now generally agreed that the Linear B texts do indeed refer to a goddess named Artemis, spelling variations notwithstanding. In PY Un 219 the name appears in a text that also refers to the god Hermes (*e-ma-a₂*) as well as the quintessential Mycenaean goddess Potnia (*po-ti-ni-ja*). In addition, the text refers to cult functionaries, such as the herald, and the highest ranking members of Mycenaean society, the king (*wa-na-ka-te* = *wanax*) and the *lawagetas* (*ra-wa-ke-ta*). A goddess would not be out of place; a named but unknown "commoner" would be. As for PY Es 650, it is well known that one category of cult functionary in Mycenaean Greece was known as the "slave of the deity" (*do-e-ro te-o-jo*). Thus, a reference to a "slave of Artemis" who, by the bye, seems to own land to the equivalent of one unit of grain, appears to indicate a cult official to the goddess in question.

One final, possible reference to Artemis appears in PY Fn 837, where the Fn refers to allocations of olive oil. Here is listed in line 5 one "*i-je-re-u a-ti*[" with the text broken after the *a-ti* signs; *i-je-re-u* is the Linear B orthography for ancient Greek *hiereus*, meaning "priest." So it is evident that we have here a reference to a priest, and the first two signs of the name following make it possible, even likely, that he is specifically a priest of Artemis.

The textual evidence thus supports the high probability that the goddess Artemis was worshipped in Bronze Age Greece, at least in the region of Pylos. As Pylos has one of the two largest Linear B archives (the other being Knossos on Crete), this may have more to do with preservation than the actual expanse of the goddess's cult. Unfortunately, the presence of Artemis' name reveals nothing about the persona of the goddess at the time, or the nature of her cult. As Françoise Rougemont noted in her study of divine names in the Linear B corpus:

> A certain number of theonyms do appear, but one must note from the start that the Mycenaean documentation does not allow one to separate the study of the gods and goddesses from the study of their names: We have no idea about their personalities, and we have only fragmentary glimpses of what their cults were like, or the rites to which they were attached.[2]

So, the documentary evidence indicates that Artemis was worshipped as early as the Late Bronze Age in Greece, but the data reveal nothing about her character or cult.

NATURE GODDESS

In addition to the textual evidence, there are also iconographic data that suggest that an Artemis-like goddess was recognized and worshipped in the Bronze Age Aegean.

One such iconographic datum is what might be termed the Aegean Nature Goddess. This image, of which there are two examples in the extant fresco repertoire with similar iconography in the glyptic, shows a young goddess in an outdoor setting. She is accompanied and/or adorned by wild animals, and, most significantly in the case of a Proto-Artemis, is associated with girls.

The most famous portrayal of an Aegean Nature Goddess is the Goddess of Building Xeste 3 (Room 3a, North Wall) at Akrotiri on the Cycladic island of Thera (Figure 1.1), dating to c. 1700 BCE.[3]

This goddess sits enthroned upon a Minoan-style tripartite shrine. Before her a blue monkey offers the goddess crocus stamens, while right behind her is a griffin with wings outstretched and tethered to a nearby window. The goddess has a full head of long hair, including a snake-like tress on the top of her head, and one well-developed breast is visible in profile. Based on what is known of the conventions of portraying age in Minoan (including Theran) art, the hairstyle plus the developed but not pendulous breast indicated that this female is in mid- to late adolescence. The Minoans shaved the heads of their children, but left a few tresses of hair growing on the scalp. These tresses were allowed to grow long even with repeated shavings, and thus older children had longer locks on an otherwise shaven scalp. Later, the rest of the hair was allowed to grow in, leading to depictions of adolescents with long locks and shorter curls. Finally, the hair grew in fully. Likewise, standard Minoan garb for females reveals the breasts. Young girls have merely dots to indicate the nipples, while older girls have more developed breasts. Grown women, presumably mothers, have

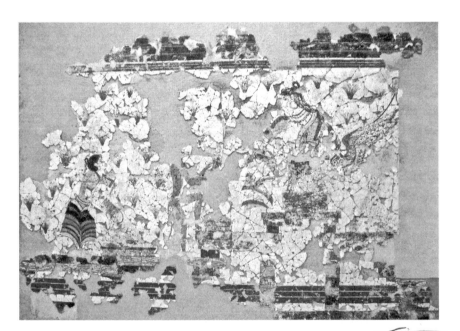

Figure 1.1 Nature Goddess of Room 3a, North Wall of Building Xeste 3, Akrotiri, c. 1700 BCE. Courtesy of the Cycladic Museum, Athens, Greece.

pendulous breasts.[4] Based on the criteria of hairstyle and breast development, the goddess of Xeste 3 seems to be in late adolescence, but not yet a fully mature woman.

Adorning this goddess is a large, lunate earring, a headband with dangling crocus (although some scholars also suggest that this crocus is a tattoo), and two necklaces, one with a line of ducks, the other with dragonflies. The vegetal and animal imagery suggest a Nature Goddess, as do the monkey and even the griffin.

Finally, and quite importantly, this goddess sits in the midst of a large, multi-wall fresco depicting numerous girls of various ages (per hairstyle and breast development), all engaged in crocus gathering. The girl closest to the goddess pours her gatherings into a pannier before the goddess, just as curly haired maiden carries a bucket of flowers toward the goddess from behind. The entire scene is one of well-dressed and bejeweled girls gathering crocuses and offering them to the goddess. Thus, we appear to have here an Artemis-like Nature Goddess involved in an outdoor ritual performed primarily, if not exclusively, by girls.

A second Nature Goddess appears on a series of frescoes from Room 14 of Royal Villa A at Haghia Triadha in southern Crete, now in the Herakleion Museum. This series, dating to Late Minoan I (c. 1600–1500 BCE), covers three walls of a small room, possibly a household shrine. The short wall opposite the entry, and thus the main focus of the composition, shows a partially crouched[5] female with arms upraised from the elbows wearing a headband, a calf-length Minoan flounced skirt and fitted bodice. Just behind this female is an architectural platform or façade reminiscent of the tripartite shrine structure supporting the Xeste 3 goddess. Both female and façade are located within a flowery meadow of what appears to be myrtle. This female faces the south wall, which depicts a rocky landscape filled with agrimi, cats, and pheasants, as well as floral motifs of crocuses, ivy, and violets. On the north wall "behind" the female in flounced skirt is another floral meadow in which another female kneels, facing the first female. This female wears a long blue dress and otherwise appears to have no adornments. Both females have chests facing forward, and thus it is difficult to reckon breast size, but in both instances it appears that the breasts are merely dots (nipples). Both females also have hair consisting of shorter curls with longer locks over the forehead and ear, suggesting an age in mid-adolescence.

The divinity of the central young female is suggested by her placement, her posture, and similarities with goddesses in other Minoan iconography, not least the goddess of Xeste 3. This girl is the focus of the composition, both in terms of the scene's layout and her placement vis-à-vis the room's entrance. She is located above a small dais, which is the only architectural embellishment in Room 14.[6] She is associated with the architectural façade, likening her to the Xeste 3 goddess and numerous female figures in the Minoan and Mycenaean glyptic that depict large (relative to other characters in the composition) females receiving offerings either from humans (typically female) or animals (see below).[7] Her arms, which extend out to either side of her body and are bent upwards at the elbows, reveals a posture typically associated with benediction both in the ancient Near East and in Minoan Crete, the latter in terms of both glyptic iconography and the later Minoan Goddess With Upraised Arms. Finally, the supernatural nature of the scene itself is suggested by the flora. As Anne Chapin notes, the flowers which are all simultaneously in bloom

stones

precious

of

relating to carving or engraving especially on ....

in the fresco normally bloom in different seasons in Crete. The fresco encapsulates the fertility of an entire year within one scene, thus depicting, "an eternal, timeless landscape expressive of the mythic fertility of the earth."[8]

Although the programs of both frescoes are quite different, the common elements of wildlife, crocus flowers, architectural platform/façade, and goddess and maiden, have led to the suggestion that they may have depicted similar religious themes, such as the "Mistress or Protector of Animals," or the "Goddess of Palace and Peak Sanctuary."[9] The religious iconographies and architecture of Akrotiri were similar enough to those of Minoan Crete to suggest at least some commonalities of cult and pantheon.

That this "Nature Goddess" is not restricted to just these two sites is suggested by the glyptic iconography, where several seals and sealings from throughout Crete show elements of the frescoes' decoration. The most direct cognate to the Xeste 3 goddess appears on a sealing from Knossos, where a female in flounced skirt sits upon an architectural façade similar in most respects to that of Xeste 3, although on the Knossos sealing Horns of Consecration (a Minoan religious symbol) are visible on the façade.[10] Before this seated female stands another female in flounced skirt who is appreciably shorter than the seated figure. This standing female offers a handled rhyton (Minoan ritual vessel) to the seated female, while the far edge of the sealing reveals another skirted female crouching away from the first two. The presence of the façade, the Horns of Consecration, the rhyton, and the difference in relative sizes all suggest that the seated female is a goddess, and the scene's composition is strongly reminiscent of the Xeste 3 fresco. A very similar sealing, although with only one mortal "devotee," comes from Zakros in southern Crete.[11] Here once again we see a larger female in flounced skirt seated upon an architectural structure being offered something (no longer visible) from a smaller female. The edge of the sealing appears to depict a rocky formation, perhaps referring to the natural world seen in the Haghia Triadha fresco.

Another close cognate to the Xeste 3 goddess appears on a sealing from Khania in western Crete.[12] Here we see a female with large breasts in a flounced skirt sitting upon an architectural structure similar to that of the Xeste 3 goddess. Before her stands a younger girl in a shorter skirt who holds what appears to be a fan and/or frond up to the goddess.

These images appear throughout Crete and even extend out into the Cyclades. Thus the Nature Goddess so depicted may have been a common fixture of Bronze Age Minoan and Cycladic cult. Her consistently close associations with the natural world, wild (even magical) animals, and women and girls all suggest that she may have been a prototype for the eventual Greek goddess Artemis.[13]

"Potnia Therôn"

The title "Potnia Therôn" brings some ambiguity to the study of the early antecedents of Artemis. The words mean "Mistress of Wild Animals,"[14] and the title is used of Artemis by Homer in his *Iliad*, Book 21, 407. However, since the late nineteenth century with the publication of E. Studniczka's *Eine Altgriechische Göttin* (1890), the term has also been used to denote an iconographic composition which depicts a goddess holding and/or mastering one or two animals.[15] The divinity of the female might be expressed through her position upon a Minoan-style architectural façade as noted above, or she may be displaying power over lions, which most people are willing to agree indicates divinity.

It is generally understood that the Potnia Therôn icon is an import from the Near East. The motif first appears in the early second millennium in Babylon and Anatolia, and becomes increasingly pervasive in the Near Eastern glyptic in the later second millennium, especially in the western regions of the Mitanni Empire, Syria, and eventually even Cyprus. The motif is thus an import into the Aegean, although this has little bearing on whether or not it could have been understood to represent a local goddess. It is entirely possible that the Near Eastern motif was used to represent a/the Goddess of Nature, or a separate being altogether.

In the Bronze Age Aegean, the Mistress of Animals appears exclusively in the glyptic, of both Minoan Crete and Mycenaean Greece. She first appears in Late Minoan (LM) I, and already she has been thoroughly Aegeanized: She wears the standard Minoan costume of flounced skirt, and, when visible, bodice. More frequently, however, her upper clothing is not depicted, and instead large breasts are visible. Several examples show close affinities with the Nature Goddess type, especially where the goddess sits upon an architectural façade. One example from Khania shows a fully dressed Minoan-style female seated upon an "altar" while she feeds a leaf to a long-horned agrimi.[16] Likewise, a flounced-skirted female sitting upon a similar seat is flanked by a pair of heraldically placed lions on a ring from the Amari Valley in central Crete.[17] Both images show very close parallels with the Goddess of Xeste 3, and it is possible, if not probable, that they depict the same goddess.

An alternate manifestation of the Potnia Therôn type, and one much closer to the original ancient Near East versions, shows a standing goddess. She may hold a pair of animals (realistic or fantastic) in her outstretched hands, or she may merely be flanked by such a pair. In some less symmetrical instances, only one animal is held. Thus a standing female with pronounced breasts holds a long-horned agrimi by the neck on a seal from Pylos in western Greece.[18] More common are the symmetrical compositions, such as a goddess with upraised arms and a labrys (double axe) above her head standing between a pair of heraldically set lions on a seal from Mycenae, or a female in flounced skirt who holds a pair of dolphins in her outstretched hands on a seal from Aidonia.[19]

Once again, one must remember that it was only in modern (relatively) times that the title Potnia Therôn was applied to the motif of a female who appears to be mastering animals. There is no reason to suppose that the ancient residents of the Aegean had a similar term for the icons discussed above, or that they would put any of these various divinities into the same category. It seems likely that the glyptic goddesses from Khania and Amari were seen as portrayals of the Xeste 3-style Nature Goddess, while the large-bosomed Mistress of Animals prevalent in the more northern glyptic was a separate character. However, it must also be kept in mind that this goddess who shows control over pointedly wild, even fantastic (such as griffins), animals might also have contributed to the eventual Greek Artemis.

A second wave of Near Eastern influence changed the portrayal of the Greek Potnia Therôn. No Bronze Age Aegean examples of this goddess show her winged, although this was a common attribute for the type in Mesopotamia and Syria. By the Archaic Age, however, the standard Mistress of Wild Animals type does have wings, as seen in Figure 1.2 from the François Vase, as well as on an early seventh-century amphora from Boiotia (where the arms are distinctly wing-like—see Chapter 3, Figure 3.1), and numerous lead figurines from the sanctuary of Artemis Ortheia in Sparta. This new appearance of wings may coordinate with a similar tendency seen on a relief pithos from seventh-century Tenos depicting the birth of Athena.[20] In this scene both Zeus and Athena appear winged, as does the attendant behind Zeus, possibly Eileithyia, an attendant at a cauldron (Hephaistos?), and another character flying before the Father of Men and Gods. None of these deities are portrayed as winged in any other contexts, and we might suppose that "winging" was a very short-term practice adopted from the Near East to indicate divinity. Although such iconography is short-lived, it does endure in the case of the Potnia Therôn.

Figure 1.2 Potnia Therôn image from the François Vase, c. 570–560 BCE, Florence Museum 4209. Drawing by Paul C. Butler, used with kind permission.

While there can be little doubt that such a mistress of wild animals does partake of Artemisian attributes, there is reason to believe that this winged Potnia Therôn was a different creature than the eventual Artemis. The best indication of this appears on the François Vase itself, which shows the winged Potnia Therôn below one of the handles, but a named (by inscription) Artemis without wings in one of the registers. Furthermore, there are no known depictions of a clearly labeled Artemis with wings in the Greek corpus. However, what does appear in the Archaic iconography is a winged Potnia Therôn type but with a distinctly gorgon's head, as on a late seventh-century dish from Kameiros, Rhodes, who holds a goose in each hand. The winged, Near Eastern Potnia Therôn type, then, clearly influenced the iconography of numerous female (and occasionally male—Zeus) deities, without necessarily representing any of the named Olympians.

By contrast, there is one early depiction of a non-winged Potnia Therôn that does express many of the elements considered here as pertaining to an early Artemis. This is an early seventh-century relief pithos from Thebes (now in the National Archaeological Museum in Athens) which shows a divinity standing *en face* with up-raised arms (Figure 1.3).[21]

She has a polos-style crown with antler-like foliate elements emerging from it. On either side of her smaller anthropomorphic beings (children?) cling to her beneath her upraised arms, while heraldically set lions stand on either side of this group facing the goddess. This image appears on the pithos neck; the body of the vase is decorated with

Figure 1.3 Relief pithos from Thebes featuring nature goddess with children, c. 675 BCE. Athens, National Archaeological Museum, 355. Drawing by Paul C. Butler, used with kind permission.

grazing deer. Thus in one object we see a crowned divinity who is associated with the vegetal word (foliate crown), wild animals (lions and deer), and, apparently, children. Her up-raised arms recall the Minoan Goddess with Up-Raised Arms who dominated Crete, and eventually Cyprus, at the end of the Bronze Age, while the heraldic lions are strongly reminiscent of Mycenaean iconography, notably the Lion Gate of Mycenae and, even more so, the Mother of the Mountain seal from LM III Knossos.[22]

Although the problem of continuity will remain, the iconography does suggest that there were strong antecedents to the goddess Artemis in the Aegean Bronze Age, specifically as a goddess of nature, children, and wildlife. Some of this iconography reemerges in the early Archaic Age, occasionally with new elements such as the wings, and often with remarkably similar attributes, such as the heraldic lions.[23]

EARLY SANCTUARIES

The search for Bronze Age antecedents to Artemis is not confined to the texts and iconography; architecture has also been brought into the fray. Two of Artemis' cult sites in particular have shown possible evidence for continuity of cult from the Bronze Age into the early Archaic Age—the Artemision on Delos and the temple of Artemis Elaphebolos in Kalapodi, ancient Hyampolis in Phokis.

Delos

The relevant structure on Delos is Building Ac, a Late Bronze Age construction beneath the Archaic Artemision. As noted by the excavator R. Vallois, this rectangular structure oriented east–west and composed of large granite blocks lies directly below the later temple and with an identical orientation.[24] The sacred nature of the structure was not only suggested because of a presumed continuity at the site, but also because discovered underneath the Bronze Age building was a foundation deposit of Mycenaean-era fine arts, including imported bronzes and ivories from Cyprus, discovered in 1928. For Hubert Gallet de Santerre, such a foundation deposit attested to the early religious nature of the site, a sanctity that endured throughout the Dark Ages and into the Greek Renaissance.[25] However, later analysis of the stratigraphy and deposit artifacts suggested rather that the cache of art objects was a collection of originally dispersed grave goods that were later, during the early Archaic period, gathered together and placed as a votive under the Archaic Artemision, with no reference to a Bronze Age cult.[26] Furthermore, Building Ac, along with several adjacent Mycenaean-age structures in the area of the later Artemision, has since been identified as a domestic unit, not a temple.[27] This accords well with the fact that the Mycenaeans rarely constructed purpose-built temples: Religious rites were carried out in the élite *megara* and open-air shrines, as at the ash altar of Zeus on Mt. Lykaion, Arkadia.[28] For these reasons, the Delian Artemision is no longer believed to show cultic continuity with the Bronze Age, and thus furnishes no evidence for a Bronze Age cult of (Proto-) Artemis that endured into the Iron Age.[29]

Kalapodi/Hyampolis

There is far greater evidence for continuity at the sanctuary at Kalapodi, ancient Hyampolis in Phokis. This sanctuary was established in the Late Helladic C period (twelfth century) and shows continuous use through to the Common Era.[30] The earliest finds at the sanctuary consist primarily of ceramic dining wares, especially open vessels such as kylikes, cups, and kraters—items that continue in use at the sanctuary throughout its long life. Such items indicate that the Hyampolis sanctuary served as a center of feasting rituals from its earliest manifestation, which accords well with the theories of both Catherine Morgan and Jeremy McInerney that the site functioned as a centralizing political core for the Phokians (at least in the Archaic and Classical periods).[31] An ash deposit with animal bones attests to an early altar associated with the temple structure.

The majority of votive items found at the sanctuary from Mycenaean until early Archaic times consists of jewelry, including fibulae, bronze pins, pendants, rings, bangles, and beads of both bronze and iron.[32] Additional votive materials consist of terracotta animals, mostly bulls, later horses, and anthropomorphic figurines, notably Mycenaean psi-style terracottas.[33] The presence of jewelry plus the psi-figurines gives evidence for the presence of a female deity revered at the sanctuary in its earliest phases.

A change occurs over the course of the Geometric period. In the nineth century, a new building was constructed north of the original Late Helladic structure, and a new altar was built. Dedications of bronze tripods, comparable to those dedicated only slightly earlier at Delphi, begin to appear in number. In the seventh and sixth centuries, the votive jewelry which typified the votives since the Mycenaean era are outnumbered by votive dedications of weapons, including iron swords and spears and bronze helmets, shields, and greaves.[34] By the mid-fifth century, dedications of jewelry cease entirely.

The archaeological evidence suggests that a single feminine deity was originally worshipped at the site, an Artemis or Proto-Artemis who would eventually become the Artemis *Elaphebolos* ("Deer-Shooter") of the Phokians. In the ninth century, Artemis was joined at her sanctuary by Apollo, whose own cult was spreading rapidly throughout Greece during this period, to judge from comparable materials in Delphi and Delos. Apollo did not displace Artemis at Hyampolis; he came to be worshipped in conjunction with his sister, possibly as Apollo of Abai, the site of a well-known oracle in the Classical period, rivaling even Delphi.[35] The two deities' names appear together in documents from the region well into the Roman period, such as a first-century BCE manumission decree freeing a woman named Eukrateia into the protection of Artemis and Apollo:

> If someone should seize Eukrateia and lead her into slavery . . . in any way or under any pretext, may he pay 30 minas of silver to Artemis and Apollo, and may it be permitted to whoever wishes to come forward and seize up to a half of this (sum from him). And may Eukrateia be free using the appellation sacred (*hiera*) to Artemis and Apollo, no longer belonging to anyone in any way.[36]

The relationship between Artemis and Apollo at Kalapodi is indicative of the rise of the Greek temples throughout Greece, when, as François de Polignac noted, these two deities, along with Hera and Athena, were the primary gods to receive temples in the early Archaic Age.[37] However, it is necessary to remember that while the early votives at Kalapodi may suggest the early presence of a female deity, very little might be deduced about that deity's persona from the cult or votive remains. As also noted by de Polignac, offerings at the early sanctuaries were highly homogenized, with each of the four deities mentioned above receiving copious quantities of tripods, fibulae, pins, and terracotta animals. All the goddesses, not just Artemis, received images of wild animals and even Potnia Therôn iconography.[38] Thus, for example, the early sanctuary of Athena Alea at Tegea in Arcadia yielded bronze birds, bronze horses, terracotta animals, nude female images, bronze pomegranates, deer figurines, a turtle pendant, copious jewelry, and several lead figurines of winged females, reminiscent of the ones from the sanctuary of Artemis Ortheia in Sparta (see below).[39] The types of objects we might think of as indicative of an Artemis-goddess are in fact more expressive of the needs and interests of the dedicators, and apply to a variety of divinities. So while it is possible to identify an early Artemis in the archaeological record, one must remain cognizant of the methodological difficulties in establishing a correspondence between offerings and persona.

Near Eastern links and influences—Artemis of Ephesos

Although there is clear evidence for many aspects of Artemis in the Bronze Age record in the Aegean, it is also evident that some aspects of the goddess and her various Greek cults derived from eastern prototypes and influence. Ancient Near Eastern goddesses were adopted by the Greeks and melded into their own conception of their virgin hunting goddess. Eventually, by the Classical period, these "foreign" goddesses were known simply as "Artemis," but with unique epithets, votives, and cult practices that inevitably betrayed their exotic origins. The most blatantly "oriental" version of Artemis is Artemis of Ephesos:

> All [cities] and men individually hold Artemis of Ephesos in honor more than they do [other] deities. It seems to me that the reasons for this are the renown of the Amazons who have the fame of having set up the cult statue, and because that sanctuary was established in most remote antiquity. Three other things in addition to these contribute to its glory—the size of the temple which excels all man-made constructions, and the primacy of the city of the Ephesians, and the renown of the goddess in that city.
>
> (Paus. 4.31.8)

The temple of the Ephesian goddess has antecedents dating back into the Late Bronze Age.[40] At this time the area was called by its Hittite name Apašas/Apasa (the origins of the name Ephesos), which was the capital of the region of Arzawa to the west of the Hittite Empire.[41] The geographical territory appears to have been called Aššuwa in the Hittite documents from the ancient capital of Hattušas (modern Boğazköy).[42]

The name of the goddess who was worshipped here is unfortunately unknown. Although she is commonly lumped in with several other almost generic Anatolian "Mother Goddesses" and may be called "Kybele" or simply "The Great Mother" in modern scholarship, Lynn Roller has argued convincingly that the goddess of Ephesos cannot be identified with Anatolian Meter ("Mother") or Kybele. At Ephesos and Lydian Sardis both Ephesian Artemis and Meter were worshipped separately, with Meter's Ephesian sanctuary being located several kilometers away from the Artemiseion.[43]

Two data give some evidence for the name of the Ephesian goddess. The Hellenistic poet Kallimakhos in his *Hymn to Artemis* recalls the tradition that the cult of Ephesian Artemis was founded by the Amazons, who called their goddess Oupis (l. 240; see also Chapter 4). This "Oupis" may be etymologically derived from Apasa, thus suggesting that the name of the town and the name of the goddess are one in the same (something like Athena, goddess of Athens).[44]

A similar result emerged when Sarah Morris considered the original identity of a deity called "Potnia Asiwiya" in the Linear B corpus from Pylos (PY Fr 1206), typically translated as "Lady of Asia." Hypothesizing (rather successfully) an eastern origin for this deity, Morris argues that the title Asiwiya (*a-si-wi-ya*) is the Hellenized form of the Hittite toponym Aššuwa.[45] Once again, then, we appear to have no personal name for the goddess other than the region where she was worshipped—"the Ephesian."

This goddess was probably worshipped at Ephesos since the Late Bronze Age. However, the earliest continuous architectural remains at the sanctuary belong to the eighth-century temple known as the *hekatompedon* (literally, "hundred-footer"). Based on the evidence of the votive remains, it appears likely that more than one divinity, even more than one goddess, was worshipped at the sanctuary at this time. It was only in the sixth century that these female divinities were syncretized into the over-arching identity of Greek Artemis.[46] It was at this time that the magnificent temple that was to become one of the Seven Wonders of the Ancient World was constructed, with no little assistance from the Lydian King Kroisos (as in "as rich as Croesus").

In spite of Greek Artemis' increasing influence over the cult, numerous Anatolian influences remained, especially in the goddess's cult statue (Figure 1.4).

The stiff frontality of the statue is typical of the Iron Age Anatolian aesthetic and appears on the cult statues of Aphrodite of Aphrodisias and Hera of Samos. The flat headdress, called a *polos*, is indicative of divinity in Greek iconography, but also partakes of more indigenous tradition—the Anatolian goddesses Kubaba and Hepat wear comparable headgear. Most distinctive of all is the goddess's pectoral decorated with numerous bulb-like protrusions. As one might imagine, it is often assumed that these are breasts, and thus indicative of a very potent fertility deity. Some Roman copies actually included nipples, a detail not present on the original.[47] But these were not breasts. Some have suggested that they were bulls' testicles, thus still within the realms of potent fertility. But the most convincing interpretation is that they are a distinctively Anatolian object known as a *kuršaš*, a leather bag that could be described as a magically fertile bag of holding. Such items, when mentioned in Hittite literature, are associated with fertility deities such as the rain god Telipinu, and are described as containing items such as grain, wine, fat, long life, and progeny

Kubsas
p. 21

Figure 1.4 Statue of Artemis of Ephesos, first century CE, Ephesus Archaeological Museum, Ephesus, Turkey. Image © Vanni Archive/Art Resource, NY (ART310475).

(KUB XVII.10, iv27–35).[48] The statue of the Carian Zeus of Labraunda wears a similar pectoral, as did zoomorphic Anatolian rhyta,[49] completely divorcing them from the realms of the mammary but bolstering their connection to the realms of the divine. All together, these attributes emphasize the strongly Anatolian background of this goddess who would eventually become Artemis.

The iconography depicted on the goddess's statue is an important key in under-standing her persona. As was typical for such Anatolian iconography, the deity was literally decorated with the attributes of her power. Thus the Aphrodisian Aphrodite was festooned with gorgeous jewelry and kallipygos Graces and frolicking sea life. For her own part, Ephesian Artemis was adorned with animals both wild (such as the lion) and domestic (such as bovines). A wreath of pollination surrounds her neck, while she stands flanked by deer and bee hives. About her chest is the zodiac (signs of a later addition), and, of course, the pendulous bags of plenty. Blooming flowers peek out

over her feet. All these call to mind Artemis' dominion over the animal kingdom and the fertility of the natural world—animal and vegetal.

The spread of Ephesian Artemis' cult throughout the Greek world was extraordinary. Realistically, of course, it began along the western coast of Asia Minor, a region in close contact with the Mycenaean kingdoms in the Bronze Age and early colonized by the Greeks in the Dark Age. But the Greeks themselves believed that the origins of this cult went farther north, to Skythia. As noted, tradition claims that the cult of the Ephesian was founded by the Amazons, specifically under their queen Hippo ("Horse"). This tradition can be traced back at least to the mid-fifth century BCE, for the Roman-era travel-writer Pausanias records that (7.2.7):

> In truth it seems to me that Pindar did not learn everything that pertains to the goddess; he says the Amazons founded the sanctuary when campaigning against Athens and Theseus. But the women from Thermodon sacrificed at that time to the Ephesian goddess, just as they knew the sanctuary of old, both when they were fleeing Herakles and even earlier when fleeing Dionysos; they came there as suppliants. [The sanctuary] was not really founded by Amazons, but by the autochthon Koresos and also Ephesos—they believe him to be the child of the river Kaustros—and these men are the founders of the sanctuary. From Ephesos the city takes its name.

Minimal archaeological evidence for the cult of Ephesian Artemis in the Black Sea region does, in fact, date back to the sixth century BCE. A small bronze votive dedicated to the goddess came to light from sixth-century Pantikapaion, while small votives—a black gloss salt cellar, a bronze lamp, and a kylix and skyphos—were found at Berezan, Olbia, and Kerkinitis respectively. An inscribed altar to the goddess came to light in Pantikapaion from the fourth century.[50]

The cult was brought to the Peloponnese by the Athenian historian-philosopher Xenophon after he had taken part in a failed *coup d'état* in Persia. As he recorded in his *Anabasis* (5.3.7–12), Xenophon settled in Skillous near Olympia while in exile from his native Athens. While there he received back a sum of money which he had entrusted to a high priest of Ephesian Artemis—the Megabyzos—and he used this money to buy a plot of land to dedicate to the goddess.

> Here [Xenophon] built an altar and a temple from the sacred silver/money, and tithing the produce of the fields ever after he offered a sacrifice to the goddess, and all the citizens, both men and women of the neighborhood, joined in the festival. And the goddess furnished those in residence with barley, bread, wine, sweets, and as well a portion of the sacred food from the sacrifice and from the hunt . . . The temple is small compared to the large size of the one in Ephesos, and the xoanon is similar, although in cypress while the one in Ephesos is of gold.
>
> (5.3.9, 12, excerpted)

To the far west, the cult of Artemis of Ephesos was established at ancient Masalia, modern Marseille, when the Côte d'Azur was colonized by Phokaians. The first-century CE geographer Strabo preserved the account in his *Geography* (4.1.4):

> Masalia is a foundation of the Phokaians . . . The Ephesion was built on the summit as well as the sanctuary of Delphic Apollo; the latter is held in common by all the Ionians, while the Ephesion is the temple of Ephesian Artemis. For they say that an oracle was given to

the Phokaians when they were quitting their homeland to consult for the voyage a leader acquired from Artemis of Ephesos. So the Phokaians, having come to Ephesos, inquired as to how to get the demanded item. Meanwhile, the goddess appeared to Aristarkhê—the most honorable of the women—in a dream and ordered her to sail away with the Phokaians, taking some model of the sacred things. Once this had happened and the colony settled, they built the sanctuary and they honored Aristarkhê most especially in appointing her priestess. And in all the daughter cities everywhere they honor above all this goddess and the image of her xoanon, and the other customs they keep the same just as they do in the mother city.

These Masalians later went on to spread the cult of the Ephesian even farther west, into Iberia. Thus Strabo records her cult in Hemeroskopeion (3.4.6):

Between Soukron and Karkhedon are three towns of the Masalians which are not far from the river; of these the most famous is Hemeroskopeion, which has on its summit a very highly honored sanctuary of Ephesian Artemis.

And Emporion and Rhodê (3.4.8):

Emporion: A Masalian foundation, some 4,000 stades distant from the Pyrenees and from the borders of Iberia and the Celtic territory. And the city is wholly fine with good harbors. There also is the town of Rhodê, a foundation of the Emporitans, although some say of the Rhodians. Both here and in Emporion they revere Ephesian Artemis.

SYNCRETISMS AND FOREIGN INFLUENCES AT HOME—ARTEMIS ORTHEIA

A wonderful case study for how the cults of Artemis evolved on Greek soil, absorbing similar local deities and spreading out from localized to panhellenic status, is the cult of Artemis Ortheia. The Romans believed that this goddess's cult statue came from Skythia; more modern scholars suggest that she herself is Levantine. When Ortheia even came to be understood as Artemis remains in debate. But as the evidence shows, Ortheia appears to be an indigenously Spartan goddess who attracted Levantine paraphernalia in her cult and ultimately came to be regarded as Olympian Artemis throughout the Greek world.

The chronology of both the archaeological remains and the epigraphy suggest that the cult of a goddess called Worthasia—eventually Ortheia—first emerged in Sparta. On the west bank of the Eurotas River was located the sanctuary of Artemis Ortheia, where the remains of the third-century CE Roman sanctuary to the goddess still partially stand. This Roman construction was built over a much earlier sanctuary where cult practice is attested as early as the ninth century BCE. Geometric pottery fragments appear near an area of burning and an ash layer where the later altar would be, serving as the earliest evidence of cult practice, which may date back to c. 850 BCE.[51] There is no evidence of cult at this site before the Geometric period, nor is the name of the deity associated with the site attested in the Linear B corpus. As such, it appears that the cult of Worthasia first emerged in the Dark Age, and has no Mycenaean precedents.[52]

At the dawn of the seventh century, the sanctuary was graced with a temenos wall, a cobble-stone pavement, and the sanctuary's first constructed altar (Altar I). It was also at this time that the first temple was built. Only the south-western long wall of this structure remains, but is appears that, in typical Greek fashion, the temple was oriented east–west, with sunbaked bricks over more waterproof stones, and an overhanging gable. A terracotta votive model of a temple found at the site may be evidence that this temple was in early Doric style, with rudimentary triglyphs and metopes.[53] Around 600 BCE the sanctuary was flooded. The site was covered with a layer of sand and a new temple and altar were constructed, dating to the first quarter of the sixth century. The more intact temple was oriented east–west with a short pronaos (vestibule) at the short, eastern end and a long narrow cella.[54] The altars—the first shorter and stouter, the second long and narrow— were some 20 meters to the east of the temple. It was this configuration that remained in use until the temple was rebuilt in the second century BCE, and then the entire sanctuary was expanded and rebuilt in the third century CE, including a stone theater where tourists could come watch Spartan boys being flogged (see Chapter 6). All in all, there is considerable continuity from c. 800 BCE until the Roman period.

The deity originally worshipped at this sanctuary does not appear to have been Artemis, but an independent deity. This is attested by the epigraphic evidence— dedications to Worthasia begin to appear in the sanctuary as early as the sixth century, but the name is not connected to the name Artemis until the first century CE in Sparta, either in the epigraphy, the literature, or even on the temple's roof tiles.[55] By the fifth century BCE at the latest, this goddess's name appears in other regions of Greece, and in some instances she is pointedly presented as a different entity than Artemis. Thus a manumission inscription from Mount Kotillion in Arkadia (*IG* V², 429) dating to c. 360 BCE relates how:

> Klenis releases Komaithos as free, and Ombria and Khoirothyon. If anyone should lay a hand on them, either Wistias or anyone else, all their goods are "sacred" [given] to Apollo Bassitas, Pan Sinoeis, Artemis of Kotillion, and Worthasia.[56]

What also becomes immediately clear when considering the epigraphy is that no one seems to have had a very good idea of how to spell the goddess's name. Inscriptions from just below the sand layer have her as Worthasia, Worthaia, and even Worphaia. By the fifth century the spelling Wortheia became more common, but not exclusive. In the third century the W was replaced by a B, leading to the spelling Bortheia, before settling on Ortheia, and eventually Orthia.[57]

Clues to the character of this goddess come from literature, epigraphy, and the copious votives unearthed at her Spartan sanctuary. Already from the seventh century we have evidence that this goddess was associated with male and female adolescents and their various competitions and games. The first datum comes from the lyric poet Alkman in his *Parthenaion* ("Maidens' Song"), where a chorus of maidens sings:

> There is some vengeance of the deities;
> He is blessed, whoever gladly
> Lives out the day
> Without tears. I sing

The light of Agido—I see
Her as the sun, which for us—
Agido bears witness—
Shines. The illustrious choregos
Does not allow me to praise
Or to blame her. For it seems she is
Preeminent, as if someone
Should set in the herds a horse
Strong, victorious, sounding-hoofed,
Of winged dreams.

Or do you not see? The Enetian
Racing horse. The flowing hair
Of my kinswoman.
Hagesikhora shines
Like unmixed gold,
And her silver face;
Why do I tell you openly?
Hagesikhora herself,
The second after Agido in beauty,
Will race like a Kolaxian horse against Ibenian.
For the Pleiades fight us
As we bring a cloak to *Orthria*
Through ambrosial night, like Sirius
Star rising.

For neither something of violet
Is enough to defend one,
Nor a colorful snake
All of gold, nor a Lydian
Headband, of young girls,
Soft-eyed, the delight.
Nor Nanno's hair,
Nor even divine-faced Areta,
Nor Sylakis and Kleësisera,
Nor going to Ainesimbrota and saying
"Astraphis—were that she were mine!"
And Philylla to glance here
And lovely Damareta and Ianthemis—
But Hagesikhora guards me.

For is fair-ankled
Hagesikhora not near here?
Doesn't she stay close to Agido
And together praise the festival?
But, deities, please receive
Our prayers. For fulfillment and
Perfection are of the deities. Chorus-leader,
If I might speak. I myself

Am a maiden; in vain from the perch I screech,
An owl. But I most of all want to delight
Aotis—of our sufferings
She was the healer.
But young girls were treading the
Lovely path from Hagesikhora.

For the trace-horse
Likewise . . .
The helmsman, one must
On a ship obey him most of all.
She is not more songstress
Than the Sirens,
For they are goddesses. But against eleven
This one of ten children sings.
It cries out like a swan on
The streams of Xenthos River.
Her lovely blond hair . . .

Clearly Orthria is yet another spelling for Ortheia, and she serves as the focus of the girls' prayers and actions.

Epigraphic evidence for Ortheia's role in adolescents' competitions appears in a fourth-century dedication discovered at the sanctuary (Artemis Orthia 1 = *IG* 5¹ 255): "To Wortheia, Arexippos, having been victorious, dedicated these things in the gathering of boys, manifest for all to see." The dedication bore five victory sickles won in competition, and similar dedications emerged at the sanctuary through the Roman period.[58] Outside of Sparta, similar evidence for Ortheia's role in games comes from nearby Messenê, where a dedication dating to c. 250 BCE (Messene Inv. No. 3587) commemorates, "Diokouridas, son of Antikles, having been an *agonothetes* ("games manager"), [dedicated this] to Artemis Ortheia."[59]

The votives from Ortheia's sanctuary present a different aspect of the goddess. These were found in *bothroi* [ditches] north and south of the temple. Prominent were dedications of gold jewelry, especially earrings and dress pins. Most copious were the lead objects, of which over 100,000 came from the sanctuary from the period between 700 and 400 BCE. The lead itself seems to come from the Laurion mines in Attika, and thus is Greek in origin. The lead votives consist of scarabs, pomegranates, rosettes, sphinxes, roosters, lions, Potniai Therôn (winged, see above), warriors, horse-riders, horses, Aeolic capitals, centaurs, gorgons, *labrydes*, and garlands.[60] The jewelry strongly suggests that the deity was female. Objects such as scarabs and sphinxes relate to the Orientalizing tendencies in Greek art during the late Archaic period. Perhaps more emblematic of the goddess's character are the copious warriors, horses, and riders, which seem to indicate that in addition to her role(s) in athletic competitions, she was also invested in the world of warfare. Items such as the Potniai Therôn, roosters, and lions give evidence for an early Artemis-type goddess, associated with command of the wilds.

Well over half (approximately 68,000 or the 100,000) of the lead votives from the sanctuary date to the sixth century, when an interesting change of iconography occurs. Fewer horses appear, and these are replaced by the new appearance of deer lead votives in the repertoire. As the deer is strongly associated with Artemis through-out Greece, it is possible, if not probable, that it is in the sixth century that Spartan Ortheia comes to syncretize with panhellenic Artemis.[61]

Such an assessment is strengthened when considering the numerous ivory and bone carvings brought to light at the sanctuary. In addition to jewelry (again), many of these small *objets d'art* were of wild animals, notably lions and goats, once again confirming the presence of an Artemis-like deity.[62] Also popular were Orientalizing images of what appears to be the goddess herself, adorned with a high polos-cap, distinctive of goddesses in Greek iconography.[63]

Far more significant in the modern study of Spartan Ortheia (and her origins) are the terracotta masks which came to light in the sanctuary's *bothroi*. Some 603 life-sized or (starting in the Hellenistic era) just under life-sized anthropomorphic masks were excavated from the sanctuary, orders of magnitude more than from any other Greek sanctuary anywhere, bar none. These masks exist in four main categories. The two smaller categories consist of gorgons (identifiable especially by their sticking-out tongues) and satyrs. The two larger categories, with approximately equal numbers, are heroes—including older (bearded) and younger (clean-shaven) heroes—and gro-tesques, with heavily furled/winkled faces. These masks first began to appear at the sanctuary c. 660 BCE.[64] Far more appear above the sand, and are most common in the first half of the sixth century, thus c. 570. They continue with some changes (such as size) well into the Hellenistic period. All are made with local fabrics, and those that are painted are done so in the same colors as appear on contemporary Lakonian pottery.[65]

In the original publication of the Ortheia Sanctuary by the British School in Athens, Guy Dickens hypothesized that the masks were used for ritual, initia-tory dances performed at the sanctuary. Based on very late texts from Pollux and Hesykhios, Dickens suggested that these were masks used in the *Baryllikon* (Pollux 4.104) or *Brydalia* (Hesykh. βρυδαλίγα) dances. In the former, it was women who danced the *baryllika* in honor of Artemis and Apollo, while in the later males donned ugly-old-woman masks and sang hymns.[66] However, as Jane Carter noted in her study of the masks, none of them are old women, nor is there any evidence as to who wore the masks. As such, the exceptionally late textual evidence based on a non-existent iconographic type must be eschewed. Instead, Carter documented the very close correspondences between both the hero masks and the grotesques and virtually identical masks from the ancient Near East, stemming back as far as Bronze Age Mesopotamia and spreading throughout the Mediterranean with Phoenician colonization in the Iron Age.[67] Considering the prominence of the votive masks at the Ortheia sanctuary, combined with a lack of Mycenaean precedents for this cult and the copious Orientalizing votives in both lead and ivory, Carter argued that the cult of Ortheia was originally established by resident Phoenicians in Lakonia, and that Ortheia was a Greek version of their own Near Eastern goddess Asherah.[68] As such, just as Ephesian Artemis was a Hellenized version of an Anatolian goddess, so too was Artemis Ortheia a Hellenized version of a Levantine goddess.

Although the Near Eastern origins of the mask styles have been well confirmed, the evidence nevertheless argues against any Phoenician origins for the deity or her cult. To begin, there is no evidence for any stable Phoenician presence in Sparta, certainly nothing comparable to their residence in places such as Attika, Euboia, and Crete during the same period.[69] It must be remembered that the masks were of *local* manufacture, and thus not brought by transient Phoenicians in honor of a cult they recognized as similar to one of their own. In this the cult of Spartan Ortheia differs significantly from larger, more cosmopolitan sanctuaries which show a high proportion of foreign—and especially Near Eastern—dedications, such as at contemporary Pherai, Perakhora, Olympia, and Samos.[70] It must also be recalled that the cult was in existence for some 150 years before the earliest attestation of masks at the site, and that the earliest items pertaining to the site were local pottery. The masks were thus a later element in the cult, not an original aspect. Finally, it is important to do the math. The masks were dedicated in the sanctuary for roughly 400 years, starting in the mid-seventh century and extending into the Hellenistic age. In some four centuries, the sanctuary produced approximately 600 masks, or 1.5 masks per annum. Such numbers pale beside the 100,000+ lead votives, or the several hundreds of ivories which R.M. Dawkins claimed to be "as far as number is concerned this excavation is probably superior to any other in Greece."[71] Thus, while it is true that the sanctuary of Ortheia produced the most important collection of ancient Near East-style masks in Greece, it cannot necessarily be stated that the masks were an exceptionally important aspect of the cult, being *relatively* few in number in regards to chronology and other votives. In the end, I do not believe that it is yet possible to suggest how the Phoenician masks came to be a typical dedication at the sanctuary, or to hypothesize as to how they were used. But it is clear that the cult itself was not founded by Phoenicians, and that Ortheia was in fact a Greek goddess, not Near Eastern.

Not that the later Greeks necessarily thought this. They seemed to prefer to think of this Spartan Artemis as some kind of northern barbarian, probably Skythian. So much comes across in the Roman-era tales told about the origins of Artemis Ortheia. According to Pausanias (3.16.7), "The place named Limnaion is sacred to Artemis Ortheia. They say that the xoanon there is the one that Orestes and Iphigenia once stole out of the Tauric land, and the Lakedaimonians say that that it was brought to their land because Orestes was king there too." Even before this, as early as the first century BCE, C. Julius Hyginus in his mythological compendium *Fabulae* reports that Orestes (§261):

> Upon obtaining an oracle because he had lost his sister, [Orestes] sought Colchis with his friend Pylades and, following the killing of Thoas, absconded with the image hidden in a bundle of wood . . . and brought it to Aricia. But because the cult's cruelty subsequently displeased the Romans, even though slaves were sacrificed, Diana was transferred to the Spartans.[72]

Part of this tendency seems to derive from a desire to distance a blood-thirsty Artemis from Greek social norms, especially in the Roman era (see Chapter 6). Additionally, as Edith Hall has discussed in detail in her work *Adventures with Iphigenia in Tauris*, the extreme popularity of Euripides' drama started a trend in the ancient world that induced numerous Greek and Roman communities to tie their own cults of Artemis/Diana to the Tauric/Skythian narrative.[73] As such, much of Spartan (et al.) Ortheia's later Skythian origins had more to do with literary trending than any early Greek beliefs about her origins.

And certainly not all Greeks thought of their version of Ortheia as Skythian. In Messenê, Ortheia appears to have had ties to Thrace and the Amazons of Ephesos. The cult of Artemis Ortheia in Messenê can be dated back to the fourth century, when the Messenians were finally freed from Spartan domination. Enough of the goddess's cult image survives to allow a picture of how the Messenians envisaged this deity. According to excavator Petros Themelis, the marble statue dating to the late fourth century as well as the votive terracottas and bronzes from the temple area all depict the goddess as a huntress, wearing a short khiton with overfold and exposed left shoulder, a deer skin (*nebris*) with belt, high leather boots, and a polos diadem.[74] On the marble cult statue, the goddess held a long torch in one hand, while a hunting hound sat by her right foot. The short khiton, *nebris*, and hunting boots were all distinctive of Thracian apparel, and this image was similar in many ways to the iconography of Bendis, a Thracian goddess who was syncretized with Artemis in Athens in the fifth century (Plato, *Republic* 1.327a–328a; *IG* II[2] 1361).

Although all the dedications at both this temple and the later, second-century BCE temple indicate that the goddess worshipped there was Artemis Ortheia (see also Chapter 4), epigraphic evidence from the Roman period shows that the goddess was also called Oupesia, a version of the Oupis cult title seen above in her cult at Ephesos. This designation appears in inscriptions pertaining to the college of men who were responsible for maintaining the temple and cult, known as the *hieroi gerontes tas Oupêsias*, "the sacred old men of Oupesia" (Messene Inv. No. 1013).[75] Further epigraphic evidence refers to honors paid to Nikeratos and Straton, both listed as *epimeletai* ("supervisors") of Oupesia, a term used in Hellenistic and later times in *thiasoi* and *orgeones*: religious "clubs" dedicated to the worship of one or two specific deities.[76] As Themelis notes, these *hieroi gerontes* emphasized their ties/descent from the Dorian hero Kresphontes, who received Messenia by lot when the Heraklids and Dorians invaded the Peloponnese (Paus. 4.3.6). Although Themelis claims that such evidence affirms the ancient and Doric origins of the cult of Ortheia, it is more likely that such links to the Doric past served to reaffirm the Messenians' Doric roots and their ties to the land, especially after several centuries of enslavement at the hands of their equally Doric Spartan neighbors.

The epithet Oupis/Oupesia later appears in the work of the twelfth-century CE scholar John Tzetzes' *On Lykophron*. Here the Byzantine author writes that (§936), "Thus Diktynna is [the name] of Artemis in Crete, Oupis in Thrace, Orthosia amongst the Arkadians."[77] Oupis was clearly regarded as a manifestation of Artemis with strong ties to the Black Sea.

Whether or not Oupesia's old men were descended from Doric invaders, the evidence from the Peloponnese in general seems to suggest that the cult of Worthasia, eventually Artemis Ortheia, first emerged and evolved in Sparta, later moving out into the rest of the Greek world. The cult is indigenous, not Phoenician, Skythian, or Thracian, although the goddess clearly adopted aspects of these latter cultures over the course of her worship in Greece. Although the evidence from Sparta is relatively late concerning Ortheia's syncretism with Artemis, evidence to this effect exists already throughout the Greek world by the fifth century. Pindar could refer to Artemis Ortheia in his victory ode (*Olymp.* 3, l. 30) to Theron of Akragas in Sicily, while Herodotos recorded how the pillars set up by Darius at the Bosporos (4.87.2) "the Byzantines later brought into their city and used for the altar of Artemis Ortheia."

OVERVIEW

There is compelling evidence to suggest that elements of the goddess known to the Greeks as Artemis appeared as early as the Bronze Age. The goddess's name appears in the Linear B corpus; a goddess of nature strongly associated with children, particularly girls, is manifest in the Minoan and Theran iconography; while a goddess shown interacting with, even dominating, wild animals—the Potnia Therôn—emerges in the Minoan-Mycenaean *koine*. At least one cult site of the goddess—Kalapodi/Hyampolis—shows continuity from the Bronze Age into the Roman era. While only the Linear B evidence might be proffered as proof for the worship of Artemis so-called in the pre-Archaic Age, the evidence does indicate that aspects of this nature goddess were revered in the Aegean since the mid-second millennium BCE.

Other aspects of the various cults of Artemis developed out of foreign influence and local syncretisms. The panhellenic, even pan-Mediterranean, cult of Ephesian Artemis began as the cult of a local, Anatolian goddess who merged with Artemis in the Iron Age, but maintained aspects of Anatolian cult and iconography well into the Roman period. Conversely, Artemis Ortheia, another panhellenic goddess, was originally a local Spartan deity who appears to have syncretized with Artemis in the sixth century and to have been imbued in later centuries with foreign origins.

NOTES

1 On Artemis in the Linear B corpus, see especially Boëlle 2004: 127–135.
2 Rougemont 2005: 326 (my translation from the French).
3 Doumas 1992: 130–167.
4 On physical manifestations of age in the Theran frescoes, see Chapin 2002: 8–16; Davis 1986: *passim.*
5 This posture is still problematic analytically. Some, such as Rehak, suggest that the goddess may be seated, or swaying, or possibly even dancing. See the debate in Rehak 1997: 174–175.
6 Ibid.: 167.
7 Ibid.: 170–171.
8 Chapin 2004: 58–59.
9 Rehak 1997: 173–174; Kontorli-Papadpoulou 1996: 101–102.
10 *Palace of Minos* (*PM*) II, 767, #498.
11 *PM* II, 768, #499.
12 *CMS* V, Suppl. 1a, #177.
13 Rehak 2007: 222; Rehak 2004: 92.

14 The term is traditionally translated "Mistress of Animals," but the word *thêr* in Greek specifically refers to wild, huntable animals, rather than the more general word *zôion* which pertains to the entire animal kingdom.

15 Barclay 2001: 373.

16 Rehak 1997: 170.

17 Ibid.: 171.

18 Younger 1988: 179.

19 Barclay 2001: Pl. CIII a and CIV f.

20 Morris 1992: 91–92.

21 Hiller 1983: 93.

22 Ibid.

23 One final image that has been implicated in the identification of an early Aegean Artemis is the boar hunt fresco from Tiryns. This restored fresco shows numerous dogs attacking a boar, with a few spear hefts visible in the scene, and a pair of females in a nearby chariot. However, the relationship between the females and the scene, their lack of divine attributes of any kind, and their multiplicity argue against any identification with an Artemisian-type goddess. For more on this identification, see Muskett 2007: *passim*.

24 Vallois 1944: 8–14.

25 Gallet de Santerre 1975: *passim*.

26 Bruneau and Ducat 2005: 208.

27 Rolley 1983: 112.

28 On the matter of Bronze Age Aegean temples and shrines, see Dickinson 2006: 224; Van Leuven 1981: *passim*.

29 Bruneau and Ducat 2005: 208; Rolley 1983: 112–114.

30 Felsch 2007: 1–27.

31 Morgan 1999: 382; McInerney 1999: 156–157.

32 Felsch 2007: 554.

33 Rudimentary female terracotta figurine with up-raised arms, thus looking like the Greek letter *psi* (ψ).

34 Felsch 2007: 554.

35 McInerney 1999: 288–289.

36 Darmezin 1999: 117–118, 153. For more on Artemis and manumission, see Chapter 7.

37 De Polignac 1995: 25.

38 Ibid.: 26.

39 Voyatzis 1998: 139.

40 Forstenpointer et al. 2008: 33.

41 Morris 2008: 57; Morris 2001: 426.

42 Morris 2001: 425.

43 Roller 1999: 127, n. 36.

44 Larson 2007: 109.

45 Morris 2001: 425.

46 Roller 1999: 127.

47 Nielsen 2009: 455; Larson 2007: 110, with citations. See also Chapter 8.

48 Morris 2001: 431.

49 Ibid.

50 Bilde 2009: 313.
51 Cartledge 2002: 310.
52 Carter 1987: 374.
53 Falb 2009: 131.
54 *AO* 14.
55 Carter 1987: 375.
56 Darmezin 1999: 22.
57 Carter 1987: 374. On the various spellings over time, see *IG* 5¹ 252, *IG* 5¹ 252a, *IG* 5¹ 255, *IG*5¹ 303, *IG*5¹ 343, *IG* 5² 429, *IG* II² 1623, and Herodotos 4.87.2.
58 *AO* 296–297. See also Kennell 1995: 126.
59 Themelis 1994: 101.
60 Falb 2009: 134–135.
61 Ibid.: 135; Larson 2007: 106.
62 *AO* 203–248.
63 See *AO* Pl. CXVIII–CXX.
64 Carter 1987: 359.
65 *AO* 169–170.
66 *AO* 172–173.
67 Carter 1987: *passim*.
68 Ibid.: 375–382.
69 Stampolides 2003: *passim*; Coldstream 1982: *passim*.
70 Kilian-Dirlmeier 1985: *passim*. In all these instances, the Greek cult revolved around Hera, the queen of the Greek pantheon. The Phoenician equivalent deity was not Asherah, but Aštart (Greek Astarte). On the syncretisms between Greek and Phoenician queen deities, see Budin 2004: *passim*, especially 137–139.
71 *AO* 203.
72 Trans. Kennell 1995: 150.
73 Hall 2013: *passim*. See also Chapter 6.
74 Themelis 1994: 105.
75 Ibid.: 115 and n. 18.
76 Ibid.
77 On Worthasia in Arkadia, see *IG* 5² 429. On Artemis Orthosia in Koroneia, Boiotia, see Schachter 1981: 100. On Artemis Orthosia in Lebadeia, Boiotia, see ibid.: 101.

2

THE CHILDHOOD AND PERPETUAL VIRGINITY OF ARTEMIS

Artemis is one of the great Olympian deities. She is the daughter of Zeus and the Titaness Leto, "most gentle of the deities." Her one full sibling is Apollo. As the daughter of Zeus she has many, many half-siblings.

CHILDHOOD

There is some ambiguity concerning where Artemis was born, and the nature of her relationship to Apollo. According to the earliest literary testimonia, Artemis was born on the isle of Ortygia in the region of Ephesos in Asia Minor. Thus the *Homeric Hymn to Apollo* (III) relates (ll. 14–16):

> Hail, O blessed Leto, since you bore glorious children,
> King Apollo and arrow-pouring Artemis,
> Her on Ortygia, him on rocky Delos.

Artemis and Apollo are siblings but not necessarily always twins; Artemis was born on Ortygia, and afterwards Apollo was born on the island of Delos. Later texts, though, bring the siblings closer together, suggesting that they were twins, both born either on Ortygia or on Delos. Thus in his *Bibliothekê* Pseudo-Apollodoros recounts how (1.3.6):

> Leto, having been with Zeus, was driven all over the earth by Hera, until coming to Delos she bore first Artemis, by whom she was mid-wifed and bore Apollo. Artemis then practiced hunting and remained a virgin.

By contrast Strabo records that both children were actually born on Ortygia, once again as Leto fled the wrath of Hera (14.1.20):

> On the same coast, a bit above the sea, is also Ortygia, a magnificent grove with every kind of tree, and most especially cypress. The Kenkhirios River flows through it, where they say that Leto bathed after her travail. For they relate that it was there where were the childbirth and the nurse Ortygia and the holy place where the birth took place, and the near-by olive tree is where they say that the goddess first rested having finished giving birth. Above the

grove is Mount Solmissos, where they say the Kouretes stationed themselves and, with the din of their weapons, drove off Hera who was jealously spying, and so helped Leto to give birth in secret.

What is consistent, however, is that Artemis and Apollo are sister and brother, and the only children of Leto and Zeus. What is also consistent is that both siblings are eternal teenagers—both Artemis and Apollo remain perpetual adolescents, forever on the cusp of adulthood without ever quite crossing that border. For Apollo, this is ultimately more academic than meaningful: His youth is manifest primarily in his lack of a beard in the arts. He also never marries (as does Zeus with Hera, Poseidon with Amphitritê, Hades with Persephonê, and even Dionysos with Ariadne). However, he does have sex with both males and females, and he has children, and thus he might be compared to Hermes, Ares in those myths where Aphrodite is the wife of Hephaistos, and even Demeter, who bears Persephonê having "mingled in love" with Zeus, but who is not considered his wife or consort. Being a youth, then, does not have a marked influence on Apollo's persona—he is a sexually initiated absentee father.

By contrast, Artemis' eternal youth is meaningful. Unlike all other goddesses, she is portrayed as a child in the arts of ancient Greece. This comes across especially well in the Theomakhy scene of Homer's *Iliad*, when Artemis squared off against the more mature goddess Hera (Book 21: 489–496, 505–513):

> Hera then seized both of Artemis' hands by the wrist with her left hand,
> And with the right hand she took hold of the bows from her shoulders;
> With these she struck Artemis on her ears, smiling,
> While Artemis twisted all about, spilling her swift arrows.
> Crying the goddess fled, slipping away just like a pigeon
> From a hawk, darting into a hollow rock-cleft
> Where it is not fated for her to be caught,
> Just so Artemis fled crying, leaving her bows there
> . . .
> Then she came to the bronze-floored house of Zeus on Olympos,
> Crying the girl sat on her father's knees,
> Her fine immortal robe trembling, and
> Father Kronides held her and asked her sweetly:
> "Who now of the heavenly ones did these things to you, dear child?
> Pointlessly, as if you'd ever blatantly do something bad!"
> And the hallowing, well-crowned one answered him:
> "Your wife hit me, Dad, white-armed Hera.
> She always doles out strife and wrangling to the immortals!"

Artemis appears even younger in her third-century BCE description in Kallimakhos' *Hymn to Artemis* when she asks the Cyclopes to make her weapons (ll. 72–78):

> Girl, even earlier, when you were three years old still,
> When Leto came bearing you with her in her arms,
> As Hephaistos requested so that he might give lovely gifts,
> Brontes sat you down on his sturdy knees,

And you seized some of the wooly hair of his great chest,
Tearing it out violently—And to this day
That mid-section of his chest remains bald.

Such portrayals are significant, for, as Lesley Beaumont has noted, while the Greek *gods* might be portrayed both literarily and iconographically as children, Greek *goddesses* almost never are.[1] Both Athena and Aphrodite are born fully grown with their powers fully manifest—Athena being born in armor, Aphrodite very distinctly nude. With the possible exception of babies being devoured by their father Kronos, Hestia, Hera, and Demeter never appear as anything but mature women. Hekatê, one of the few virgin goddesses in the literature, is also a kourotrophos and a member of the older generation of deities, according to Hesiod's *Theogony*. Only Persephonê is briefly presented as a young girl in the *Homeric Hymn to Demeter*, no doubt for the literary purpose of contrasting her pre-married, virginal state with her status as fully fledged Queen of the Dead and Wife of Hades.

But then there is Artemis, who playfully crawls upon the lap of a Cyclops and rips out a handful of his chest hair, who gets her ears boxed by Hera and goes sobbing off to daddy. Her childishness is not relegated exclusively to literary accounts: Unlike the other Greek goddesses, Artemis might also appear in the visual arts as a child. This is certainly rare. One of the earliest known such portrayal is on an early fourth-century red-figure amphora of Athenian or Apulian manufacture. Here the goddess Leto appears holding her two infant children in her two arms while running from a giant snake, clearly Pytho.

A similar late fifth–early fourth century inscribed stele now in the Michael C. Carlos Museum at Emory University (Figure 2.1) shows the mother Leto running

Figure 2.1 Relief with Leto escaping from Pytho with her twins, Artemis and Apollo, fourth–third century BCE, 2003.23.6. Image © Michael C. Carlos Museum, Emory University. Photo by Bruce M. White, 2011.

from Pytho while holding one toddler-aged child in her arms, another (presumably Apollo Python-slayer) running just behind her. In the three-dimensional arts, Pliny in his *Natural History* (34.19) documents a bronze statue by the fourth-century BCE painter and sculptor Euphranor which depicts Leto carrying Artemis and Apollo as infants in her arms. In the passage cited above from Strabo (14.1.20) about the birth of Artemis and Apollo on Ortygia, the geographer continued his narrative with the description of a sculpture by the late fourth-century artist Skopas, who made a statue depicting Leto and the personification of Ortygia itself as a nurse holding in her arms the twins Artemis and Apollo as small children. Such images may be reflected in a Rhodian-style terracotta votive from a sanctuary on the acropolis of Gortyn in Crete which depicts an adult female with two children. Standing to her right is a small, nude male child holding the woman's right hand. On her left shoulder the woman carries a dressed child, presumably female by her clothing. The similarity of the iconography with those described plus the sacral nature of the find spot strongly suggest that this is a portrayal of Leto, Apollo, and Artemis, the latter two as children.[2]

Once again, it is important to note that there is nothing especially different or strange about the appearance of Apollo as an infant. He is clearly portrayed as an infant in his *Homeric Hymn* before boldly breaking his golden swaddling band. Hermes spends his entire *Homeric Hymn* as a new-born baby, cattle-rustling, inventing the lyre, and blatantly lying to his father within his first 24 hours of life. Zeus' infancy is a significant aspect of his cult especially in Crete, where he was hidden from his cannibalistic father, guarded by the Korybantes, and nursed by the goat Amaltheia. This aspect of his persona and cult appears to date back well into the Bronze Age. The semi-divine Herakles presages his later exploits by strangling serpents in his cradle and later, perhaps inauspiciously, bludgeoning his music teacher to death. Even Dionysos gets younger over time, losing his Archaic Age beard in the red-figure pottery tradition and appearing as a tiny baby in Hermes' arms in a famous sculpture by Praxiteles in the fourth century.

But apart from Artemis, goddesses are not portrayed as children in the ancient Greek art. Beaumont has suggested, certainly correctly, that this is because to render a goddess as a child would have the inevitable result of disempowering her in the Greek ideology. Especially in the Athenian world view of the fifth century BCE, for which we are the best informed, females were deemed considerably inferior to males in terms of physicality, intellect, and even morality. Likewise adults were superior to children in these qualities. As Aristotle noted in the fourth century in his *Politics* (1.1260a):

> For it is a different manner by which the free rules over the slave, the male over the female, and the man over the child. In all of these a portion of the soul is present, but present differently. For the slave is wholly without the deliberative faculty; the female has it, but it is without authority; and the child has it, but it is not yet fully developed.

To be a child, then, is to be weak. To be female is to be weak. To be a female child is to be weakest of all. Such a state was thus antithetical to the supremacy associated with divinity in ancient Greece. Apparently it was possible for the Greeks to conceive of their deities as having a single factor of weakness, and thus it was not difficult to imagine a male god as an infant. If anything, showing the gods performing their "natural" functions even as babies enhanced their power, and thus Hermes, for example, thieving as a neonate. Goddesses were by definition already dealing with a weakness category; to add another would functionally be an affront to, even a contradiction of, their divinity. Thus, tactfully to avoid the awkward nature of their innate imperfection, goddesses were never rendered doubly weak: female *and* child.

The one goddess who could break this unspoken rule was Artemis. Apparently her close ties with youth in general, and her own perpetual adolescence allowed for a rendering of the goddess in childhood guise that did not diminish her glory. Artemis was the consummately powerful girl: portraying her as such was not a threat to her divinity, or to the world view of the Greeks. Nevertheless, as Beaumont noted, portrayals of Artemis as a small child—Kallimakhos, Euphranor —mainly begin to appear in the fourth century, when women see a boost in status with the disintegration of the polis-based society and the rise of the Hellenistic kingdoms, and when there is a new appreciation of small children perceptible in the arts. In short, it is only when the categories of female and child improve that the girl goddess might be more comfortably portrayed as a girl. The other goddesses, Athena, Aphrodite, Hera, etc., maintain their robust maturity.[3]

VIRGINITY

One of the most important aspects of Artemis' persona was her perpetual virginity. Her lack of sexual initiation was atypical in ancient Greek ideology, where the choice to remain celibate was rarely offered (and rarely taken) amongst mortals, and exceptionally rare amongst the deities. Certainly no male deities are currently on the books as foregoing sex. According to the *Homeric Hymn to Aphrodite* V, only three deities were immune to the powers of the Kyprian (7–33):

> Three minds she cannot persuade nor deceive:
> The daughter of Aegis-bearing Zeus, Owl-Eyed Athena,
> For the works of golden Aphrodite do not please her,
> But rather wars and the deeds of Ares do,
> And combat and battle and preparing shining works,
> She was first to teach crafts to earthly men,
> To make chariots and decorous bronze war wagons,
> And to delicate maidens in their halls she
> Taught shining works, putting them into the minds of each.
> Nor ever hallowing Artemis of the golden spindle
> Can laughter-loving Aphrodite tame in love.
> For truly the bow delights her and slaying beasts in the mountains,
> And lyres and choruses and piercing cries
> And shadowy groves and cities of just men.
> Nor do the works of Aphrodite please the reverend maiden
> Hestia, whom crooked-minded Kronos bore first
> And last by the will of Aegis-Bearing Zeus.
> Lady, whom Poseidon and Apollo courted,
> But she was not interested and firmly declined.

She swore a great oath which is indeed fulfilled—
Having grasped the head of Aegis-Bearing father Zeus—
To be a virgin for all days, goddess of goddesses.
To her Father Zeus gave a fair gift in the place of a wedding,
And in the middle of the house she sits and received the best things.
In all temples of the deities she has honor
And amongst all mortals she is foremost of the gods.
Of these [Aphrodite] cannot persuade the mind, nor deceive.

A fourth goddess is Hekatê, who is also presented as an ongoing virgin in the Greek mythological corpus. The three goddesses mentioned in the *Hymn* each preserve their virginity for important reasons pertaining to their roles in Greek ideology. On one level, Athena, as the protector of the citadel, maintains her virginity as a symbolic reference to the inviolability of the *polis*: Just as she is not penetrated, neither are the city walls.[4] Perhaps more significantly, Athena's character is functionally androgynous; that is to say, while her sex is female, her gender is strongly masculine. Although she does partake of the feminine task of weaving especially, she is a goddess of warfare and strategy, and protector of the citadel. In the mundane lives of the Greek mortals, such activities were properly in the realm of men. Athena, then, had a strong masculine overlay upon her female sex, such that it was not conceivable for her to submit to a male sexually, or to be distracted with pregnancy and maternity. Furthermore, as she herself states to the audience in Aeschylus' *Eumenides* (ll. 735–738), "I approve the male in all things—except marriage—with all my heart." Athena is a guide and comrade to the male, his companion in the field and, one might say, at the drawing board. But she cannot fulfill such a function *and* be liable to eroticism: She does not submit to males, sexually or otherwise, because she is one of them, and their superior at that, being a goddess.

Hestia must remain a virgin because of her embodiment of stability. Her role as virgin tender of the fire is important for understanding ancient Greek conceptions of the family. The Greeks were patriarchal and patrilocal, meaning men wielded greater control in politics, law, and economics, and that women left their natal families upon marriage to join their husbands' families. There was always a certain distrust of wives, strangers in the paternal household who could still have loyalties to their own families, or who could form greater bonds with their children than with a husband and his clan. Furthermore, there was a general anxiety present in same-sex familial relationships. Sons inevitably enforce the notion of the father's mortality, and sons or grandsons often cause a (grand)father's death in literature, like Oidipous and his father Laius. Mothers and daughters might form close bonds, but those bonds are inevitably severed when the daughter leaves her family to join a husband's household, as with Demeter and Persephonê. Thus, the closest familial bonds are between mother and son, and father and daughter. However, as with the mother–daughter bond, the father–daughter bond is constrained by the daughter's need to leave home upon marriage. In human life, then, a father's closest familial ally is temporary. The lives of the gods, however, were not so constrained, and in Hestia existed the ideal paternal ally: the daughter who did not marry but who clung to the paternal hearth, ultimately loyal to the paternal line. Just as the hearth is the solid center of the household, the virgin daughter, on the divine plane, is the solid center of the family. Hestia, being both, is more than just a hearth goddess for the Greeks: She is the personification of stability.[5]

Artemis is forever a virgin because she, like her brother, never grows up. She is the perpetually nubile maiden, always just on the verge of fertile maturity, but never passing the threshold into domestic maternity. She is not asexual, like Athena or Hestia, but eternally on the cutting edge of sexuality without going over. As Helen King once put it:

> It is logically difficult to make the *parthenos* wholly asexual, because every *parthenos* is a potential *gynê*. Similarly, every *gynê* was once a *parthenos* . . . Artemis is the exception to the rule that all *parthenoi* are potential *gynaikes*; the true *parthenos*, she throws into greater relief the nature of her opposite pole, the true *gynê*, yet it is nevertheless the eternal *parthenos* who presides over the creation of new *gynaikes*.[6]

It has been suggested that Artemis (and Athena) are actually homosexual, and that references to their sexuality are passed over in the literature because of the dearth of references to lesbian eroticism in the male-dominated sources of ancient Greece and Rome. This is certainly not the case for Athena, but at least in the Roman period Ovid made some references to potentials for erotic encounters between Artemis' nymphs and a Jupiter *disguised* as Artemis (*Metamorphoses* 2.420–425). Perhaps closer to the Greek reality, as a perpetual adolescent, Artemis remained in that phase of life when homosocial and homoerotic behaviors were considered normal for both males and females. Considering the above-mentioned lack of reference to lesbianism in Greek literature, it is at least possible to suggest that Artemis *may* have been understood to experience such feelings with her female hunting mates.

Artemis' virginity also established her position in the divine hierarchy. One might argue that Artemis could not engage in (heterosexual) intercourse because, as the goddess of the wilds and wild animals, she herself could not be tamed (*damazô*) by sex, as other females in the Greek literature, and especially brides, were said to be. However, the Greek nymphs routinely engaged in what might be called sexually promiscuous behavior, either with gods or mortal males, bearing and raising children, with no sense of their being bound to any overpowering individuals, or with any reference to their loss of freedom or autonomy. Put simply, they were free to have sex with whomever they pleased.[7] Such freedom was, perhaps paradoxically (unless one considers the pointedly patriarchal nature of the Greek pantheon), unavailable to the Olympian goddesses. Hera and Aphrodite must be married, and Aphrodite's extra-marital affairs are considered to be adultery and result in her shame and punishment (with Ares in *Odyssey* book VIII, with the Trojan prince Ankhises in *Homeric Hymn* V). Demeter, a former mate of Zeus and with him parent to Persephonê, can in fact be raped, as she is by Poseidon in the regional mythology of Arkadia, where the god raped the goddess in equine form, siring the nature goddess Despoina (Paus. 8.42.1). Other goddesses might be *threatened* with rape, as was Hera by Ixion (Apollodoros E20) and Leto by Tityos (*Od.* 11.576 sqq.), but these attempts end in disaster for their mortal assailants. For Hera and Leto and Demeter, then, there are no additional tales of sexual exploits and maternities of goddesses after they have mixed in love with one of the Olympian gods, especially Zeus (excluding the atypical equine rape just mentioned). Unlike the nymphs, Olympian goddesses have only two options before them: to be tamed by sex and be bound, to one extent or another, to a male mate, or to eschew sexuality altogether and remain free (by which I mean still under the authority of Zeus, but not having to sleep with him). Artemis, the goddess of the wilds, was still constrained by the Olympian code of female sexuality. She chose the path of virginity.

The goddess's self-dedication to virginity is recorded as early as the sixth century BCE in a fragment of lyric poetry ascribed to the Lesbian poet Sappho (fr. 44a, ll. 4–11):

> Artemis swore a great oath of the deities, "By your head indeed I shall be a virgin untamed, hunting in the peaks of sheep-rearing mountains. Come and nod to this for me, please." So she spoke, and the father of the blessed gods nodded.

> "Maiden, deer-shooting, wild," deities and humans call her, a great name. Limb-loosening Eros never approaches her.

Such a sentiment was echoed in the third-century BCE *Hymn to Artemis* composed by Kallimakhos, who described how the goddess, still functionally a toddler, asked her father to grant her everlasting maidenhood (Kall. 3.5).

Perhaps one of the most intriguing references to Artemis' virginity appears in her cult at Kondylea near Kaphyai in Arkadia. Here, according to Pausanias (8.23.6–7):

> Kaphyai is about one stade away from the region of Kondylea; there is a grove and temple there of Artemis, originally called "Kondyleatis." They say the goddess got a new name for this reason: Children were playing around the sanctuary—they don't remember how many—and they came upon a cord, and tying this cord around the statue's throat they said that Artemis was strangled. The Kaphyans having discovered what was done by the children stoned them. And then a plague fell upon the women, such that their fetuses died in utero and were expelled. The Pythia ordered them to honor the children and to offer sacrifices to them annually, for they killed them unjustly. The Kaphyans did these things and similar according to the oracle, both then and now, and amongst the Kondyleans the goddess—for they say this was also commanded by the oracle—she is called "Strangled" since then.

The apparently weird notion that the goddess is strangled was originally ascribed to a misunderstanding of an earlier ritual, whereby images of females—specifically vegetation deities—were hung from trees (*apankhomenê* has the meaning of "hanged" as well as "strangled").[8] However, it is now interpreted as a reference to the goddess's virginity. Specifically, Helen King has argued that the death offered by strangulation/hanging is bloodless, in contrast to acts of bodily penetration that result in bleeding, be this the bloody sacrifice of an animal or the defloration of a virgin on her wedding night (or, often in the mythology, rape). For a female to hang herself is to avoid penetration, and thus suicide by hanging is the "standard" means (or threat) of suicide for virgins attempting to avoid unwanted intercourse (Aesch. *Suppl.* 465 and 788; Lactantius *Theb.* 4.225 on the Karyatids; less sincerely, Eur. *Hippolytos* 776–785). "Strangulation can therefore be culturally opposed to unwanted sex."[9] As the "Strangled One," Artemis thus reaffirms her unpenetrated, virginal nature.

An additional element might also be brought into play in this regard. The ancient Greeks recognized a parallelism between the vagina and the throat, both culminating in a mouth (cervix) and lips (labia).[10] It was believed that upon defloration, a woman's neck expanded, as her upper neck mirrored the opening experienced by her lower "neck." Concomitantly, the newly deflowered girl's voice deepened and became darker, in contrast to virgins' voices which remained high and "pure" (*hagnai*) (Aesch, *Agam.* 244). Strangulation is, of course, the forceful closing off of the throat. By being "strangled" Artemis emphasizes the biological reality of her perpetual virginity—just as her upper throat is bound and closed off, so too is her lower "throat," her vagina. Being strangled then not only provides a symbolic reference to her resistance to intercourse, it is also a biological reference to her unpenetrated vagina.

Just as Artemis remained a virgin so too did she expect the maidens who hunted with her in myth or served her in real life to remain chaste as well. Penalties for non-compliance could be severe. Mythically the most famous example of a lapsed virgin is Kallisto. The most popular version of this myth is that related by Ovid in his *Metamorphoses* (2.420–425), but the tale was popular in Greece at least since the late Archaic Age—Kallisto appears in Pseudo-Hesiod's *Catalogue of Women* and a fragment from a lost tragedy of Aeschylus called *Kallisto*.[11] In this myth, the maiden Kallisto was either raped by Zeus or, in later versions at least, seduced by the King of Men and Gods when he was disguised as Artemis. Upon discovering that her hunting partner was pregnant, Artemis turned her into a bear, that most maternal of creatures in ancient Greek ideology.

Somewhat more "historically" by Greek standards is the tale of Komaitho of Patrai in Akhaia, although this tale recounted by Pausanias (7.19.2) is more likely a foundation myth for the cult rituals of Artemis Triklaria than history per se. According to this story an exceptionally beautiful virgin named Komaitho was made priestess of Artemis Triklaria. She caught the eye of Melanippos, who was the best looking youth in Patrai at the time. They fell madly in love, gave in to their desires, and had sex in Artemis' sanctuary. In this they were doubly at fault. First, Komaitho broke her period of chastity during her term as priestess (as Pausanias noted, the girls served in this capacity until it was time for them "to be given to a man." Perpetual virginity was not at issue, merely a temporary state already associated with girls of that age). Second, the couple had sex in a sanctuary, a serious *miasma* (religious pollution) by Greek standards.[12] In retaliation, Artemis sent the worst plague that the region had ever experienced, causing the death of crops and vicious diseases for the human population. Consulting Delphi, the people were told that they must not only sacrifice Komaitho and Melanippos, but also must continue to sacrifice one beautiful boy and girl every year to appease the wrath of the goddess. The river by which they were sacrificed near the sanctuary came to be called "Implacable."

Such plagues, discussed in greater detail in Chapter 6, are not exclusive to Artemis. The earliest description of a plague was that sent by Apollo at the beginning of the *Iliad* (1.1–15). The plague that afflicted the residents of Thebes during the reign of Oidipous for Oidipous' *miasma* of patricide as recounted by Sophokles was sent by no specific deity as expressed. Nevertheless, the "sin" of sexuality is more closely associated with Artemis than other deities, and plague was more in her (and her brother Apollo's) repertoire than was necessarily the case with other deities. As such, the dynamic between lost chastity and plague is typical of the virgin goddess.

Virginity as a liminal state

It is important to remember, though, that mortal Greek girls did not remain virgins; they had to grow up, marry, and hopefully have children, just as boys had to grow up, marry, and protect their families and cities. Artemis could remain in the liminal state of nubile virgin only because she was a goddess. An important function of the goddess especially in literature, then, was to help girls on their way out of the virginal state. The word "help" here is perhaps a bit of a misnomer, however. The most frequent leitmotif we have in this respect is the motif of the virgin girl dancing in the chorus of Artemis, who is then abducted and raped, forcibly initiated into the world of adult sexuality.

Perhaps the most shocking potential victim of such an attack was Artemis herself. According to Pausanias (6.22.9) in ancient Elis the river (god) Alpheios fell in love with Artemis. Knowing full well that she would never marry him, he decided to try to rape her. One night the goddess was celebrating a festival with a group of nymphs at Letrinoi, and Alpheios arrived to join in their festivities. Suspecting something, Artemis covered both her own face and those of the nymphs with mud, such that the river god could not tell who was who. Rather than going through the effort of seeking out the goddess, he left with his aims unfulfilled. The tale probably served as a foundation myth for later rituals associated with the goddess (including possible mineral mud facials for the adolescent girls of Elis).

As ever, Artemis gets to hold on to her virginity in a way that is not feasible for other girls. More typically, nymphs and mortal girls playing/dancing with/for Artemis succumb to rape or seduction. Already mentioned was Kallisto, who was a hunting companion of Artemis until Zeus seduced her. In Homer's *Iliad* (16.181 ff.), the maiden Polymelê caught the eye of Hermes when she was dancing "in the choir for clamorous Artemis of the golden distaff." Hermes later snuck into her bedroom and had sex with the girl, fathering the hero Eudoros. Fortunately, her father was very understanding, and she later married a nobleman names Ekhekles. In his *Life of Theseus* (31.2), Plutarch records how Theseus together with Peirithoos went to Sparta and attacked a group of girls dancing at the sanctuary of Artemis Ortheia. They seized Helen of Sparta and fled to Tegea in Arkadia, casting lots to see which one would get to marry her. Theseus won, but recognized that Helen was still too young for marriage and left her with his mother. Before he could consummate the marriage, the girl was rescued by her brothers who brought war to Athens.

More historically (a bit), Pausanias records the story of the sanctuary of Artemis Limnatis on the border between Lakonia and Messenê (4.4.2):

> There is on the border of Messenia a sanctuary of Artemis Limnatis—only the Dorians share it, both the Messenians and the Lakedaimonians. Now the Lakedaimonians say that their maidens were once heading out to a festival and men of the Messenians raped them, and that they

even killed their king when he tried to stop them—Telekles son of Arkhelaos son of Agesilaos son of Doryssos son of Labotas son of Ekhestratos son of Agis—and what's more they say that the maidens who were raped killed themselves for shame.

This is not the only case of Messenians violating Lakonian girls. Once again according to Pausanias (4.16.9), King Aristomenes of Messenê once invaded Sparta and ambushed a group of girls who were dancing for Artemis at Karyai, several of whom were from noble, affluent families. They were technically only supposed to be held for ransom, but several of the soldiers (possibly drunk) began to rape the girls. To his credit, King Aristomenes punished the rapists with death, and returned the girls to their families (for large ransoms).

Even the goddess Persephonê was out playing with Artemis, Athena, and the various nymphs when she was forcibly seized by her future husband Hades. A touch more comically, in her lying tale to Ankhises, Aphrodite claimed that she was but an innocent Phrygian maiden (*Homeric Hymn to Aphrodite* V, 116–126):

> "But now Argeiphontes of the golden wand seized me
> From the chorus of hallowing Artemis of the golden spindle.
> Many nymphs and much courted maidens,
> We were playing, and around us a huge crowd stood about.
> Then gold-wanded Argeiphontes seized me,
> He led me over many an untouched and unapportioned land, through which beasts,
> Flesh-eaters! roam in shady glens.
> I was thinking that I'd never touch the life-growing earth with my feet.
> And he told me that I should be called the wife of Ankhises,
> To bear for you glorious children."

The chorus of Artemis, then, was a paradoxical place. In theory, it was where girls should have been the most protected and secure, being surrounded by age-mates. But it was ultimately not possible for girls to remain girls: They had to grow up, and it was in Artemis' purview to assist them in this process: it was she who functionally handed them over to adulthood.

Hippolytos

Artemis' role as she who helps children make the transition to adulthood comes across most clearly when that transition fails, most notably in the case of Hippolytos. The popular version of this myth as preserved in Euripides' tragedy *Hippolytos* is a variation on the "Potiphar's Wife" folkloric motif, whereby an older married woman attempts to seduce a younger man in her household, is rejected and caught, and blames the targeted youth of having attempted to seduce or rape her. Thus in Euripides' tragedy the eponymous hero's stepmother Phaidra (who, in this instance, is not necessarily older than her stepson, although as a stepmother is *generationally* older) is forced to fall in love with her stepson through the machinations of Aphrodite. Hippolytos, who is dedicated to Artemis and virginity to such an extent that in modern times we would diagnose him with clinical frigidity, is appalled by his stepmother's attractions and has a conniption fit onstage. Phaidra in turn commits suicide by hanging, having accused Hippolytos of ravishing her, and thus brings her husband Theseus' curses down upon Hippolytos who dies having been trampled by his horses who were themselves frightened mad by a giant bull sent from the sea by Poseidon. One simply has to wonder how well Theseus knew his son, seeing as he could believe that Mr. Anti-Sex himself could rape anyone.

There is a not wholly irrational desire to hold Artemis at least partially responsible for Hippolytos' fate. This is not in that she orchestrated his demise, but because his "sin" was his extreme devotion to her and virginity to the complete exclusion of any reverence for Aphrodite and the pleasures of sex. Furthermore, in spite of this devotion, Artemis did nothing to save her acolyte. Euripides himself appears to need to explain this fact, arguing in the character of his Artemis that the deities do not cross each other's intentions (l. 1330), but merely seek revenge for slights against each other's "pet" mortals (l. 1420). Such a rationale is perhaps easy to accept uncritically when there is a general predisposition in modern times to view the Greek deities as immoral and irrational.

However, such a reaction does not take into account the significance of Hippolytos' "crime" or the long-term effects of his excessive devotion to the hunting goddess. The problem was perhaps best framed by Robert Segal in his analysis of what at first appears to be the anti-hero most antithetical to Hippolytos: Adonis. Consider his argument:

> The myth . . . is a political myth: it dramatizes the prerequisites for membership in the polis. But it does so negatively, by presenting the life of one least equipped for the responsibility entailed by citizenship. One learns what to do by seeing a model of what not to do. Adonis is ill suited for life in the polis because he is ill suited for its cornerstone, the family. His life involves the severest violations of family life: incest, murder, license, possessiveness, celibacy, and childlessness.

> The myth serves as a warning to those who identify themselves with the puer archetype [the boy who does not grow up, like Peter Pan]. To live as a puer, the way Adonis does, is to live as a psychological infant and, ultimately, as a fetus. The life of a puer in myth invariably ends in premature death.[13]

This analysis could just as easily apply to Hippolytos. Like the hero Adonis who is content to be the plaything of Aphrodite and Persephonê, spending his life hunting in the wilds rather than working in the fields, those both of a farm and of a wife's womb, Hippolytos too is an avid hunter who remains in the wilds at an aristocrat's pastime. He shuns women, marriage, and sex, and thus reproduction, the maintenance of the household and the polis. Put simply, Hippolytos is not merely frigid; he is an irresponsible citizen.

It is right for children to cling to Artemis. But Artemis herself is a goddess of transitions, and thus to refuse to make the transition, to try to cling to her indefinitely, is not only an egregious case of excess (already anathema to the Greeks), but also a denial of the goddess's persona and function. One might argue that not only did Hippolytos malign Aphrodite, but he also ultimately refused Artemis herself. It is in this light that one must see the death of Hippolytos and understand Artemis' apparent lack of sympathy.

In the end, Hippolytos was made an object lesson, as a cult was established for him in Troizen (the location of Euripides' play) where girls went to offer a lock of hair as they prepared themselves for marriage. Thus proclaimed Euripides' goddess (ll. 1424–1429):

> "For you, o suffering one, in recompense for these evils
> Great honors in the city of Troizen
> I shall give; for unwed girls before their weddings
> Will cut their hair for you, who for a long age
> Will cull the great sorrow of their tears.
> Always will you be recalled in the music-making of maidens."

This practice, which occurred at a sanctuary dedicated to Hippolytos in the city of Troizen, was recorded as late as the second century CE by Pausanias (2.32.1):

> There is a most notable temenos dedicated to Hippolytos son of Theseus, with a temple in it and an ancient statue. They say that Diomedes made these and additionally that he was the first to sacrifice to Hippolytos. Amongst the Troizenians is a priest of Hippolytos who serves for his entire life, and they offer sacrifices annually. And this other thing they do: Every maiden cuts a tress for him before marriage, and bringing it to the temple dedicates it.

It is often the case that ritual serves to correct what went wrong in myth. The Athenian Arrephoroi delivered an unopened package from the Acropolis to compensate for the daughters of Kekrops who opened a box entrusted to them by Athena which they were ordered never to open. Little girls at Brauron play the bear for Artemis (see Chapter 4) in recompense for a bear which was unjustly killed after scratching a little girl. Every year two maidens from Lokris must travel to Troy to serve in the temple of Athena because their ancestor Ajax once raped a girl in that very temple. Women throughout Greece rave all night like mainads because their ancestors denied the divinity of Dionysos, god of mainads.

Hippolytos is the same. He was the youth who refused to grow up. Like Peter Pan he lived in the wild word, a world of fantasy, surrounding himself with young men and a single female who was herself virginal and wild. He rejected the responsibilities of adulthood, including marriage and fatherhood. He was destroyed, and henceforth girls mourn him and learn from his negative example, passing by him to leave a token symbol of childhood on their way to reproductive adulthood. They did not allow young men anywhere near him, apparently.

OVERVIEW

Artemis' perpetual childhood and virginity stand like a fulcrum around which she will lead mortal girls who must eventually make the transition from girl to woman and mother. Artemis herself remains eternally at the threshold of sexual maturity without ever quite passing over. She is the only girl in the Greek pantheon, wielding power in spite of, or even because of, her eternal youthfulness. Part of this feminine youthfulness is her ongoing virginity. Unlike Athena and Hestia, who are adults in spite of their chastity, Artemis embodies a *potential* nubility that ultimately contributes to her wild, untamed nature and her role as a goddess of sylvan fertility.

[handwritten annotation: associated with woods, trees.]

NOTES

1 Beaumont 1998: *passim.*
2 Hadzisteliou Price 1978: 88 and Fig. 35.
3 Beaumont 1998: *passim.*
4 Hanson 1990: 326.
5 Vernant 1963: 20.
6 King 1983: 124–125.
7 Larson 2001: 64–71, 87–90.
8 Cole 2004: 206–207.
9 King 1983: 119.
10 See Hanson 1990: 328, esp. n. 96 for references in the medical corpora.
11 Cole 2004: 204, n. 34. With additional references.
12 Parker 1983: ch. 3.
13 Segal 1991: 64 and 74.

ARTEMIS OF THE WILDS

GODDESS OF WILD SPACES AND HUNTING

Divine huntress

Consistent with Artemis' role as a goddess of transitions, hunting is an activity that marks a midway point between animal and human. In structuralist terminology, it is literally where the "raw" meets the "cooked." At the one end of this raw–cooked spectrum are agriculturally grown and processed foods; for the ancient Greeks these were mainly grain for bread, grapes for wine, and olives for oil. Unlike horticulturally grown foods (fruits, vegetables, technically milk), these products require extensive preparation and labor to grow and additional labor to process into their edible and drinkable forms. As multi-step processes requiring carefully honed techniques and considerable delayed gratification, these comestibles represent a pinnacle of human civilization.

At the other end of the spectrum is hunting. At its core, hunting is the killing of wild animals for food; in this the human hunter is no different than a lion or a baboon or a wolf. However, unlike most animals, the human hunter uses tools to hunt—bow and arrows, spear, nets, traps, and even other animals, specifically dogs. Thus what separates man the hunter from the other hunting animals is his identity as "Man the Tool User."[1] A human hunter who does not use tools in many respects reverts back to bestial status, a reversion seen when Herakles needed to kill the Nemean Lion with his bare hands, because no weapon could harm the creature. That is to say, the lion could only be killed by another animal, not a human, even a hero.

If one were to apply the Olympian deities to this spectrum, at the "raw" end would be deities such as Poseidon or Zeus, who represent/embody/dominate the raw forces of nature—the sea, sky, and storm. At the "cooked" end are the deities Demeter and Dionysos, representing bread and wine respectively (and perhaps Athena for her olives). In the middle are Hermes, Hekatê, and Artemis. The first two are associated with domesticated flocks (Hesiod, *Theogony* 444–447), and thus represent the "agricultural" side of animal husbandry, where time, planning, tools, and technique are applied to acquiring food and other products (milk and dairy products, wool and textiles) from non-wild animals. For her part, Artemis is the huntress, the being who uses human tools and skills to kill wild animals in the wild.

Artemis as huntress is the dominant image we get of the goddess in the Greek literature, well before she became a goddess of childbirth (Chapter 5), a kourotrophos (Chapter 4), or a Skythian (Chapter 7). It is the image we see consistently from the works of the epic poets down through Greek antiquity. A minimal character at best in Hesiod, Artemis appears in Homer very specifically as the huntress. In the *Odyssey* we read how (6.102–108):

> Like arrow-pouring Artemis in the mountains,
> By tall Taygetos or Erymanthus,
> Rejoicing in boars and swift deer,
> And with her nymphs, daughters of Aegis-bearing Zeus,
> Wild, they play, delighting the mind of Leto,
> Artemis' head and brow above all others,
> And easily moves the illustrious one, but all are lovely.

Later in the Archaic Age her primary *Homeric Hymn* (27) revolves almost exclusively around this aspect of the goddess's persona:

> I sing of hallowing Artemis of the golden shaft,
> August maiden, deer-shooter, arrow-pouring,
> Sister of Apollo of the golden sword.
> She amongst shadowy mountains and airy peaks
> Rejoicing in the hunt draws her golden bow,
> Shooting painful arrows. The peaks of the high
> Mountains tremble, and the thick-shaded forest cries about
> With the dread clamor of wild beasts, and the earth shudders
> As well as the fishy sea. And she being strong of heart
> Puts all to flight, slaughtering the race of beasts.
> But whenever the arrow-shooter is sated with looking for prey,
> Content in her mind, having slackened the well-wrought bow
> She comes to the house of her dear brother
> Phoibos Apollo, in the rich land of Delphi,
> Where the Muses and Graces prepare a lovely chorus.
> There, having hung up the recurve bow and arrows,
> She leads at the head of the graceful dance
> Having a fair appearance, and they raise ambrosial voices
> Singing of fair-ankled Leto, how she bore children
> Preeminent amongst the immortals in counsel and deeds.
> Hail, child of Zeus and fair-haired Leto!
> But I shall recall yet even another song.

So too does she appear as the huntress in the works of the lyric poets. Alkman claimed:

> I am your servant, Artemis.
> You draw your long bow at night,
> Clothed in the skins of wild beats.[2]

While Anakreon insisted:

> I supplicate you, Elaphebolos,
> Shining-haired daughter of Zeus, mistress
> Of wild animals, Artemis.
> And now how upon the city
> Of brave-hearted men by whirling Lethaios
> You look rejoicing
> For the citizens (you see) are not
> Savage flocks.

Artemis is not a common character in the preserved works of the Athenian playwrights. Her most prominent dramatic role was in Euripides' *Hippolytos,* where emphasis was upon her status as pure, virgin huntress. When speaking of the goddess directly, the Nurse asks (145–150):

> Are you possessed, O Miss,
> Either by Pan or Hekatê,
> Or the reverend, roaming Kourybantes,
> Or the Mother of the Mountains?
> Or did you sin against Diktynna[3]
> Surrounded by wild beasts,
> Unholy, neglecting a libation, and she wears you away?
> For she roams through marsh
> And upon dry land and
> The watery, eddying sea-spray.

More emblematic of Artemis is "Phaidra's Song," where the play's protagonist imagines herself in the guise of the goddess (209–231):

> Ai, ai!
> How I would draw a drink of pure
> Waters from a dewy spring,
> And rest reclining in a grassy
> Meadow beneath poplar trees.
> . . .
> Send me to the mountain, I go to the forest
> Amongst pine trees, where beast-killing
> Dogs tread
> Chasing dappled deer.
> By the gods, I want to call out to the dogs
> And tossing aside my flowing, shining hair
> Cast a Thessalian javelin, holding the sharp-
> Pointed weapon in my hand.
> . . .
> Mistress Artemis of the salty marsh
> And training ground of horses,
> O how I would be on your fields
> Taming Enetean ponies!

In addition to the literary portrayals, Artemis also appeared more "practically" as the patroness of hunting. In his manual *On Hunting*, the polymath Xenophon pointedly declared both Artemis and Apollo as the inventors of the hunting arts, and advised his readers to invoke them when in the field:

> 1.1: It was the invention of the deities—of Apollo and Artemis—to hunt with dogs. And they gave it to Kheiron and so honored him for his extreme righteousness.

> 13.18: Not only are all the men who love to hunt good, but so too are the women to whom the goddess Artemis has given the art—Atalanta and Prokris and some other.

> 6.15: After this place the net-watcher on guard; he then takes the dogs and sets out to the game's retreat. Promising to split the game with Apollo and Artemis Agrotera, release one dog, whichever one is best at tracking.

Many apparently took Xenophon's advice, to judge from the thanksgiving dedications offered to the goddess as preserved in the *Greek Anthology*.

> 6.105 (Apollonides): A red mullet from the charcoal grill and
> Seaweed to you, Artemis
> Limnatis, I Menis the fisherman offer,
> And pure wine, mixed to the brim, and a morsel of bread,
> Dried, broken into it. This poor sacrifice
> In exchange for which grant me always nets full of prey.
> To you, blessed one, are given all fishing lines.

> 6.111 (Antipater): The deer who fed at Ladon and about the Erimathion waters
> And the ridge of beast-tending Pholoas,
> The child of Thearidas—Lykormas—
> Has struck down with the rhomboid butt-end of a spear
> And the skin and two horns from the peak of its brow
> Having removed them, I dedicated to the Maiden Agrotera.

> 6.268 (Mnasalkas): For you, Goddess Artemis, this statue Kleonymos set up,
> This one. And you protect this headland of many beasts
> Whenever in the mountains with shimmering leaves you tread,
> Lady, with your feet,
> Running fiercely after eager hounds.

> 6.326 (Leonidas of Alexandria) A Lyktian quiver and a recurve bow, to Artemis
> Nikis son of Lysimakhos, a Libyan, dedicated.
> For he has emptied the quiver ever full of arrows
> Into the flanks of roe and dappled deer.

Pertaining to more group-oriented activities, Artemis served as a patron of hunting associations, as is evident on a mid-second-century BCE decree from Haliartos in Boiotia (*IG* VII 2850):

In Athens in the archonship of Nikodemos and in Haliartos in the secretariat of Antagoros son of Antagoros of Otrynes, the priest of Artemis Kallistratê declared: Antagoros son of Antagoros the Otrynean, when appointed as treasurer of the association of hunters, rendered his accounts properly and justly, and while appointed also applied himself to the task of restoring the (club-) house properly and justly, making it more useful for the association of hunters. For all these things they praise Antagoros son of Antagoros, and it has seemed best to the association of hunters to crown him with a gold crown.

Even *baby* bunnies?

What is especially ironic about all this is that Artemis is also known for loving wild animals, especially the young. In his *Agamemnon*, Aeschylus says of her (140–143):

How very kindly, lovely she is
to the young and weak of devouring lions,
and she rejoices in the breast-loving young of all wild creatures.

And Xenophon notes in his hunting treatise that (5.14), "Sportsmen, however, leave the very young ones to the goddess. Yearlings go very fast in the first run, but then lag, being agile, but weak."

So, "Love 'em then kill 'em" seems to be the goddess's motto. One might likewise suggest that the nature goddess had an interest in sustainability. By leaving the young to mature and, hopefully, reproduce, there would be continued wildlife to hunt later on.

The iconographic corpus replicates what is seen in the textual. No version of Artemis in the *Lexicon Iconographicum Mythologiae Classicae* (*LIMC*) shows greater proliferation and variety than do the various types of hunting Artemis and the related Potnia Therôn motif (see Chapter 1). This latter motif already appears prominently in the Bronze Age and may be indicative of an early version of Artemis in the Mycenaean era. The motif reemerges in the seventh century. In central Greece—Boiotia and Corinthia—winged, unwinged, and "semi-winged" Potniai Therôn appear on the local pottery. One such example appears on a Boiotian amphora that depicts an *en face* female with wing-like arms standing in the midst of several animals of diverse species (see Figure 3.1). The wide spectrum of animals—birds for the air, lions for the earth, a fish for the sea—indicates a significant role throughout the animal realm, while the bovine head to the right of the Potnia suggests sacrificial ritual, and thus the divinity of the female in question.

Beginning in the sixth century Artemis as Potnia Therôn and as huntress appears in the vase painting of Attika. In her more violent role, Artemis is shown bow-hunting, most frequently hunting deer in her role as Elaphebolos ("Deer-Shooter"). So she appears on a mid-fifth-century white-ground lekythos from Locri attributed to the Karlsruhe Painter (see Figure 3.2).

This iconography became popular in sculpture in the Classical and Hellenistic eras, with perhaps the most famous version being the "Diane de Versailles," a

Figure 3.1 Boiotian pithos-amphora depicting a nature goddess, c. 680–670 BCE. Athens, National Archaeological Museum, A00220. Drawing by Paul C. Butler, used with kind permission.

Roman copy of a Greek original dated to c. 325 BCE and attributed to Leokhares, now in the Louvre Museum.

Complementing the Potnia Therôn motif where the goddess dominates animals, and the "Artemis as Huntress" motif where she kills them, is the motif of Artemis as caretaker of creatures (Figures 3.3 and 3.4). In such depictions, even where the goddess is shown with bow or quiver, the emphasis of the iconography is the

Figure 3.2 White-ground lekythos of Artemis hunting, attributed to the Karlsruhe Painter, from Locri, c. 460–450 BCE. Bibliothèque nationale de France, Department of Coins, Medals, and Antiquities, Paris, De Ridder 494. Image © Bibliothèque nationale de France.

Figure 3.3 White-ground lekythos of Artemis feeding a swan, attributed to the Pan Painter, c. 490 BCE. Saint Petersburg, The State Hermitage Museum, B.2363. Image © The State Hermitage Museum, Saint Petersburg.

Figure 3.4 Terracotta figurine of Artemis holding a fawn. Korkyran workshop, c. 480 BCE. Athens, National Archaeological Museum, 1120. Drawing by Paul C. Butler, used with kind permission.

goddess nurturing wild animals. Most famous in this respect is a white-ground lekythos dated the beginning of the fifth century, attributed to the Pan Painter and now in the Hermitage Museum (Figure 3.3). This delicate rendering shows the goddess in a full khiton with a quiver upon her back and a phialê (ritual cup) in her left hand. Rather than hunting, though, the goddess uses her right hand to stroke the chin of a large white swan or goose, possibly feeding it. Likewise, the terracotta votive from Korkyra (modern Corfu, Figure 3.4) shows the goddess with a bow in her left hand while cradling a fawn in her right arm. The threat of the huntress is always present, but so too is her love of the wild young.

Artemis as the goddess of wild animals is a persistent theme in the goddess's votives. Terracottas from three sites in Sicily and Italy are indicative in this respect. Already mentioned are the finds from Scala Graeca in Syracuse (see Introduction), where the votive deposit brought to light images of Artemis with bow and arrows, panthers and lions, petting (hunting-)dogs by her legs, and deer either held to her bosôm (the nurturing role) or grasped by tail or legs—the Potnia Therôn.[4] The Spartan colony of Taras on the mainland revealed Classical era terracottas depicting the goddess wearing lion skins or fawn skins, with dogs or fawns at her feet, holding bow and quiver, riding deer, or holding a goose upon her lap. Artemis' cult in the region is attested by a late sixth to early fifth-century inscription naming *Artamitos Hagrateras*—a dialectical form of Agrotera, "Wild One."[5] The Artemision at San Biagio dates back to the seventh century and has a votive deposit dating to the sixth. Here were found images of Artemis as a winged Potnia Therôn carrying water fowl by the neck, or mammals (deer? goats?) in her arms, or as an unwinged enthroned goddess holding water fowl in her lap.[6]

Similar data come from the Greek mainland, islands, and Anatolia, although certain details should be kept in mind. For one, not all Artemisian sanctuaries show a similar concern with the goddess's rapport with animals. All Greek deities show variety in their manifestations and cults from place to place, and Artemis is no exception. The main Artemisia where bestial votives appear are the sanctuary of Artemis Ortheia at Sparta, at Ephesos, in Arkadian Lousoi, in Kalydon, at Brauron in Attika, and on the islands of Delos and Thasos, with a lesser number appearing at Hyampolis/Kalapodi in Phokis and the northern site of Pherai.[7]

The data from the Spartan Ortheia sanctuary are fascinating for the light they cast on the emerging cult of Artemis at the site. As noted in Chapter 1, Artemis was probably not the original goddess worshipped there. Rather, a goddess called some permutation of Worthasia was the local goddess, and it appears that she only syncretized with Artemis in the late Archaic Age. It cannot be denied that the sanctuary of Ortheia brought to light more animal votives than any other Artemision. The reckoning given in Elinor Bevan's 1985 dissertation on *Representations of Animals in Sanctuaries of Artemis and Other Olympian Deities* reveals 3 bears, 120 birds, 3+ boars, over 30 bovines, about 50 lions (some mauling prey), numerous deer, 41 dogs, 6+ fish, 4 frogs, 7 tortoises, 15+ goats, 2 hares, well over 100 horses (not including close to 30 images of people riding horses, and 7+ depictions of horse-drawn chariots), 106 rams and sheep, 3 snakes, 6 scorpions, and a spider. These votives appeared in terracotta, bone, gold, bronze, iron, lead, ivory, faience, silver, on pieces of jewelry and on seals.

And the grand majority of them date to the period before the syncretism between Worthasia and Artemis technically took place.[8] As such, what we see at this Spartan sanctuary of "Artemis" is the strong correlation between animals and the goddess with whom Artemis would eventually merge.

The osteological remains from the altar of Artemis at Ephesos shed light on the kinds of animals offered to the goddess of the hunt. Here were found bones from chickens, pigs, bovines, deer, a single gazelle, dogs, sheep, horses, and the bones and horns of sacrificial goats—an impressively large range of animals by Greek standards. While part of this diversity probably derives from the cosmopolitan scope of the sanctuary, the nature of the goddess there worshipped also contributed to this skeletal zoo.

WILD SPACES

When not on Mt. Olympos, Artemis is in the wilds. As she tells her father Zeus in Kallimakhos' *Hymn to Artemis* (19–23):

> Give to me all the mountains, and grant some city,
> Whichever you wish, for it is seldom that Artemis goes down to a city;
> I shall inhabit the hills, and I shall visit the cities of men
> Only when women in sharp labor pangs, suffering,
> Call for aid.

The ancient Greeks certainly conceived of Artemis as inhabiting regions far from men (less so women). As noted by Susan Cole in her chapter "Landscapes of Artemis":

> Pausanias mentions or describes eighty-six of her sanctuaries, forty-nine of which were in the Peloponnese. Four fifths of the total eighty-six [approximately seventy] were located far from settled areas, and of the forty-nine Peloponnesian sites, at least twenty-nine lay outside a city, with eighteen situated on a road between two cites or at a boundary between territories.[9]

Referring once again to the Peloponnese, E.L. Brulotte reported on no fewer than 175 sanctuaries of Artemis, the majority of which were located in extra-urban environments, some in territories that not only did not belong to a city proper, but were in regions that could not even be claimed by a city.[10] This is not to say that Artemis was never worshipped in an urban setting: As noted in Chapter 7, Artemis could serve as a city goddess and have temples and sanctuaries in urban settings, too. But this was the exception, and even when going to town the goddess tended to have her sacred places reflect elements of her wilder nature, such as being located on rocky outcrops, or with prominent bodies of water present.

Water

Water was a significant aspect of Artemis' sanctuaries, and those sanctuaries that did not have them naturally had them added manually. Artemisia were typified by the presence of springs, wetlands, rivers, and wells.[11] Artemis' sanctuary at Brauron was located by a spring that formed a small reservoir before joining the Erasinos River to the west of the sanctuary. On the far side of the Gulf of Euboia was Artemis' sanctuary at Amarynthos, which was also founded at the site of a natural spring. To the south in Lakonia the goddess was worshipped in sanctuaries such as Dereion and Karyai (source of the famous "Caryatids"), typified by springs, wild trees, and an altar, but with no evidence of any temple. A rustic Artemision on Mount Megalovouni consisted of a grotto with a spring providing cold, fresh water. In Anatolia, the sanctuary of Artemis Pythia located equidistant between Miletos and Didyma was founded upon a rock face concealing spring water which the keepers of the sanctuary dug reservoirs to collect.

Some of Artemis' most famous sanctuaries were positioned near wetlands, most notably her grand temple in Ephesos. Nothing of the temple remains today save for a single column, atop which is a stork nest and beneath which are numerous turtles. Artemis probably would have liked it that way, actually. Artemis Saronia (of the Saronic Gulf) was worshipped next to the lagoon of Troizen, while on Cyprus Artemis Paralia ("by the sea") was revered in Kition in a sanctuary located by the marsh. At Aulis, site of the "sacrifice" of Iphigeneia, Artemis' sanctuary was located to the west of an ancient wetland whose waters were accessible via a fountain house constructed in the fifth century and located directly between the wetland and the temple.

Wetlands were often located near rivers, and so were the goddess's cult sites. The temple of Artemis Ortheia in Sparta is located in boggy terrain next to the Eurotas River, earning the goddess the additional epithet of *Limnatis* (*limen* = "marsh" or "wetland"). The waters of the goddess's sanctuary at Lousoi (literally "Baths") in Arkadia were especially famous for their perceived healing qualities. In Akhaia the Alphaios River was said to have been in love with Artemis (see Chapter 2), while the former Ameilikhios ("unassuageable") River was the site of human sacrifices to Artemis before Dionysos came and changed the rite from one of sacrifice to one of ritual bathing, causing the river to become Meilikhios (see Chapter 4).

Just as artificial means were used at Aulis and Asia Minor to access the waters prevalent at the goddess's sanctuaries, so too were wells dug to reach underground sources. Such was the case at ancient Hyampolis at the sanctuary of Artemis Elaphebolos. More amazing are the waters of the goddess's shrine at Mothonê, where, as Pausanias tells us (4.35.8), "And there is a sanctuary of Artemis there and water in a well, mixed with pitch, looking very much like unguents from Kyzikos. And the water furnishes every color and scent."

Epithets

Many of Artemis' epithets also emphasize her "wild" qualities. In the literature and the epigraphy the goddess appears as Agrotera (wild), Agrotis (wild), Agrota (wild), Philagrotis (loving the wild), Polyboia (many flocks), Maloessa (sheepy), Hippikê (horsey), Tauro (bullish), Tauropolos (bull-tamer), Polo (pony), Elaphia (deerish), Khelytis (tortoise), Batrakhis (froggy), Kedreatis (cedar), Karyatis (nut-tree), Kyparissia (cypress), Baïane (palm-tree), Daphnia (laurel), Phakêlitis (reed bundle), Lygodesma (bound with *agnus castus*), Thermaia (hot springs), Limnatis (wetland), Limnêtis (wetland), Limnaia (wetland), Limnênoskopos (with a view of wetlands), Heleia (marsh), Potamia (rivery), and Paralia (seaside). Complementing these are epithets that express the goddess's proclivity for the hunt, such as Toxia (of the bow), Toxodamos (subduing with a bow), Klytotoxos (bow-famous), Elaphebolos (deer-shooter), Lykeia (wolfy), Kaprophagos (boar-eater), and Taurophagos (bull-eater).[12] Over half of all of Artemis' epithets pertain to her relationship with the wilds.

Liminality

Artemis' proclivity for the wilds meant that her sanctuaries tended to be located in what might be termed "out-of-the-way" locations, in what François de Polignac referred to as periurban and extraurban areas. "Periurban" (or "suburban") sanctuaries are those located on the margins of the poleis or just beyond, and they served, amongst other things, to help demarcate the area of the polis itself. Extraurban sanctuaries were located well outside of the poleis, often from 5 to 15 kilometers outside of the city walls. Such sanctuaries of Artemis include her Attik temenê at Brauron and Mounykhia, her mountain sanctuary at Kombothekra in Elis, Bolimos in Lakonia, Arkadian Lousoi, and her temple at Hyampolis/Kalapodi in Phokis.[13] Artemis was not the only Greek deity to be worshipped so far from the city: Zeus, Hera, Apollo, and Poseidon had similarly extraurban cults.

Just as the periurban temples helped to define the boundaries of the polis, the extraurban sanctuaries expressed the very real limits of a city's power. That is to say, a polis indicated how far it could extend its defense and influence by maintaining control over a territory that far from its city limits. This was especially the case when the extraurban sanctuaries in question were the loci of cults that focused on young girls, such as at Brauron. In such instances, the polis advertised its ability to protect the most vulnerable of its citizens by routinely sending them "out into the wilderness" to worship the deities, more often than not Artemis.

Thus Artemis' role as a goddess of transitions was also expressed in the location of her sanctuaries. As Albert Schachter noted:

> It may be observed that her sanctuaries . . . share the same common feature of being in areas of transition: near the juncture of land and water, as at Aulis, Halai Araphenides, Delos, Cape Artemision, Amarynthos; in marshy land which shares the characteristics of both land and water, as at Sparta, Stymphalos, Brauron, Ephesos; in ill-defined and disputed boundary areas as at Gorgopis, Hyampolis, Karyai, Limnai; on high ground in far reaches of the chora, as at Lousoi and Kombothekra; in neutral territory, as at Amarynthos and Patrai; between city and chora, as at Kalydon and Sparta; in the centre of a newly-founded colonies, which are themselves at the uncertain edge of the extended territory of the mother city, as at Thasos, Korkyra, and Ortygia; between the sacred and profane, as the gateways of larger sanctuaries, as at Eleusis, Didyma, and Epidauros.[14]

WAR GODDESS?

One significant result of this liminal location of her sanctuaries combined with her role as a huntress is that Artemis has come to be seen as a war goddess in much modern scholarship. The current consensus is best summarized by Jean-Pierre Vernant:

> Artemis plays her part fully in the conduct of war, although she is not a warrior goddess. Her interventions in this domain are not of a bellicose kind. Artemis is not a combatant; she is there to guide and to save, both Hegemone ["leader"] and Soteira ["savior"]. She is invoked as a savior in critical situations, when a conflict threatens the city's continued existence, at a time when it is threatened with total destruction. Artemis is mobilized when too much violence is used during a military engagement, when warfare abandons the civilized codes through which the rules of martial struggle are maintained and moves brutally into the realm of savagery.
>
> In these extreme cases, the goddess does not have recourse to either physical or military force in order to bring deliverance. Rather, she acts by means of supernatural manifestation that muddles the normal arena of combat in order to destroy the aggressors and give the advantage to those under her protection. The former she blinds, leading them astray on the roads or troubling their minds with confusion and panic. To the others she offers a kind of hyperlucidity by guiding them miraculously through the dark or by illuminating their minds with sudden inspiration.[15]

As the data will show, this consensus is wrong. Artemis did have a minimal role to play in warfare, mainly in Sparta. But she was no war goddess of any caliber, and the modern construct is based upon methodological error.

Sacrifices to Artemis Agrotera

So, just what role did Artemis play in ancient Greek warfare? Artemis appears in military guise mainly in her manifestation as Artemis Agrotera—"Wild" or "Rustic." The Spartans sacrificed goats to Agrotera before the commencement of battle, as recorded by Xenophon (*Hell.* 4.2.20) when the Spartans under King Agesilaos faced a joint army of Athenians and Arkadian Tegeans at the Battle of Nemea in the early fourth century:

> Not being quite a stade away, the Lakedaimonians sacrificed to Agrotera, as is customary, a she-goat, and drove against the enemy encircling the overlying wing.

The Spartan ritual of pre-battle goat sacrifice appears in other contexts, and the usual belief is that these, too, were offered to Agrotera. Thus in his *Constitution of the Lakedaimonians* (13.8), Xenophon mentions that the Spartan law-giver Lykourgos established that all Spartans present at the pre-battle goat sacrifice should be garlanded, a detail later remembered by Plutarch in his *Life of Lykourgos* (22.2). No divine recipient is explicitly named in these passages, but the strong correlation between goat sacrifice and Artemis make it likely that it was she.

The Athenians also revered Artemis Agrotera, not so much with a preliminary ritual but specifically in thanksgiving for the victory at the Battle of Marathon. According to Xenophon (*Anab.* 3.2.11–12):

> For when the Persians were coming and those with them in a full complement to destroy the Athenians completely, those same Athenians daring to withstand [the attack] defeated them. And swearing to Artemis to sacrifice as many she-goats to the goddess as they struck down of the enemy, when the time came they could not find enough goats, so it seemed best to them to sacrifice 500 annually, and they still do so to this day.

Pseudo-Aristotle in his *Constitution of the Athenians* (§58) does indeed note that one of the duties of the Athenian General-in-Chief, the Polemarkhos, was to offer sacrifices to Artemis Agrotera and Enyalios, an epithet of Ares. Aristophanes makes a humorous reference to sacrificing goats to Agrotera in his *Knights* (ll. 660–662), which adds one more slight datum to the ancient Greek pile.

This is actually the sum total of evidence we have from Classical Greece (as opposed to Roman sources projected back onto ancient Greece) pertaining to the role(s) of Artemis in warfare. There are a few epigrams recording dedications of weapons to the goddess (including hunting weapons), and some of the epigraphic evidence mentions young warriors engaging in rituals for the goddess, or the goddess's temples receiving monies from the ransom of war prisoners. But these data occur in the midst of lists and decrees that mention the same for all the other deities of the city pantheon. Thus, there is nothing that specifically makes Artemis out to be associated with warfare any more so than, say, Demeter, or Hermes.

So, then, where does the war goddess construct come from? Mainly from the Romans. Excluding the brief references given by Xenophon (and Pseudo-Aristotle and Aristophanes), most of the evidence for Artemis' aid to warriors comes from Roman-period authors, mainly Plutarch and Pausanias. As the data will show, there is such a heavy emphasis on nocturnal (moon)light that it becomes immediately evident that it is not so much Greek Artemis as lunar Diana who has influenced these narratives, even though (as we shall see) the narratives themselves are set in Classical Greek history.

So that is part of the problem. The other part, the part contributed by modern scholars, is the creation of a concatenation of "common denominators" that supposedly connects the later Roman accounts with those of Xenophon. That is to say, we note certain key details in the war stories pertaining to Artemis (e.g. goats). We then see some of the same or similar details in other stories, so we infer a common meaning based on the shared similarities. New details in *those* stories are then made part of the concatenation (e.g. darkness), so additional tales are brought into the corpus. Drift occurs, such that the original details (goats) are no longer necessary to identify the recognized construct, so long as the later details (darkness) are present. More accounts with similar data are pulled into the fray until it appears that we have a full corpus of narratives pertaining to Artemis' military exploits, when in fact Artemis herself had long since stopped being a subject in the tales, and the links are based solely on the other, distantly connected details.

The core data for the eventual idea of Artemis as war goddess appear above in the very brief references to the Spartans and Marathon. The critical details are: Artemis, battle, goat sacrifice. How did these two stories and three details then get spun into the construct of Artemis-as-war-goddess?

Consider two tales from Pausanias. In Pausanias 7.26.2–3, we read how the city of Aigeira, formerly "Hyperesia," got its name:

> In the epics of Homer it is called Hyperesia; the name it has now comes from the Ionian settlement and it got it for this reason: An army of Sikyonians was about to engage them in hostilities over the land, but they [the Hyperesians]—for they didn't think that they were a match for the Sikyonians— they muster goats, as many as they have in the country, and collecting them together they tied torches onto their horns, and far into the night, they light the torches. Now the Sikyonians—for they feared that allies set out on behalf of the Hyperesians and that the flame was from allies' fire—they went back home and the Hyperesians bestowed upon the city the name it now has from the goats [*aiges* in Greek]. And where the most beautiful goat who led the others sat down they made a sanctuary of Artemis Agrotera, believing that the trick against the Sikyonians came to them not without Artemis.

It is immediately easy to see how this story became connected to the accounts in Xenophon. All three feature Artemis, battle, and goats, and while these goats are not being sacrificed per se in the Hyperesian narrative, tying torches to their horns was not necessarily conducive to their overall well-being. Additional elements that appear in are the nocturnal setting, the use of light at night (the torches, also associated with Artemis generally), and the idea of the ruse. It is these latter details—night, light, ruse—that then appear in the second passage from Pausanias, also pertaining to Artemis and warfare. This text relates how Artemis once helped to annihilate a contingent of Persians in 479 BCE (1.40.2–3):

> Not far from this spring is an ancient sanctuary, and in our day likenesses stand in it of Roman kings, and there is a bronze statue of Artemis, called "Savior" [*Sôteira*]. They say that men of Mardonios' army, when ravaging the Megarid, wanted to head back towards Mardonios in Thebes, but by a notion of Artemis it turned to night for the travelers, and mistaking the road they went into the mountainous part of the country. Attempting to see if an enemy army was nearby, they set off arrows, and a nearby rock being struck groaned, and they began to shoot in full earnest. In the end they used up all of their arrows thinking that they were shooting the enemy in full earnest. When day appeared the Megarians set out, armed men fighting men unarmed and no longer provided with arrows, and they killed many of them. And on account of this a statue was made of Artemis Sôteira.

There are some differences between this narrative and those previous, especially insofar as there are no goats to speak of, and Artemis is called Sôteira rather than Agrotera. Nevertheless, the emphasis on Artemis, night, and light in addition to a pre-battle context is sufficiently similar to Pausanias' Hyperesian narrative, which was sufficiently similar to Xenophon's accounts, that we accept it as part of the war goddess construct, now featuring (unexpected) darkness and trickery (neither of which, please recall, appeared in Xenophon). We have lost the goats entirely.

Additional data are introduced in Plutarch. When referring to the Battle of Salamis, Plutarch, in his *De Herodoti Malignitate* (869d=37) and his *Life of Themistokles* (22.1), claimed that the Athenian strategist Themistokles dedicated a temple in Melitê to Artemis Aristoboulê, "Best Counsel," after the battle of Salamis, apparently insofar as it was she who inspired him to use trickery to instigate the battle.[16] As a follow-up, Plutarch in his *On the Glories of the Athenians* (349f) records that: "The sixteenth of Mounykhion they [the Athenians] dedicated to Artemis, for on that day the goddess shone with full moon upon the Greeks as they were victorious at Salamis." On this day they brought to Artemis offerings of *amphiphôn* ("light on both sides") cakes—a flat, round cake decorated all-around with lighted candles (Athenaios 14.645). Thus it was in gratitude for the light and, presumably, accompanying divine favor that the Athenians made their dedications.

So now we see battle preparations, trickiness, and lunar light, as well as references to Artemis, and thus these narratives are added into the evidence pile.

But the attentive reader will notice that all these narratives come from Roman-age authors. All these details, such as the reference to amphiphôn cakes, (the full moon at) Salamis, and Themistokles' dedication to Artemis Aristoboulê, are from the Common Era, and the association with moonlight strongly betrays Dianic influence. Significantly, when accounts of these very events appear in the more contemporary Greek sources, there are no references to Artemis or to the details that were used to form the war goddess construct. When describing Mardonios' romp through Megara, Herodotos simply writes (9.14):

> Mardonios then carefully withdrew, and while on the road there came to him another message that there was an army ahead of him heading to Megara—1,000 Lakedaimonians. And hearing these things he considered how he might attack them first. Having turned the army around he headed to Megara, and the cavalry went forth and trampled the Megarid country. This indeed was the farthest westwards in Europe the Persian army ever came.

No arrows, no night, no Artemis. Herodotos makes no reference at all to Artemis in his account of Themistokles' trickery at Salamis. Additionally, as Robert Parker notes, "The moonshine during (*sic*) the battle mentioned by Plutarch (*De Glor. Ath.* 349f) *but not Aeschylus or Herodotus* looks like aetiological fiction . . . More simply, note that the goddess was associated with the land on both sides of the straits of Salamis (Hdt. 8.77)."[17]

So references to Artemis as a tricky, illuminating war goddess actually begin in the Roman age. For reasons pertaining more to moonlit Diana than Artemis, Roman-period authors saw far more military assistance from their hunting goddess than did their Greek predecessors. This may be partially due to the various syncretisms that affected Artemis over the course of the Hellenistic and Roman ages as discussed in the first chapter.[18] For example, Artemis' syncretism with the Persian-Armenian goddess Anaïtis/Anahita. This Anaïtis/Anahita/Anahit emerged through a Zororastrian adoption and adaptation of the Mesopotamian goddess Ištar, goddess of war and love. However, she also absorbed the attributes of a local water goddess, and came ultimately to known as *anahita*, the "Immaculate One."[19] The Greek deity to whom she was most often compared was Artemis in the function of a "pure" fertility goddess. So much is attested in Plutarch's *Lucullus* (§24), the *Annals* of Tacitus (3.63),[20] and the Anatolian epithets of Artemis *Anaïtis* and possibly *Persikê*.[21] Like Ištar, Anahita had a militaristic side, and the goddess received at her temple in Staxr the severed heads of enemies killed in battle.[22]

Nevertheless, we have very few examples of Greek Artemis as a war goddess, and these are mostly contradicted by the actual Greek sources. In spite of this, in the modern scholarship all of these accounts, regardless of chronology, are considered together, and a pattern is recognized: At some point before the commencement of a battle trickery and darkness and night-time illumination are mentioned, and Artemis is named.[23] As the thinking goes, once you have enough of these common denominators together, you do not necessarily need all of them to argue that the full construct is implied.

So consider another datum used to argue for Artemis' war persona. This oblique reference to Artemis as leader and savior appears in the writings of Clement of Alexandria when discussing the attempted overthrow of the Athenian democracy. Here Clement recalls how Thrasyboulos was leading the democrats out of exile when an unexpected snowstorm aided their efforts (*Stromate* I, 24, 163): "They were making their war on a moonless night in bad weather when a flame appeared before them and led them flawlessly to Mounykhia, where it left them. In this place the altar of the goddess Phosphoros still stands."[24] The combination of Mounykhia, famous site of one of Artemis' sanctuaries, and the epithet Phosphoros ("light-bearer," see below) links the narrative with Artemis as well as the notion of light in darkness.

But when Xenophon describes the return of Thrasyboulos, he merely has him claim in his pep-talk to the democrats (Xen. *Hell.* 2.4.14):

> And the deities are now clearly our allies. For even in fine weather they make a snow storm, whatever is useful to us, and whatever we might attempt, even being many against few, they grant to us to erect trophies.

No flame, altar, or Phosphoros. As with Plutarch and Pausanias, Clement is adding a Roman overlay to a Greek narrative that did not in any way implicate the goddess of the hunt. Nevertheless, his version includes familiar elements such as men in civic hostilities, night, and illumination, and thus it gets pulled into the growing pattern of Artemis as war goddess.

Next, we might consider the tale of the "Phokian Desperation" as recorded by Plutarch in his *Virtues of Women* (2: Phokis):

> The war of the Thessalians against the Phokians was without treaty; for [the Phokians] in one day had killed all the [Thessalian] rulers and despots in the Phokian cities, so that the Thessalians slaughtered 250 hostages, then with full army invaded by way of Lokris, having established a decree that no one should spare anyone of fighting age, and to enslave the children and women. Therefore Daiphontes son of Bathyllos, the third of the leaders, persuaded the Phokians on the one hand to fight the Thessalians until they themselves were wholly destroyed, and on the other hand having gathered together the women along with the children from throughout all of Phokis into one place, both to pile up a pyre of wood and

to leave behind guards, giving them a command that should they hear that the Phokians were defeated, with all speed they were to ignite the wood and cast onto it the bodies [of the women and children]. The others voted for these things, but one man standing apart said that it was only right to see if these things were acceptable to the women or not, if they would accept them and not be forced. So when the plan was brought to the women, they, gathering amongst themselves, voted in favor of them and crowned Daiphontes, as these were the best things for Phokis. And they say that even the children for their own part had a council and voted for this plan. These things being accomplished, the Phokians engaging in battle near Kleonia of Hyampolis won, and the Greeks thus called the vote of the Phokians the "Desperation." And to this day they [the Phokians] celebrate the Elaphebolia, the greatest of all their festivals, for Artemis [in honor] of that victory.

Once again we have a Roman-period narrative that discusses the eve of a battle where the underdog wins and Artemis is referred to at the end. One might notice that the only reason that Artemis appears in the "Phokian Desperation" is because after the event the Hyampolians celebrated their victory annually at the sanctuary of Artemis Elaphebolos. There is no statement that Artemis assisted the citizens in any way in their battle for freedom, whereas the local geography makes it likely that that sanctuary was picked out for special notice because it was located near the border between Phokis and Thessaly. So Artemis served as goddess of liminal spaces, but there is no evidence, even in Plutarch, that she in any way functioned as any kind of war goddess. The tale even lacks the standard common denominators which to this point have been used to argue for the Artemis-as-war-goddess paradigm—night/darkness, light/moon, trickiness, goats. Nevertheless, not only does the "Phokian Desperation" get used as evidence of the war aspect of Artemis' persona, it is used to add new elements to the pattern, specifically the notion of a war of desperation and overwhelming odds.[25]

And once scholars have determined that Artemis is the tricky war goddess who saves desperate people during night-time wars of annihilation, other examples can be thrown into the fray, *even with no reference to Artemis at all*. For example, in his 1984 article "Les Ruses de Guerre d'Artémis" ("Artemis' Wartime Tricks"), Pierre Ellinger lists four complementary battle narratives that supposedly pertain to Artemis. In the first (Herodotos 8.27), in a battle between the Phokians and Thessalians, the Phokians made a night-time raid having covered their bodies with white chalk so as to appear like spirits, and they determined to kill anyone they came across not all white. In the darkness, the Thessalians panicked at the strange apparition, lost their nerve, and were slaughtered. The victorious Phokians dedicated 4,000 captured shields to Abai and Delphi (both sanctuaries of Apollo[26]). In the complementary tale as recounted in Pausanias (10.1.5–6), the Thessalians killed the Phokians in a night-time rout, when the Phokians tried to hide in the dark but did not engage the enemy. In the third narrative (Herodotos 7.176), the Phokians, to prevent the Thessalians from entering their land, diverted hot spring water onto a mountain road so that it would become impassable for the ravines carved, while simultaneously building a defensive wall. Neither tactic was successful. By contrast, when the Phokians dug a trench, filled it with broken pottery and covered it up, the Thessalian cavalry was stopped when their horses fell into the trench and broke their legs (Hdt. 8.28).

Even Ellinger admits that none of these accounts at first appear to have anything to do with Artemis.[27] But then he goes on to enumerate the many common denominators between these tales and those that "clearly" pertain to Artemis, such as the story of how Aigeira got its name, the story about Mardonios' army, and Clement's Thrasyboulos narrative: night, trickery, confusion, the threat of total annihilation averted,[28] just as discussed by Vernant above. All of these, of course, are parts of the overarching pattern of Artemis as war goddess. If enough of these are present (the thinking goes), the pattern is firmly established, and thus Artemis might be inferred. So, narratives that have nothing to do with Artemis suddenly are used as evidence for her martial persona.

In spite of these weaknesses, the construct is widely published. Vernant writes a chapter on "Artemis and Preliminary Sacrifice in Combat," where he basically cites all the same references given by Ellinger.[29] Susan G. Cole agrees with both scholars, and has sections on "Boundaries and Combat" and "Epiphany and Crisis" in her chapter on "Landscapes of Artemis," where she, too, repeats the standard litany of "evidence."[30] By this point you have several "ancient" references to Artemis as war goddess as well as at least three well-known, very highly respected scholars concurring on the subject, so it becomes the received wisdom. Now, any reference to a night-time battle, a cunning strategy, or even moonlight can be used to strengthen the perceived construct. And any time we are at a loss as to why Artemis might be called "Savior" or "Phosphoros" we can simply invoke the martial aspect: The argument has already been made, the pattern recognized. Thus, when writing of the mysteries of Ephesian Artemis and her epithet *Sôteira* ("Savior"), Guy MacLean Rogers can simply state that, "Rather, Artemis the Savior was sculpted out of military victory, and it may very well have been as a deity who could provide salvation in the form of military victory that she was conceptualized."[31] Now, in addition to Sparta, Athens, and Phokis, one might find Artemis the war goddess in Ephesos, and the pattern continues.

But one must recall that the only actual Greek evidence we have for Artemis' role in war is the scant handful of references mentioned at the beginning of this section—Xenophon's Agrotera, confirmed by Aristophanes and Pseudo-Aristotle. Everything else is either a Roman Dianic add-on or false pattern recognition in modern academes. Artemis was not a war goddess.

More epithets

That said, let us consider some of the epithets used of Artemis in her "military guise." The least belligerent, so to speak, is the epithet that appears in Clement of Alexandria's narrative—*Phosphoros*. This is one of a number of related epithets applied to the goddess since the fifth century at the latest. We have Phosphoros, "Light-Bearer" attested in Euripides' *Iphigeneia Amongst the Tauroi*, line 11, while the synonym *Phaesophoria* appears in line 11 of Kallimakhos' *Hymn to Artemis*. *Amphipyron*—"With Fire in Both [Hands]" or, perhaps a bit more likely, "With a Torch in Both [Hands]"—appears in Sophokles' *Trakkhiniai*, line 214. In addition, Phosphoros served as a cult epithet of the goddess, most notably in Messenê (see Chapter 4), where the cult statue of

Artemis Phosphoros was sculpted by Damophon in the second century BCE (Paus. 4.31.10). Based on the terracotta votives found at the site, the image of this statue can be tentatively reconstructed:

> Most of the terracotta figurines of both deposits represent Artemis wearing a short chiton with overfold and topped with an animal skin (*nebris*), wrapped around the body and bound with a belt; the tail of the animal hangs downwards between the thighs; one of her breasts and the corresponding shoulder are left bare. She wears high leather boots and has a polos-like diadem on her head; she is holding a very tall torch (λαμπάς) close to her left side; a dog seated by her right foot turns its head upwards.[32]

So why was Artemis a light-bearer? Part of the answer might be related to her role as hunting goddess. As the poem from Alkman given above mentions, Artemis "draws her long bow at night." Of course, it is exceptionally difficult, not to mention dangerous, to draw a bow when one is holding a flaming torch, and so there are shortcoming to the huntress hypothesis. More likely is that the torch-bearing aspect of Artemis was adopted when the goddess began her syncretism with the goddess Hekatê, for whom torch-bearing was an attribute. One of this goddess's most significant roles in early Greek literature is as the one who helped Demeter to look for and greet Persephonê in the Homeric *Hymn to Demeter*. Torch-bearing is a common theme in the iconography of Eleusis, related to the night-time search for the missing Korê and rites pertaining to the Underworld more generally. Epigraphic evidence from Athens, Boiotia, and the island of Thasos show that Artemis and Hekatê began to merge identities no later than the fifth century (see Chapter 6), and thus a sharing of iconographic attributes is to be expected from this period.

Hegemonê means "leader," and is in all respects inappropriate for Artemis in military matters. As noted by Vernant inter alia regarding the goddess's role in warfare, she does not appear in the ranks, much less the front lines. She is supposedly the "tricky" goddess, winning by mostly night-time stealth and cunning. Artemis does, in fact, bear the epithet Hegemonê, and her iconography can overlap with that of Artemis Phosphoros. At the sanctuary of Despoina[33] in Lykosoura in Arkadia, Pausanias describes the cult statue of Artemis as (8.37.1):

> Four stades distant from Akakinos is the sanctuary of Despoina. The first thing there is a temple of Artemis Hegemonê and a bronze statue holding a torch—we reckon it to be six feet at most; it is there at the entrance of the sacred precinct.

As is typical with epithets, Artemis is not the only goddess to be called by this title. Also sharing the denomination of "Leader" is the god Hermes, the goddess Aphrodite (twice), and Hegemonê is also the name of one of the Charites worshipped in Attika (if not Hesiod, *Theog.* l. 907). As noted by Jenny Wallensten, one common factor shared amongst Artemis, Hermes, and the Attik Charites is that they are all concerned with the care of the young, Artemis serving as "kourotrophos" of older adolescents (see Chapter 4), Hermes as god of games and athletes, and Hegemonê the Grace as a goddess who aids in the physical growth of children.[34] When Aphrodite is invoked as Hegemonê, once it is in context with the Charites

(*IG* II² 2798) and once in honor of Nikomakhos, a man whose father's name was Aineas (thus with symbolic links to Aphrodite) and who held command over a garrison of ephebes.³⁵ As such, both examples pull the title back into the realm of the young. Considering the use of the Hegemonê epithet/name when dealing with youth, it is more logical to see Artemis' epithet as referencing her role as kourotrophos, rather than as anything pertaining to battle.

Finally, let us look at *Sôteira*—"Savior." This title applies to so many deities that it quickly becomes evident that no specific meaning might be derived from it beyond a rather generalized compliment in praise of the power of the divinity. The epithet Sôteira is shared by Artemis, Demeter, Persephonê, Athena, Hekatê, Tykhê (Luck), Themis (Divine Justice), Eunomia (Good Custom), and Rhea, while the masculine *Sôter* belongs to Zeus, Helios, Apollo, Hermes, Asklepios, and the Dioskouroi. All deities might save someone from something (Demeter from famine, Asklepios from illness), and thus there is no need to suggest that for Artemis specifically it refers to a role of military savior.

As a final detail, it is worth noting that not even the Orphic Hymn to Artemis refers to warfare in its otherwise extensive list of the goddess's attributes and function (see "Why Artemis?"). Neither, for that matter, does Kallimakhos.

In the end, we can see that Artemis served a very limited function in war. The Spartans sacrificed goats to her on the cusp of battle, just as they sacrificed sheep to Zeus and Athena when crossing borders in warfare. The Athenians credited her for help during the Persian Invasions, sacrificing 500 goats to her for the success at Marathon. A temple at Melitê in Attika *might* be associated with her presence at the Battle of Salamis as well. Such dedications are in no way remarkable, and do not warrant giving the title of "War Goddess" to Artemis. It is only in later years, possibly under Roman influence, that further, but still limited, tales of Artemis' aid in battle become popular.

OVERVIEW

Artemis was first and foremost a goddess of the wilds and the hunt. The grand majority of her epithets pertain to hunting and the natural world, just as most of her iconography shows her with bow and quiver, often dominating one or more wild animals. From Greece's earliest literature she is portrayed as the tall, beautiful huntress—the dominant theme in her best preserved Homeric Hymn and her exclusive role in the extant drama. Numerous dedicatory epigrams pertain to her help on the hunt, just as many thanked the goddess for her help in childbirth (see Chapter 5).

For all this, Artemis was not a war goddess, in spite of much modern scholarship that claims that she was. As a goddess of transitions, it is perhaps reasonable that Spartans would sacrifice to her when entering into battle, and the Athenians would credit her help in defending threatened borders. But Artemis was neither a warrior nor an assistant to warriors, certainly not like we see of Athena, and Apollo, and even Hera in the *Iliad* and elsewhere. Perhaps there is a lesson in this, that the Greeks were less likely to condone wildness in warfare than we credit them.

NOTES

1   I realize that women can hunt too, and that my description here is somewhat sexist in terminology. However, as males were the dominant hunters in ancient Greece, and as the anthropological terminology itself evolved in a less gender-enlightened age, I use the original language as chronologically accurate.

2   Trans. Barnestone 1988: 52.

3   An epithet of Artemis associated with Crete.

4   Orsi 1900: 366–376.

5   Fischer-Hansen 2009: 237.

6   Ibid.: 242.

7   Bevan 1985: Appendix 8.

8   Ibid.

9   Cole 2004: 180.

10   Brulotte 2002: *passim.*

11   For all references, see Morizot 1994.

12   Brulé 1998: 23–25.

13   De Polignac 1995: 22–23.

14   Schachter 1992: 50.

15   Vernant 1991: 203.

16   As recorded by Herodotos (8.75), when Themistokles could not get the various Greek generals to agree to a battle strategy (namely his), he sent his slave to go tell the Persians that the Greeks were in the process of retreat, and that they should attack at once. In so doing the Persians not only got the Greek generals to find consensus quite quickly, but also lost their advantage of numbers in the close quarters of the straits.

17   Parker 1996: 155, n. 10. My emphasis. The "(*sic*)" is in the original.

18   Greek Aphrodite went through a similar change. In the Greek materials she is only armed ("Hoplismenê") in Sparta in Greece, and possibly nearby Kythera. In the Roman period, she becomes the far more martial Venus Victrix.

19   Boyce 1987: 61.

20   Garsoïan 1989: 347.

21   Brosius 1998: *passim.*

22   Chaumont 1965: 172.

23   There are, however, fewer and fewer goats.

24   Vernant 1991: 248.

25   This is especially the case in the works of Pierre Ellinger.

26   Apollo. Not Artemis.

27   Ellinger 1984: 56.

28   Ibid.: 56–60.

29   Vernant 1991: 244–257.

30   Cole 2004: 188–191.

31   MacLean Rogers 2012: 267.

32   Themelis 1994: 105. All things considered, she actually sounds a bit like a dominatrix.

33   "Mistress," an otherwise rarely attested daughter of Demeter. In the local myths of Lykosoura, Artemis was the daughter of Demeter, and she and Despoina were sisters.

34   Wallensten 2003: 69, with references.

35   Ibid.; Budin 2010: 92–94.

4

ARTEMIS AND CHILDREN

Perhaps one of the best-known aspects of Artemis is that she is the protectress of children. In modern scholarship any number of her cults throughout ancient Greece have been associated with aspects of initiation, child cult functionaries, and the dedication of infants and small children to her care. In the modern literature the goddess is frequently referred to as *kourotrophos*, "nurturer of children."

However, as the evidence below indicates, there is some ambiguity regarding this aspect of the goddess. Artemis is far less concerned with, or protective of, small children than her modern kourotrophic reputation indicates, and she is more likely to demand the death of children than she is to guard them, at least according to the ancient sources. Thus Artemis' rapport with children is one area of her cult and persona in considerable need of reconsideration.

KOUROTROPHIC ARTEMIS(?)

They say that Artemis discovered the proper care of infants and the nourishment appropriate for their nature, and for this reason she is called *kourotrophos*.

(Diodorus Siculus 5.73.5–6)

Artemis is the Kourotrophos par excellence. She takes all the little ones in charge, both animal and human, whether male or female. Her function is to nurture them, to make them grow and mature until they become fully adult. With human offspring, she leads them to the threshold of adolescence.

(J.-P. Vernant 1991: 198)

Such is the modern understanding of Artemis' relationship with infants and small children. She is known as the *kourotrophos*, literally the "nurturer (*trophos*) of boys (*kouroi*)," although her nurturing functions pertain to young girls as well, if not more so. Artemis is not alone in either this function or this epithet: The word applied to numerous deities in the Greek pantheon, including Hekatê (*Theogony.* 450–452), Gaia (Pausanias 1.22.3), Demeter (*IG²*, 5131, 5152–3), Aphrodite (*Greek Anthology* VI, 318), Peace (*Works and Days* 228), Apollo (Kallimakhos *Delos* 2.276), the nymphs, as well as being the independent goddess Kourotrophos.[1] As references to the virginal Artemis, as well as Hekatê and Apollo (non-virgin male) make evident, the relationship between a kourotrophos and child was not that of mother and offspring, but rather one of caretaker and child. More specifically, the term "kourotrophos" in the modern literature refers to one who tends to the young, especially nursing infants, caring for their physical needs and protecting them. In the iconography, the word "kourotrophos" refers to an image of an adult female (divine or mortal) who holds an infant and for whom the previous relationship tends to be inferred.

Kourotrophic epithets

However, the data for Artemis' role as a kourotrophos are more ambivalent than may at first appear. All of the literary texts are Roman in date. Thus there is the passage from Diodorus Siculus given above. In the *Orphic Hymn* to Artemis discussed in the Introduction she is addressed as *brotôn kourotrophe daimon*, "divine kourotrophos of mortals" (*OH* 36, 8), while Pausanias, writing in the second century CE records that in the polis of Koronê (4.34.6), "The gods who have temples here are Artemis, called 'Paidotrophos' ('child-nurturer'), Dionysos, and Asklepios." On the island of Knidos Artemis was worshipped as Hiakynthotrophos, a bit of a misspelling for the later corrected Hyakinthotrophos, suggesting that the goddess was at least responsible for tending to either the hero Hyakinthos or to her brother Apollo with that epithet. The inscription naming Artemis Hyakinthotrophos dates to the first century BCE.[2] Finally, in the third century CE Athenaios wrote of Sparta that (*Deipnosophistai* 4.16 = D139a):

> In the city [Sparta] they celebrate the Kopis [Cleaver] and also a festival called the Tithenidos [Suckling] on behalf of the children. For the nurses bring the little boys at the proper time into the country to Artemis called Korythalia [Blooming Youth], whose sanctuary is by the so-called Tiassos in the region of Kleta. And they celebrate the Kopis in the same way as those mentioned. And they sacrifice suckling pigs and they serve as well oven-baked bread at the feast.

Kourotrophic iconography

The artistic evidence for a kourotrophic Artemis is older, but care is necessary in determining how to interpret these data. Specifically, there are four separate categories of iconographic evidence for Artemis' rapport with children—Artemis herself shown with children; depictions of kourotrophoi (adult females holding a child); reliefs showing families with children before Artemis; and sculptures of small children from Artemis' sanctuaries.

Of the literally hundreds of depictions in Lily Kahil's article on Artemis in the *Lexicon Iconographicum Mythologiae Classicae* (*LIMC*), only two stand out as portraying the goddess in kourotrophic guise (#s 723 and 723a). Both come from Korkyra on the island of Corfu, and they depict the goddess standing upright, wearing a polos crown and holding a hunting bow in her left hand (Figure 4.1).

Standing directly in front of the goddess—in fact, standing right on Artemis' *feet*[3]—is a girl who is as tall as Artemis' hips and who reaches her arms upwards toward the

Figure 4.1 Terracotta figurine of Artemis with a small girl. Korkyran workshop, c. 480 BCE. Athens, National Archaeological Museum, 1112. Drawing by Paul C. Butler, used with kind permission.

goddess. Both terracottas date to the fifth century BCE.[4] The iconography from Corfu is quite explicit, and gives no cause for doubt that the deity with the child is in fact Artemis.

In contrast to such explicit Artemisian iconography are the numerous kourotrophic figurines that have come to light in Artemis' sanctuaries throughout the Greek world that appear to represent not the goddess herself, but her worshippers. Thus from the sanctuary of Artemis Paralia in Kition, Cyprus came numerous kourotrophic figurines, some dating as early as the Archaic Age. Likewise, two sixth-century kourotrophoi came to light at an Artemiseion in Kamelarga, Cyprus. The sanctuary of Artemis at Brauron revealed terracotta figurines of seated kourotrophoi, many depicted as veiled and holding an infant up to the chest (see *LIMC* 721). So too were terracotta statuettes depicting veiled kourotrophoi of a distinctly Ionian-Rhodian type dating from the first half of the fourth century found at the sanctuary of Artemis at Ephesos. To the north, the island of Thasos brought to light a group of kourotrophic statuettes from the sanctuary of Artemis.[5]

The Brauron votives are a good case in point. One example dating to the mid-fifth century depicts a mature female wearing a veil and holding a small child in her arms against her chest. The child is not nursing, but rather looks up at the kourotrophos and raises its right hand upwards toward the woman's face.[6] The Brauronian location certainly suggests Artemis. However, the mature female bears no signs of divinity, such as a polos crown, much less such distinctive features as a bow or quiver. Furthermore, the presence of a veil in Greek iconography was typically associated with married women, which Artemis most assuredly was not. As such, there are more arguments to be made that this kourotrophic female was not Artemis, but rather the image of a recent mother with child, dedicated at the sanctuary.

Family reliefs

So much might also be said for the relief dedications discovered in Artemis' sanctuaries. Brauron has brought to light several marble reliefs showing relatively large families in procession before Artemis, whose identity and divinity are manifest in her much larger scale and attributes such as a deer or archery bow. At least one family member will be carrying a *kistos*—a box containing items necessary for a sacrifice, and in some instances a sacrificial animal such as a bull will be present. Similar reliefs, as well as reliefs depicting pregnant women standing before the goddess, have also come to light from Mount Kynthos on the island of Delos.[7] In no case, however, is there any indication that any special relationship exists between Artemis and the small children in the scene: The composition consists of Artemis as the receiver of worship, and the family group or mother who worships her.

This rapport between Artemis, child, and mother/family is well expressed on a marble relief dating to the late fourth century from ancient Ekhinos in Phthiotis and now in the Lamia Museum, discovered in 1979 on the southern side of the city acropolis (Figure 4.2).[8]

This marble panel (68 × 120 centimeters) depicts the female members of a family presenting an infant to Artemis. The goddess herself stands to the right of the panel, facing the family approaching her. She wears a polos crown and carries a flaming torch in her right hand, thus emphasizing her role as "Phosphoros." Her left arm rests upon a pedestal. She wears a Doric style peplos, with a himation falling from her left

Figure 4.2 Marble votive relief to Artemis from Ekhinos in Phthiotis, late fourth century BCE, Lamia Archaeological Museum, 1041. Courtesy of the Lamia Archaeological Museum, Ministry of Culture and Sport.

shoulder to cover the pedestal behind her. Barely visible behind her left shoulder is her quiver. However, the artist seems to have forgotten to include a strap, so the quiver rather floats in midair behind the goddess.[9] Immediately in front of Artemis is a small altar, before which stands the only male in the picture, who is rendered at a much smaller scale than anyone else in the depiction. This tiny male, possibly a slave per his size, leads forward a tiny horned bovine with his left hand while he holds a knife in his right. Clearly a sacrifice is about to take place. Behind the bovine is presumably the mother, a mature woman with her hair pulled back in a chignon and who wears a peplos similar to the goddess's. She holds forth the baby whose hair and dress indicate female sex;[10] the baby herself stretches forward both hands toward the goddess, possibly to beg Artemis not to let them kill the nice cow.[11] This infant with her forward reach is the center of the composition, and thus the focal point of the scene. Behind "Mom" is a young girl carrying a plate of offerings upon her head. It is possible that she, too, is a servant/slave, but her scale relative to the male instead suggests an identification as either the infants' older sister or perhaps the mother's younger sister. The offerings consist of an apple, a pomegranate, grapes, myrtle branches and triangular shapes that are either honey cakes or, possibly, cheese. The girl carries a small *askos* in her right hand down by her thigh. The final character in the panel is an older woman of a scale similar to that of the goddess herself. Her face has been damaged, but she wears a veil and carries a small pyxis in her hand (unguents?). Behind this line of family members is a line from which are hung shoes, tunics, and various textiles, just as are recorded for Artemis sanctuaries in Attika and elsewhere (see Chapter 5).[12]

The interpretation offered for this scene is one of thanksgiving. Specifically, it depicts a sacrificial offering the family (or at least its female members) makes to Artemis in gratitude for the safe delivery of the child who takes center stage in the composition.[13] Considering the importance of Artemis in childbirth (see Chapter 5), this is hardly surprising, and it negates any need to see this panel as dedicatory—the family specifically placing the infant under Artemis' protection.

Children in stone and clay

Finally, there are the statues of children that have come to light in Artemis' sanctuaries. By far the most notable collection of statues of small children has been excavated at Artemis' sanctuary at Brauron, the majority of the images dating to the fourth century BCE.[14] Here are found both little girls in elaborate khitons as well as nude little boys. Similar collections have also come to light in sanctuaries of Asklepios, the god of healing, and by the late fourth century terracotta versions appeared throughout the Greek world.[15] In the case of Asklepios, it is likely that the statues of children represent either children whom the god had healed in his sanctuary, or possibly offspring provided by the god to petitioning families. For that which concerns Brauron, the inscriptions on the statue bases in the sanctuary indicate that the images represent children of parents grateful for successful parturition and healthy offspring,[16] as well as depictions of girls who had served as "little bears" in the Arkteia ritual (see below), and thus are memorials of former temporary cult functionaries.[17]

A similar scenario occurs in the sanctuary of Artemis Phosphoros in Messenê in the Peloponnese.[18] This early second-century BCE temple with its cult statue of Artemis wrought by Damophon replaced the earlier sanctuary of Artemis Ortheia (not to be confused with the Spartan Ortheia!) located just to the north of the new structure, and the goddess was worshipped with both epithets at the new sanctuary.[19] Within the *cella* of the Hellenistic–Roman temple were discovered eleven stone bases, five of which were inscribed, that held votive statues of women and girls set in a semi-circle around the statue of Artemis. Also discovered in the temple were four marble and one sandstone life-sized statues of little girls who appear to have served as cult-functionaries of Artemis at the sanctuary. It is clear that the various statues were originally set on the bases, inscribed and otherwise, and thus we have a series of inscribed votives from which to learn about the cult.

The most complete evidence involves the girl Mego, whose relatively lengthy inscriptions survives in addition to her statue. The inscription (*SEG* 23.220), dating to the first century BCE reads:

> [Damonikos, son of . . .] and Timarkhis, daughter of Damarkhidas, having been priests, [dedicate Mego] their daughter. To you Maiden, Lady Ortheia, Damonikos and his noble-born wife Timarkhis dedicated me, their child Mego, who, Artemis, carried in my hand your image (*bretas*), and the also the torch which I stretched out before your altar. May I also be permitted to give thanks to my parents, as it is proper that children honor their parents in their turn.

Mego's statue as preserved shows the lower body (breasts to feet) of a girl nearing adolescence. She has long limbs, but relatively small breasts. An arm with qualities and scale similar to that of the statue has been connected with Mego's sculpture, and depicts an arm with bracelets and armlets holding up the bottom corner of a small statue, probably the *bretas* of Artemis mentioned in the inscription. It is interesting to note that additional evidence that such priest(ess)hoods of Artemis ran in families comes from a dedication in the *Greek Anthology* (6.356) where Pankrates wrote:

> Two children of Kleio—Aristodikê and Ameinô—
> Cretan girls, to you, Lady Artemis, are dedicated
> By their mother, your priestess (*Neokoros*). O Queen, you see
> What good children they are, and may you make of them two Neokoroi from one.

Another statue and inscription pairing pertained to the girl Timareta. Her first-century BCE inscription (*SEG* 23.221) reads simply, "Thiotas and Sopharkhis (dedicate) Timareta, their daughter, to Artemis." The statue itself is similar to Mego's in most respects: It is missing the head and arms, but the body is quite tall, with narrow hips and small breasts (as preserved). What may be a later (first century CE?) statue depicts what appears to be an even younger girl. Once again the head and arms are missing, but the legs visible under the folds of her khiton are shorter and a bit stockier than those of Mego and Timareta, and her breasts are even smaller. Clearly there was a desire to show the youth of the young girls who attended to Artemis in her sanctuary at Messenê.

Artemis kourotrophos reconsidered

What becomes increasingly clear is that there is very little evidence, either textual or iconographic, for an Artemis who tends to or protects small children and infants, the typical understanding of the term "kourotrophos." The literary evidence is late, even Roman in date, while the kourotrophic iconography that appears in her sanctuaries—as well as the sanctuaries of deities such as Demeter, Hera, Aphrodite, Eileithyia, and Persephonê amongst others—pertains more to grateful mothers with their own offspring than Artemis holding any actual babies. Likewise, the votive reliefs show families offering thanksgiving to Artemis for successful births. The child statues in her sanctuaries—amongst other deities—appear to be memorials of young servitors in her cult rather than children placed under her protection and care.

Considering the general paucity of evidence for an early, distinctively baby-tending Artemis, the question emerges as to why the goddess has been deemed "the Kourotrophos par excellence" in the words of Jean-Pierre Vernant, the Classicist par excellence. Part of the answer is surely theoretical. A kourotrophic aspect of Artemis' persona would fit well in line with her role in Greek religion and mythology generally. As the goddess who oversees and aids transitions, she is the virgin goddess who assists others through the perilous process of parturition (see Chapter 5). Just as Artemis herself does not really grow up (see Chapter 2), she instead helps mortal children to survive this most dangerous time of life (infant mortality was ridiculously high in the ancient world). Finally, children were understood to be rather wild, on the very far end of the continuum between civilized humans and savage beasts. As the goddess of savage beasts, it was ultimately appropriate for Artemis to watch over the wild human beasts as well.

Furthermore, one must consider the matter of chronology in Artemis' kourotrophic role. As noted above, all of the goddess's kourotrophic epithets are Roman in date, thus quite late by Greek standards. While images of mortal women with their babies found in Artemis' sanctuaries (amongst others) go back to the fifth century at least, the prevalence of statues of small children in her sanctuaries (amongst others) only dates back to the late fourth century, and collections such as at Messenê are late Hellenistic to Roman in date. This correlates with the findings of Leslie Beaumont, who notes a distinct change in attitudes toward small children over the course of Greek history. It is only in the late Hellenistic period and later that the Greeks display a sentimental and even affectionate attitude toward their children. As she puts it, "[T]he image of children and childhood was now sentimentalized and idealized, both through the representation of cute childish behavior and physical attitudes and through the iconographic adoption of physically charming childish anatomy."[20] It is possible, then, that Artemis' care of *infants* is a later development that had more to do with a new-found fondness for babies amongst mortals than it necessarily did with the goddess's persona over the ages.

It is also important to note that other goddesses in the Greek repertoire were more closely associated with human infants than was Artemis, and from much earlier. First of all there was Hekatê, the first goddess to be called "kourotrophos" in Greek literature in the eighth–seventh century BCE (*Theogony* 450–452):

And Kronides made her kourotrophos; they[21] afterwards
see with their eyes the light of much-seeing Eos.
And so from the beginning she is kourotrophos, and these are her honors.

This aspect of Hekatê's persona is expressed artistically on a second-century BCE frieze of the goddess's temple in Lagina, where the seated goddess holds a new-born infant.[22]

There is also the goddess Hestia to consider. It was she who, in Attika, inducted new children into the family through the *amphidromia*, a ritual wherein fathers walked or ran around the hearth holding a new baby, thus incorporating the infant into the family.[23] Babies not so inducted were viewed as strangers and could be exposed without guilt. Furthermore, as the goddess most involved with familial transitions, Hestia was ultimately a protectress of home and family. In Euripides' *Alkestis*, when the queen is about to die, she goes to the hearth to pray to Hestia to look after her children (ll. 163–169):

Mistress, as I proceed beneath the earth,
for the last time I shall beseech you in supplication,
to care for my orphaned children, to join my son in
marriage to a dear wife, my daughter to a noble husband.
Nor let them, as their mother was destroyed,
die as children, before their time, but happily
give them a joyful life in their fatherland.

Finally, there were the nymphs. Just as Hekatê was the first goddess to be called kourotrophos by Hesiod, so too were the Okeanid nymphs given the task of rearing the young in the *Theogony* (346–348):

[Tethys] bore a holy race of daughters, who throughout the earth
Rear boys with Lord Apollo
And the Rivers. This portion they have from Zeus.

The mountain nymphs performed a similar function at the end of the *Homeric Hymn to Aphrodite*, when the goddess tells Ankhises (ll. 256–258 and 273):

"As for him [Aeneas], when indeed he first sees the light of the sun,
Deep-bosomed mountain nymphs will raise him,
Who dwell on this great and sacred mountain . . .
They will keep my son with them and raise him."

Similar references occur in Sophokles' *King Oedipus* (l. 680) and Euripides' *Electra* (l. 626) and *Rhesos*.[24] It is these goddesses, more so than Artemis, who are shown to care for infants and small children in the literature.

Rather than seeing Artemis as a "protector of infants," it might perhaps be better to understand that the goddess cared for humans, and especially female humans, *on either side of the infant stage*, and especially as the deity who helped adolescents make the transition into adulthood. As Claude Calame once put it referring to

Artemis' role as kourotrophos, "This term has too often been used to refer exclusively to her influence over early childhood; however, *kourotrophos* does not stand just for the care given to nursing infants, but implies divine supervision over the whole of the child's education until he or she passes into adulthood."[25] As the goddess most closely linked to parturition from the fifth century onwards (even to the point of being wholly syncretized with the birth goddess Eileithyia; see Chapter 5), Artemis presided over new mothers and their neonates, and thus received their gratitude. At the far end of the childhood spectrum, Artemis helped adolescents evolve into young adults, which for girls involved marriage, pregnancy, and parturition. Such a cycle is well expressed in a dedication from the *Greek Anthology*, where Artemis is asked to protect not a small child, but a girl on the threshold of womanhood (6.280):

> Timareta before her marriage dedicated her tambourine, her
> Beloved ball, her hair-guarding snood,
> And her dolls to [Artemis] Limnatis, girl to girl, as is fit,
> And the dolls' dresses to Artemis.
> Daughter of Leto, set your hand over the child Timareta,
> And purely save her purity.

THE BEARS OF ARTEMIS

This is not to say, however, that Artemis had nothing to do with small children. As the evidence from Messenê indicates, girls did play important functions in her cults. Perhaps nowhere is this more so than in Attika in a ritual known as the *Arkteia*, where little girls "played the bear" for Artemis at her sanctuary at Brauron and probably a few other locations as well. These girls were, logically enough, called "bears" (*arktoi*).

The usual understanding in the modern scholarship on this ritual is that girls aged 5 to 10, or possibly aged 13 to 15, danced and raced in saffron-colored robes (*krokota*) which they may have taken off at some point and then performed in the nude. The rite was some kind of initiation ritual that helped to transform the little girls into future mothers, and the origin texts indicate that no girl could get married before "playing the bear" for Artemis.

The main problem with this analysis, and the *Arkteia* in general, is that we have remarkably little information about what the ritual actually consisted of, or what "playing the bear" meant. The evidence comes from various textual sources all written centuries after the ritual went out of use, and the iconographic sources are more ambiguous than they may at first appear. More recent scholarship on the *Arkteia* has shown that there were in fact at least two *separate Arkteia* rituals—one for little girls and one for older adolescents. Neither of them necessarily served as initiation rituals, but were rather rites of appeasement for the angry goddess.

The earliest evidence we have for "playing the bear" comes from a line in Aristophanes' late fifth-century comedy *Lysistrata*, when the women of Greece go on a sex strike to get their husbands to end a war. At lines 645–646 the women of Athens claim:

I bore the holy vessels at seven, then
I pounded barley at the age of ten,
And clad in yellow robes, soon after this,
I was little bear for Brauronian Artemis;
Then necklaced with figs, grown tall and pretty, I was a Basket-bearer . . .

Thus we have evidence from the fifth century that girls "played the bear" for Artemis at Brauron, although with no other details save for the saffron robes. The actual origin stories comes from much later—some as late as the tenth century CE—and a careful reading shows that two separate traditions were involved. I give here a representative sampling.[26]

Suda: "I was a bear at the Brauronia":

S1: They used to celebrate a festival to Artemis by "playing the bear" and by wearing a saffron robe (*krokoton*), neither being older than ten nor younger than five, and by placating the goddess.

S2: Once a wild bear was wandering about the deme of the Philaidai and was wreaking havoc. (They say) that the bear, once it had been tamed, became a companion to humans, and that a *parthenos* (maiden) was playing with it, and when the child treated it roughly, the bear was provoked and scratched the *parthenos*. And because of this, her brothers shot it down.

S3: And for this reason a plague fell upon the Athenians. And when they petitioned the oracle, it said that there would be a release from these misfortunes if as payment for the slain bear they forced their own *parthenoi* to "play the bear." And the Athenians voted that a *parthenos* could not live together with her husband, until she had played the bear for the goddess.

Scholion to *Lysistrata*:

L1: When females used to perform the secret rite, they imitated a bear. Those "playing the bear" for the goddess used to wear a saffron robe and together perform the sacrifice for Artemis of Brauron and Artemis of Mounykhia, *parthenoi* who were selected and neither older than ten nor younger than five. And the girls also performed the sacrifice placating the goddess, since the Athenians had once encountered a famine after they had killed a tame bear to the displeasure of the goddess.

Bekker *Anedota Graeca*: *arkteusai*:

Lysias mentioned that the term "to play the bear" refers to how maidens are dedicated to Artemis before their weddings. And *parthenoi* who play the bear are called "bears", as Euripides and Aristophanes say. Otherwise it is said that "to play the bear" means "to expiate oneself" and "to sacrifice" to Artemis. This is said because once a bear appeared in Piraeus and harmed many people, and afterwards it was killed by some young men and a plague ensued, and the god [Apollo] ordered them in an oracle to honor Artemis and to sacrifice a girl for the bear. And when, therefore, the Athenians were considering how to follow the oracle, one man would not prevent it, saying that he himself would perform the sacrifice. He got a goat and called it "daughter" and sacrificed it in secret. And the disease stopped. And when the citizens were in his confidence, he told them to question the god further. And when the god said that whoever claimed to have made the sacrifice should do it in this way also in the future, the man revealed what happened in secret. And from this, girls before their wedding did not hesitate to play the bear, as if they were expiating themselves for the killing of the animal.

Eustathius *ad Iliad* 2.772:

> A man named Embaros played a subtle trick in prayer. For he set up the sanctuary of Mounykhian Artemis. And a bear appeared in it and was slain by the Athenians, and so a plague arose. And from this the god proclaimed that there would be a release if someone should sacrifice his daughter to Artemis. And Embaros promised he would so this on the condition that his family should have the priesthood for life. Dressing up his daughter completely, he hid her in the inner recess of the temple and adorning a goat in clothing, he sacrificed it as if it were his daughter.

So we have two separate traditions here. In the one, it is a tame bear who hurts a young girl, is killed by her brother(s), which leads to a plague. The people send to Apollo's oracle at Delphi and are told that they must have their daughters "play the bear" for Artemis at some point between the ages of five and ten. No girl may cohabitate with a husband unless she has "played the bear." In the second account, a wild bear shows up at the main harbor of Athens, kills/mauls a few people, and is killed by some Athenian males. Once again a plague ensues, so once again they send to Delphi, where the god tells them to sacrifice one daughter to placate Artemis. One man is willing to do so, but only by hiding his daughter in Artemis' temple in Mounykhia and sacrificing a goat instead. Apparently Artemis was satisfied with this, and so the tradition endured.

These two separate origin stories correlate with two *separate* rituals. In the first, deriving from the first story, little girls aged five to ten must somehow play the bear for Artemis, at least in Brauron but possibly in other locations as well: The ritual is not tied exclusively to Brauron in any of the sources, merely performed there by the women in the *Lysistrata*. The idea that all the girls of Attika must perform this rite at some point is suggested by the fact that they are not permitted to marry without having "played the bear." In the second ritual, deriving from the second origin myth, older girls before marriage must spend time in Artemis' temple at Mounykhia, and possibly Brauron as well, and sacrifice a goat to the goddess.

The iconographic evidence has not shed much more light on these rituals. Most of the evidence comes from a series of little mixing bowls called *krateriskoi*, which came to light at Brauron, Mounykhia, the Athenian Agora (marketplace), and even on the city's acropolis. They depict females of various ages, including naked little girls, engaged in activities such as racing and dancing. Thus it was thought that these *krateriskoi* must be pictures of the *Arkteia*, and show little girls "playing the bear."

The problem is that the details on the krateriskoi are both broad and general. To quote Richard Hamilton on the kind of details they provide:

> The participants range from very young girls to adults; their garments, if they wear any, can reach to the ankles, to knees, midthigh, or the hips; the garments can be plain or decorated with white stripes or a white border, sleeved or sleeveless, belted or without belt. The figures' hair can be long, shoulder length, short, or tied in a bun. The females most often are racing but can be depicted dancing, processing, or standing, and they can hold torch, garland, basket, staff, or laurel branches.[27]

Or, to put it another way, they depict female rituals generally, with many ages and many activities portrayed. None of them can specifically be ascribed to the *Arkteia*, or any other particular rite.

And so we know that there were two rituals in Attika where girls "played the bear" for Artemis. In the one little girls called bears, aged five to ten, somehow "played the bear" in saffron-colored robes, possibly even tromping around pretending to be bears. In the other, girls on the verge of marriage also donned saffron robes and sacrificed to Artemis in her temple(s), possibly serving for some time at the sanctuary. They too were called bears.

Neither rite necessarily functioned as an initiation ritual, as is common in the modern scholarship. The girls in the first ritual were aged five to ten, and thus both too old and too young for initiations—they are too old for any rituals such as the Athenian *Khoes*, where three-year-old boys had their first sip of wine; and too young for menstrual or marital rituals. The second rite dealt with older girls on the eve of marriage. However, rather than seeing their *Arkteia* as an initiation per se, one might argue that by "playing the bear" and serving in Artemis' temple, they assuaged the goddess's potential anger over the fact that they were soon to leave her chorus and to lose their virginity, actions that provoked violent responses in the goddess (see below). So much is mentioned in a scholion to Theokritos (2.66), where the commentator notes that the *arktoi* "placate the goddess for their virginity so that they would not be the objects of her revenge." More generally, in the *Suda* it is claimed that the *arktoi* "soothe (*apomeilisomenai*) the goddess."[28]

AND THE FAUNS

Attika was not the only place where girls took on an animal identity to please Artemis, and bears were not the only animal. To the north, in Thessaly, epigraphic evidence dating from the third and second centuries BCE indicates that there girls played the fawn for Artemis. Like the case for Brauron, there appears to be some mythological precedent to this ritual: In Euripides' drama *Helen* the eponymous heroine mentions at line 380 the unnamed daughter of Merops, whom Artemis turned into a deer because of her excessive beauty. As such, as with Brauron, there was some affront to Artemis that was rectified by young girls "playing" the animal in question.

The majority of the inscriptions, all on marble stelai or diminutive temple sculptures, come from the close-set cities of Atrax, Larisa, and Phayttos, but at least one comes from the farther area of Demetrias, suggesting a broader spread of the tradition.[29] The ancient Greek word for "fawn" is *nebros*, and the inscriptions state that these girls *nebeusasa* ("acted as/played the fawn") for Artemis. Thus we have:[30]

> . . . daughter of Damokhares, to Artemis, having played the fawn.
>
> (Atrax, c. 300–200 BCE, *SEG* 46.636)

> To Artemis, Thaumareta daughter of Eudamides, having played the fawn.
>
> (Atrax, c. 300–200 BCE, *SEG* 49.602)

> To Artemis, Agis daughter of Astokrates, having played the fawn.
>
> (Phayttos, 300–200 BCE, *SEG* 51.732)

Nikê daughter of Nikagoras, having played the fawn.

(From Atrax, c. 200 BCE, *SEG* 34.489)

To Artemis, Aikhelokhis daughter of Pythagoras, having played the fawn, dedicated.

(Atrax, c. 200 BCE, *SEG* 34.493)

Antipatra daughter of Kleugenes, to Artemis, having played the fawn.

(Atrax, 200–150 BCE, *SEG* 42.240)

Laukrita daughter of Philonikos, having played the fawn.

(Atrax, c. 200–100 BCE, *SEG* 46.633)

Dynatis daughter of Melanthios, to Artemis Pagasitis, after having played the fawn.

(Demetrias, c. 100 BCE, *SEG* 44:456)

And finally:

To Artemis Throsia, Hippolokhos son of Hippolokhos, on behalf of Eubioteia, daughter of Alexippos, who played the fawn, recompense.

(Larisa)[31]

Unfortunately, the inscriptions give no evidence as to the age or marital status of the females playing the fawn, and it is entirely possible that the "fawns" were in fact older, married women. As we shall see in Chapter 5, the adult priestess of Artemis in Cyrenê was called *arkos*, "bear," and thus a comparable term might have been in use in Thessaly. However, the fact that the term "fawn" is used, rather than the adult *elaphos*, "deer," may indicate a more youthful role. Furthermore, all the "fawns" are listed as daughters rather than wives, which would indicate a more youthful age and unmarried status for the functionaries. As was the case with the bears in Attika, we have no idea as to their actual function, what "playing the fawn" really entailed.

ARTEMIS AND THE CHORUS

If Artemis' rapport with small children is more ambiguous than commonly assumed, her role in the lives of adolescents is on much firmer ground. Specifically, the dancing grounds of the chorus, where Artemis herself enjoyed the song and dance, and where humans entertained the goddess with their own lithe steps.

The singer of her *Homeric Hymn* (27) is most emphatic about Artemis' role in the dance. After a day of hunting (ll. 11–20):

whenever the arrow-shooter is sated with looking for prey,
Content in her mind, having slackened the well-wrought bow
She comes to the house of her dear brother
Phoibos Apollo, in the rich land of Delphi,
Where the Muses and Graces prepare a lovely chorus.

> There, having hung up the recurve bow and arrows,
> She leads at the head of the graceful dance
> Having a fair appearance, and they raise ambrosial voices.

The author of the *Homeric Hymn to Aphrodite* notes that the sylvan goddess enjoys the lyre and chorus as much as the mountains and hunt, all to the exclusion of the works of Aphrodite (l. 19). For Kallimakhos in his *Hymn to Artemis,* the goddess dances with the nymphs after a successful day's shooting, be that in Egypt, Greece, or even Skythia (ll. 170 ff.). In *Proverb* 9 the ancient Greek fable teller Aesop once went so far as to ask, "For where did Artemis *not* dance?" in reference to the goddess's predilection for the chorus.

Just as Artemis loved to dance, so too did young maidens and youths dance in her honor and at her festivals. In Euripides' *Iphigeneia at Aulis* (ll. 1480–1481), the young heroine asks the chorus of young maidens (*neanides*) to "Dance the circle for Artemis, Queen Artemis the blessed, around her shrine and altar," while in Euripides' *Trojan Women* the maidens of the chorus recount how they were singing and dancing in choruses around the house in honor of "the maiden of the hills, the child of Zeus" when the Akhaians invaded Troy (ll. 553–555). In later years Pausanias recorded how in Lakonia (3.10.7), "Karyai is a region sacred to Artemis and the nymphs, and here stands in the open-air an image of Artemis Karyatis. Here every year the Lakedaimonian maidens hold chorus-dances, and they have a traditional native dance."

One site especially famous for its choruses dedicated to Artemis was Ephesos. According to the Hellenistic poet Kallimakhos, this custom was established by Amazons who founded the cult by dancing around a wooden image of the goddess. Lines 237–247 of his *Hymn to Artemis* relate how:

> For you too the Amazons keen for war
> Once dedicated a wooden statue on the Ephesian shore
> Under an oak trunk; Hippo performed the rite for you.
> And they, Queen Oupis, around the statue danced a war dance first,
> In armor, bearing shields; and then again
> Stationed in a circle, dancing a broad chorus. And the whistling
> Pipes accompanied in fine form, so that
> They might begin the beating dance.

Later this ritual was taken up by the girls of Ephesos, as described by the Athenian comic poet Autokrates in his play *Tympanistai* ("Drum-Players") as quoted in the Roman scholar Aelian's *De Natura Animalium* (12.9):

> How the dear maiden
> Girls of the Lydians dance,
> Nimbly leaping, and pushing back
> Their long hair with their hands,
> Beside Ephesian Artemis
> Most beautiful, and their hips
> Dipping and then again
> Rising up, just like a leaping wagtail bird.

If this dance was alluded to by Aristophanes in his comedy *Clouds*, when the play-wright summons (ll. 599–600) "You blessed goddess who has the all-golden house of Ephesos, in which Lydian girls greatly revere you," then we have evidence that this cult practice dates back into the fifth century BCE at the least.

Artemis was not the only deity who took part in the chorus or was worshipped with dance. Just as maidens (and boys: see below) danced for Artemis, young men danced for Apollo as early as the composition of the Homeric epics; Hera, Aphrodite, Athena, and Demeter had their choral entertainments; and all choral dance in Athenian drama was by its very nature dedicated to Dionysos. Among the host of Olympos it was Apollo who was the *choregos* ("chorus-leader") extraordinaire, typically playing for the Muses who entertained the Olympians.

Nevertheless, Artemis dancing with her maiden nymphs, or adolescents dancing for Artemis, were prominent images in the ancient Greek imagination. A large part of this is because in ancient Greece the chorus was not only a religious practice, but also a means of education, and thus part of the process by which children metamorphosed into adults. This is explicitly described by the fifth-century Athenian philosopher Plato in his *Laws* (664b–665a):

> We spoke, if we recall, at the start of our talk about how the nature of all the young is fiery, not the sort to keep quiet either in the body or voice, but they always blather randomly and leap about; and the perception of the order of both of these [body and voice] does not pertain to other living beings, but only to humans alone. Indeed, to the ordering of movement the name "rhythm" is given, and that of voice—when the sharp is mixed with the deep—the name offered is "harmony." The two together is called "chorustry."

Artemis is especially well suited to this aspect of Greek artistic culture because it is she who presides over this development. As the goddess of the young, then, Artemis uses the chorus to educate her charges and turn them into educated, well-formed adults.

On the darker side, as noted in Chapter 3, it was often in Artemis' choruses, myth-ological or real, that young girls were seduced or raped, and thus forcibly shifted from girlhood into womanhood. As the goddess of transitions, Artemis naturally presided over this aspect of ancient Greek life. Often times we are expected to feel sympathy for these victims of rape, but, as we shall see, Artemis herself was not always so understanding.

SEX AND PUNISHMENT

One of the themes that reappear frequently in the study of Artemis is that the moment of transition from virgin to no-longer-virgin for females was dangerous and often violent. As noted in Chapter 3, although Artemis herself remained a perpetual virgin, the girls, nymphs, and even goddesses dancing with her in the chorus were often raped, as Persephonê and the Lakonian girls at Karyai, or seduced, as with Polymelê. Although the former theme is more popular—that of violent abduction—the matter of seduction was also critically dangerous, for maidens who could not control themselves were punished by Artemis.

Kallisto

The most famous example of Artemis' wrath against her unchaste companions is the tale of Kallisto. Although most of the references to her are late (such as Apollodoros, Pausanias (8.3.6-7), and Ovid (*Metamorphoses* 2.405-531), all Roman in date), Apollodoros claims that Hesiod discussed her, while the fifth-century playwright Aeschylus has a lost play called *Kallisto*, and thus we do have evidence that her tale goes very far back in Greek mythology. According to Apollodoros' account in his *Bibliothekê* (*Library*, 3.8.2), Kallisto was either a nymph or mortal girl who joined Artemis' hunting band, dressing like the goddess and vowing to remain a virgin. However, Zeus either seduced or, according to the majority of sources, raped the girl, having approached her by disguising himself either as Artemis herself or her brother Apollo. Then, to hide his deed, he turned Kallisto, now pregnant, into a bear to hide her from his wife. In other versions of the tale, it is Artemis who turns the girl into a beast. Eventually Artemis shot the girl-turned-bear, either to please Hera or to punish the girl for having lost her virginity. With some modicum of compassion, Zeus placed Kallisto in the heavens, where she is the constellation Ursa Major (The Great Bear). He also saved the son with whom she was pregnant—Arktos, "Bear," who went on to become the forefather of the Arkadians.

The story is painfully distasteful to modern readers, as it punishes a victim for being raped. Nevertheless it does express clearly the dangers involved in a girls' transition into heterosexuality. The common themes are that it is frightening and violent, the girl's volition is irrelevant, pregnancy is mostly inevitable, but that in the end a prize is received, typically socially acceptable marriage (as was the case with Persephonê), but in this instance catasterism and immortality. And a son.

Artemis Triklaria of Patrai

Such benefits are rare for Artemis' victims. They tend to die, either via shame-induced suicide or, in the case of Komaitho and Melanippos, divinely sanctioned execution by sacrifice. According to Pausanias (7.19.1-20.2), once upon a time the shrine of Triklarian Artemis in Patrai in Akhaia was tended by a virgin girl until it was time to marry her off. One of these virgin priestesses was Komaitho, the most beautiful girl in Patrai of her day. She, of course, fell madly in love with Melanippos, the handsomest youth in town. Alas, their parents refused to let them marry, and so the couple indulged their passion in Artemis' shrine. In revenge, Artemis sent a plague to the entire town, withering the crops and sickening the people. Finally the citizens sent to Delphi to find out how to end the plague, and the Pythia instructed the Patrians to sacrifice Komaitho and Melanippos to Artemis, and henceforth to sacrifice the most beautiful maid and youth to the goddesses every year. The river by the shrine where the sacrifices took place came to be known as Ameilikhios, "Implacable."

Later, the oracle at Delphi sent a further message: The sacrifices would stop when a strange king brought a strange god to Patrai. Meanwhile, Eurypolos, King of Olenos, was leaving Troy after the war when he received an image of Dionysos made by Hephaistos in a box. Upon opening the box and seeing the image, he went mad. During periods of lucidity, he made his way to Delphi, where the oracle told him that he would be cured when he reached a place in Greece where they were performing a foreign sacrifice and he dedicated the god-in-a-box there. Eurypolos came to Patrai, where they were performing a very un-Greek human sacrifice to Artemis. There he established worship of Dionysos Aisymnestos [Dictator], and the sacrifices came to an end. According to Pausanias (7.20.1–2):

> This same night has received this mark of honor—the children, as many as are in the region, walk down to the Meilikhios River with crowns of wheat-shafts on their heads. They were so bedecked even in the old times, those whom they led to be sacrificed to Artemis. But in our day they put aside the garlands of wheat before the goddess, and bathing in the river and immediately taking on new garlands of ivy they go to the sanctuary of [Dionysos] Aisymnestos. These things they established for them to do.

The practice of sacrificing adolescents was replaced by a ritual where younger children bathe in the river by Artemis' shrine. They descend decked out like the former victims, but upon emerging from the stream they don the regalia of Dionysos—the ivy. There is some debate as to whether the *paides* who perform the ritual are of both sexes or just boys.[32] As the word *pais* (sing. for *paides*) is functionally gender neutral and refers specifically to young children of either sex (as opposed to, say, *parthenos*, which designates an adolescent female), both sexes are certainly possibly. Furthermore, as the ritual implicated both the males and the females of Patrai, it is more likely that the *paides* are both boys and girls.

Although Dionysos is most popularly known as the god of wine, for which we love him dearly, he is more generally a deity of liminality, of the (temporary) crossing of boundaries such as sane and mad (thus intoxication), male and female, human and animal. He steps in to remedy a situation that had gone totally wrong by Greek standards. Komaitho and Melanippos inappropriately made the transition from child to adult by way of sexuality, for they had sex outside of marriage and inside of a shrine, known as a *miasma* or ritual impurity in Greek. Their transgression brought disaster to the entire town and led to the annual sacrifice of a girl and boy. When Dionysos arrived he corrected the rite by providing an alternate means of crossing that boundary. Now younger children, before their hormones kick in, as we might say, literally went to take a cold bath and place themselves under the protection of Dionysos, a deity who, much like Artemis, was instrumental in crossing boundaries. Dionysos could help them to channel (not suppress!) their wilder impulses and thus refrain from offending the virgin goddess.

Eurypolos was returning from the Trojan War when he helped to bring an end to the "barbaric" (meaning un-Greek) ritual of human sacrifice, so it is clear that the origins of this tale are shrouded deep in mythological time, and there was probably never an actual period when the human sacrifice portion of the myth took place. What is important is that the residents of Patrai believed that their practice—bringing children to the River Meilikhios—was a correction for the ancient problem, and that Dionysos helped to protect their children from the wrath of Artemis.

THE ILLNESS OF VIRGINS

The inverse of young women inadvertently losing their virginity and being punished by Artemis in myth is young women not losing their virginity soon enough and being punished by their own bodies and being saved by Artemis in real life. So much is recorded in the medical texts of the fourth century BCE, as recorded in the Hippokratic "On Virgins" (VIII.466). This is a document written by men expressing their own belief on how the female body functioned (or did not) in late adolescence. Although the author takes a "scientific" perspective, he does indicate that the common populace recognized the role of Artemis in curing adolescent girls who went crazy when sexual maturity came upon them.

> As a result of visions, many people choke to death, more women than men . . . And virgins who do not take a husband at the appropriate time for marriage experience these visions more frequently, especially at the time of their first monthly period, although previously they have had no such bad dreams of this sort. For later the blood collects in the womb in preparation to flow out; but when the mouth of the egress is not opened up, and more blood flows into the womb on account of the body's nourishment of it and its growth, then the blood which has no place to flow out, because of its abundance, rushes up to the heart and to the lungs; and when these are filled with blood, the heart becomes sluggish and then, because of the sluggishness, numb, and then, because of the numbness, insanity takes hold of the women . . . When these places are filled with blood, shivering sets in with fevers . . . When this is the state of affairs, the girl goes crazy because of the violent inflammation, and she becomes murderous because of the decay, and is afraid and fearful because of the darkness. The girls try to choke themselves because of the pressure on their hearts; their will, distraught and anguished because of the bad condition of the blood, forces evil in itself. In some cases the girl says dreadful things; [the visions] order her to jump up and throw herself into wells and drown, as if this were good for her and served some useful purpose. When a girl does not have visions, a desire sets in which compels her to love death as if it were a form of good. When this person returns to her right mind, women give to Artemis various offerings, especially the most valuable of women's robes, following the orders of oracles.[33]

As we shall see in the following chapter, dedicating clothing to Artemis was also practiced by women who successfully gave birth. Thus, there was a common rite for thanking the goddess on either side of the transition into full womanhood.

The illness of other virgins

The medical corpus is not the only place where we find information about Artemis' healing abilities. Although more commonly known as a goddess of plague (see Chapter 6), Artemis also appears in the mythology as a healing deity, although not to the extent shown by her brother Paian Apollo. The most famous example of this function of the goddess appears in Bakkhylides' *11th Epinician*, where he recounts how the goddess cured the daughters of King Proitos of insanity by her sanctuary at Lousoi in Arkadia (*Epinician* 11, ll 37–58, 92–119):

And now Artemis Agrotera
Of the golden shaft, gentle one,
Bow-famous, gave lasting victory.
To her once the son of Abas set up
An altar sought with many prayers,
Along with his fair-clothed daughters.
Them all-powerful Hera scared
From the lovely, high-roofed halls
Of Proitos, saddling their minds
With powerful, constraining blows,
For while still in maidenly
Spirit they went to the temenos
Of the purple-belted goddess
Saying that their father
Excelled in wealth the shining consort
Of reverend, wide-reigning Zeus.
In anger at them
[Hera] cast a thought back into their chests
To flee to the fluttering-leaved mountain,
Sending forth terrible cries,
Leaving the city of Tiryns
And its god-built paths.
. . .
Thirteen full months they suffered throughout the thick-shaded forest.
And then they fled to sheep-pasturing
Arkadia; but when indeed
Their father came to the fair-flowing river Lousos,
Then washing his skin he
Called on the ox-eyed daughter
Of purple-veiled Leto—
Stretching his hands toward the rays
Of the swift-chariot sun—
To remove the wretched, raving madness
From his children.
"I shall sacrifice twenty red bulls
Unbroken."
The beast-hunter of excellent father
Heard the praying man, and she persuaded Hera
To stop driving mad the girls
With blossoming crowns.
And they immediately stained your temenos and built altar
With the blood of sheep
And set up a women's chorus.
And then you approached the Ares-loving
Men of the horse-rearing city of Akhaia,
And with good fortune
You inhabit Metaponton, O
Golden Mistress of the people,
And for you is a lovely grove
By well-watered Kasas.

BOYS TO MEN

Artemis is less visible in the transition from boyhood to manhood in ancient Greece. This is probably because the transition was far more drawn out, and, in contrast to what it was for girls, more social than physical. For girls, the progression from girl to woman was mostly biological—a girl is an unmarried *parthenos*, whereas a woman (*gynê*) is a wife (also *gynê*) and a mother (see Chapter 5). The whole process takes about a year, and is usually completed before the girl turns 19 years of age at the oldest.

For boys, the process is comparatively long. At 18 years of age, Athenian males, for whom we have the best evidence, could inherit, represent themselves in the law courts, and orphans were declared independent of state care. They became ephebes in military training, just as Spartan boys joined the krypteia at this age. Nevertheless, men aged 20 to 30 were still thought of as quite young, *neoi* in Athens (literally "new ones") and *hebontes* in Sparta (literally "young ones").[34] Spartan males married at this point, but they were not free to live with their families until age 30. Most other Greek males married between ages 30 and 36. Since most men only began having children around age 30, by the time a man turned 30 years of age himself his father was probably dead, meaning that one acquired a wife and one's inheritance at roughly the same time. And so, in the eyes of the law and state, one was officially a man.

As Robert Garland noted in his *The Greek Way of Life*, the maturation process for males was an intensely social process. For his archetypal Telemakhos, becoming a man meant imposing his will on his mother, confronting the suitors who were depleting his paternal estate, going out in the world to establish ties with his father's allies, and making new *xenia*-relationships on his own. For less mythic lads, rites of passage included the military training mentioned above, participation in social-bonding rituals such as the Koureôtis, and taking part in the governmental apparatus. The range of changes involved numerous deities, those who protect the civic body, the clan, the military, the institution of marriage. Any role of Artemis diminishes under the length and complication of the male maturation process.

Nevertheless, it was still Artemis who presided over the chorus, boys' as well as girls'. Boys on the cusp of manhood dedicated locks of hair to Artemis, as did girls (see Chapter 5).

Furthermore, the evidence indicates that Artemis took an active concern in the survival of boys, and in this regard two data are worthy of note. In his *Constitution of the Lakedaimonians* (2.9), Xenophon tells us that Lykourgos, the Spartan law-giver, established it as a "noble thing" for starving Spartan boys to steal as many cheeses as possible from Ortheia.[35] Likewise, Herodotos recalls how once (3.48):

> Periandros son of Kypselos [of Corinth] sent off three hundred sons of the most eminent men of the Korkyrians to Sardis, to Alyattes, for castration. When the Corinthians bringing the boys docked at Samos, the Samians learned of the story—how they were taking them to Sardis. First they instructed the boys to take hold of the sanctuary of Artemis, and then they did not allow them to drag the suppliants from the sanctuary. Then when the Corinthians denied them food, the Samians had a festival, which is still held even now in the same way. For at night, so long

as the boys were suppliants, they set up choruses of maidens and youths, and they officially established that the choruses should carry cakes of sesame and honey, so that the Korkyrian boys, snatching them, might have food. And this took place until such time as the Corinthian guards left for home. Then the Samians returned the boys to Korkyra.

In both instances we have either a ritual in honor of Artemis (Samos) or a practice that seems to take place in her sanctuary (Sparta), where starving boys steal her food in her temenos. The Samian ritual was set up precisely so these boys could steal the food, but it must be noted that the boys are nevertheless not technically part of the ritual. In all other known contexts with all other deities, stealing anything from the sanctuary would be deemed *asebês*—impious. In these two instances, it is not, and is actually encouraged (even if the Spartan boys get nominally flogged for it). This indicates that the Greeks understood that it was permissible for these suppliants to steal "religious" food in a non-religious/non-ritual way. Both examples pertain to Artemis, and both pertain to boys who are desperate. So it would appear that some aspect of Artemis' persona/cult specifically and panhellenically permitted the "hunting" of food in her sanctuaries to those in such desperate straits that they had to. I believe this, more than anything else, expresses the goddess's concern for the well-being of boys.

Furthermore, one might note that by keeping the boys from being castrated, Artemis allowed them to make the transition from boys to men, a transition that would have been physically impossible had the castration taken place. As Claude Calame summarized Artemis' role in the narrative, "It looks as if the consumption of foods, associated in ancient Greece with the consummation of the marriage, would rescue the adolescents from the symbolic death represented in the founding event by the castration."[36]

OVERVIEW

Although in modern times we tend to think of Artemis as the goddess who protects and guides children, the evidence indicates that the situation was far more complicated in ancient Greece. Many tales of her cults throughout Greece, as in Attika and Patrai, refer to the demanded sacrifice of children, both young and adolescent. Rituals such as playing the bear emerged not as initiation rites with the goddess presiding over the growth of her young charges, but as means of assuaging Artemis' divine anger against her presumed charges.

Evidence for a kourotrophic Artemis who tends to *small* children is late in the ancient literature, and may have more to do with growing sentimentality than to any aspect of the Greek goddess's persona. The iconography indicates that it was probably not so much infants who were dedicated to Artemis, but rather thanksgiving votives from older females who were grateful for a successful parturition. As such, the kourotrophic figurines and reliefs from Artemis' sanctuaries say more about the goddess's role in the lives of mothers than in that of babies.

Our evidence becomes better when we look at the place of Artemis in the lives of adolescents, those who are about to make the transition from childhood to adulthood.

In the chorus especially, Artemis reveled and received the worship of girls and boys, teaching them good form and commensality. And yet even here a dark side lingered. Those girls led to the edge of womanhood in Artemis' choruses were often violently thrown over the divide, and the goddess could be remarkably cold-hearted to those who landed on the other side. Things were medically just as bad for those who did not make the transition.

Unlike with girls, Artemis did not preside entirely over the long process that turned boys into men. Social and military matters belonged more in the realms of deities such as Apollo, Herakles, and Athena. Nevertheless, in a stroke of amazing sympathy, Artemis showed pity on desperate boys and shared her food with them.

NOTES

1 Pirenne-Delforge 2004: *passim*; Hadzisteliou Price 1978: 189–195.
2 Hadzisteliou Price 1978: 160.
3 This part of the votive is reconstructed, but the placement seems confirmed by the location of the girl's head.
4 *LIMC* Artemis 723 and 723a.
5 Hadzisteliou Price 1978: 96–164.
6 *LIMC* Artemis 721.
7 Hadzisteliou Price 1978: 151–152.
8 Dakoronia and Gounaropoulou 1992: 217.
9 Ibid.: 218.
10 Ibid.: 220.
11 Sorry: a bit of vegan humor there.
12 Cole 2004: 213.
13 Dakoronia and Gounaropoulou 1992: 220; Cole 2004: 213.
14 Beaumont 2003: 78.
15 Ibid.
16 Demand 1994: 89 and n.14, with references.
17 Lundgreen 2009: 122.
18 Themelis 1994: *passim*. See also Connelly 2007: 147–157.
19 Themelis 1994: 107–111.
20 Beaumont 2003: 79.
21 The "they" refers to the children she cares for.
22 Hadzisteliou Price 1978: 159.
23 Burkert 1985: 255.
24 Larson 2001: 42–43.
25 Calame 2001: 100–101.
26 For all of the sources, and an excellent analysis, see Faraone 2003: 51–61. See also Sale 1975: *passim* and Osborne 1985: 161–164. All translations excerpted from Faraone.
27 Hamilton 1989: 453.
28 Cole 2004: 210–211.
29 Graninger 2007: 155.

30 Ibid.: 155, n. 27.
31 Ibid.: 157.
32 Redfield 1990: 119–120.
33 Translation excerpted from Lefkowitz and Fant 1992: 242–243. Many of the symptoms are similar to those of rape survivors.
34 Garland 1990: 200–201.
35 See Chapter 6 for a full study of this practice.
36 Calame 2001: 98.

5

ARTEMIS AND WOMEN

As a goddess of transitions, one important role for Artemis was turning girls into women. As discussed in Chapters 2 and 4, Artemis presided over the chorus, where in literature and historiography nubile maidens were snatched away to become brides or rape victims, and thus initiated one way or another into the realms of sexuality. Artemis herself was free from such threats; nevertheless, it was she, along with Hera and Aphrodite, who helped girls to make the transformation from maiden to bride to mother. It was only when a female had given birth to her first child in wedlock that she was truly considered to be a woman.

A few words on terminology. The word often translated as "maiden" is *parthenos* in Greek. The word "maiden" is preferred to "virgin" because a *parthenos* need not be a physical virgin in the modern understanding. Instead, one might understand a *parthenos* to be a female who is not yet socially recognized as a mother. Thus, in Euripides' *Ion*, the hero's mother Kreusa—who was raped by Apollo, hid her pregnancy, and exposed the child at birth—is still called a *parthenos* by the chorus, for she is not yet a socially recognized mother of children to her husband Xouthos.

Ideally, a *parthenos* loses her virginity on her wedding night (or, at worst, pretty close to that time). As such, a newly wed female is called a *nymphê*, translated as "bride." This is a female who is probably no longer a physical virgin as we would understand it, but who has not yet given birth to a child. She is in a liminal state that lasts until the birth of her first born.

Once a socially recognized wife and mother, a female becomes a *gynê*, a word which means both "wife" and "woman" in ancient Greek.

Artemis is most important in the lives of *parthenoi* and *gynaikes* (pl. of *gynê*). She is the kourotrophos who helped to bring the maidens to the edge of adulthood. In return, maidens had to assuage the goddess's possible anger over the impending loss of their virginity so that they would not suffer as did the huntress Kallisto or the priestess Komaitho. Rituals such as the older girls' *Arkteia* in Athens were of this caliber. For *gynaikes*, Artemis was especially important during parturition, when she functioned as the divine midwife who helped bring the new child into the world or, possibly, killed the mother in the process.

Of course, Artemis was far less involved in the sex that physically transformed the maiden into a mother, which was the domain of Aphrodite. Nevertheless, the evidence indicates that even the liminal bride was involved in rites to Artemis, mainly so that, when the moment of childbirth grew near, the goddess was more likely to serve as midwife than huntress.

FROM *PARTHENOS* TO *NYMPHÊ*

A common way for girls-becoming-women to pay their respects to Artemis was through the dedication of a lock of hair. To be sure, Artemis was not the exclusive recipient of such dedications: Most ancient Greek deities from Apollo through Zeus, as well as various river lords and several heroes and heroines, received them. Our earliest evidence for this practice dates back to Homer's *Iliad* and Akhilleus' vow to dedicate a lock of his hair to his home town river deity Sperkheus upon his (non-existent) return (*Il*. 23.141). Although the dedication of a tress in fulfillment of a vow was a common ritual practice in ancient Greece and extended well into the Roman period,[1] it was also an extremely common rite-of-passage, especially for girls passing from girlhood into adult status by way of marriage. Thus on Delos we read (Herodotos 4.35):

> And these things indeed I know that they do for those same maidens who came from the Hyperboreans and died on Delos—both the girls and the boys of the Delians cut their hair. The girls before marriage cut off a tress and wrap it around a spindle and place it on the tomb (the tomb is within the Artemision precinct on the left, where the olive tree grows); the Delian boys wrap the hair around some green shoot and they lay it on the tomb.

Identical practices are still recorded in the writings of Pausanias. Thus, concerning the "Delian Maidens" he writes (1.43.4), "It is established for girls to bring libations and to dedicate a tress of hair on the tomb of Iphianoê before their wedding, just as the daughters of the Delians once cut their hair for Hekaergê and Opis." Likewise the cult of Hippolytos in Troizen (2.32.1): "Every maiden cuts off a tress of hair for him before her wedding, and bringing it to the temple dedicates it." In the *Greek Anthology* we read of a Hellenistic dedication to Artemis as composed by Damagetos (*GA* 6.277):

> To Artemis, allotted the bow and arrow-prowess,
> To you this tress of her own hair has Arsinoê left
> By the fragrant temple, the maiden [daughter] of Ptolemy
> Having shorn the lovely lock.

Other items representing childhood could also be dedicated to Artemis as the child became an adult. In Antipater's epigram, we read how the girl Hippê on the eve of marriage dedicated her toy dice to the goddess (*GA* 6.276):

> The thick-haired maiden Hippê has put up her curly
> Tresses, wiping clean her fragrant temples;
> For already the fulfillment of her marriage has come,
> And the scarf upon her temples demands maidenly hair.
> Artemis, to you for the sake of marriage and progeny
> For the child of Lykomedes, who has abandoned her knuckle-bones [dice].

These pre-nuptial rites were called *proteleia* in Greek. Another ritual in honor of Artemis engaged in by maidens on the cusp of marriage—at least those living in parts of Sicily—was to bear a *kaneon* (the basket in which sacrificial implements were kept) to the goddess. The evidence for this appears in a *scholion* to Theokritos and a Hellenistic marble relief dedication to the goddess. As the scholiast explained the Sicilian rite (Scholion to Theokritos II 66–67):

> For they hold it customary to carry a (sacrificial) basket to Artemis—those females about to be married—as an expiation for their maidenhood (*parthenias*), lest they be resented by her . . . And those females of an age to wed used to bear sacrificial baskets to Artemis as an apology for their maidenhood to the goddess, so that she might not be angry.

Clearly the girls involved were trying to avoid a fate similar to that of Kallisto. An iconographic portrayal of such a practice appears on a third-century BCE marble votive from Tyndaris in Sicily, now in the Ny Carlsberg Glyptotek in Copenhagen (Figure 5.1).

The inscription reads: *Prôtos and Menippê to Artemis Eupraxia* ("Good Work"). The image, however, shows three humans before the goddess: Protos in front, followed by his equally sized wife, both of whom are followed by a smaller female. Since its earliest

Figure 5.1 Marble votive relief to Artemis from Tyndaris, Sicily, third century BCE. Ny Carlsberg Glyptotek, Copenhagen, 516. Image © Ny Carlsberg Glyptotek, Copenhagen. Photo by Ole Haupt.

publication in 1849 the interpretation of this image has been that the parents Protos and Menippê offered this votive to Artemis in thanksgiving for the successful marriage of their unnamed daughter.[2] The three-lobed item in Artemis' left hand is the *kaneon* she apparently just received from the daughter-bride.

NYMPHÊ TO MATER

Artemis was not absent when young brides began their careers as new wives. Although this time when girls were newly inducted into the rites of sexuality appears to be a period when the former virgins turn their backs on Artemis, a fourth-century inscription pertaining to purity regulations from Cyrenê in northern Africa indicates that these young brides were still quite focused on the goddess of their youth. Here we read (*SEG* IX 72 = *LSCG* 115, B, ll. 1–23):

> a bride (*nympham*) comes to the bed-chamber (*koitatêrion*), she must bring a p[enalty] to Artemis, and she herself may not be under the same roof as her man/husband and must not be polluted until she comes to Artemis. She who has not done these things is willingly polluted; having purified the Artamition (temple of Artemis) let her sacrifice an adult animal as penalty, and then go to the bed-chamber. If she is unwillingly polluted, let her purify the sanctuary.

> A bride must go down to the *nympheion* to Artemis whenever she wishes during the Artemitia, but the sooner the better. She who does not go down, let her sacrifice to Artemis what is customary at the Artemitia; as one who has not gone down let her purify the sanctuary and sacrifice in addition an adult animal as penalty.

> A pregnant bride (*nympha kuoisa* = a first-time mother) before giving birth shall go down to the *nympheion* to Artemis . . . let her give to the Arkos ("bear" = priestess of Artemis) the feet and the head and the skin. If she does not go down before giving birth, let her go down with an adult animal. Let her who has gone down be pure the seventh, eighth, and ninth (days), and may she who has not gone down be pure these same days. If she is polluted, having purified herself may she purify the sanctuary and sacrifice in addition an adult animal as penalty.

The broken, fragmentary state of the inscription makes it extremely difficult to derive much meaning from it. It seems that two distinct locations are involved—the *koitatêrion* of the first clause and the *nympheion* in clauses two and three. According to the wording of the text, one simply goes "to" the *koitatêrion* ("bed-chamber"; think "coitus" perhaps?), whereas one goes "down to" the *nympheion*.

Considering the context, it would appear that the *kotatêrion* is simply the bridal bedroom, the place where a girl will lose her virginity to her husband and thus become an official *nymphê*. According to the dictates of the inscription, the girl must pay a penalty to Artemis before losing her virginity. The "penalty" is unknown but may be similar to the other pre-marital rites we have seen, ranging from the dedication of a lock of hair or a childhood toy, to some service/sacrifice in the sanctuary as with the cults of the older "bears" in Attika, to the formal offering of a "recompense" (*lytra*) as on the inscription from Larisa made by Hippolokhos son of Hippolokhos on behalf of his bride (?) Eubioteia (see Chapter 4).[3]

If she goes to this room and "is under the same roof with" (i.e. "has sex with") her husband before offering the appropriate offering to Artemis, she must pay as penalty the sacrifice of an (expensive) adult animal. The girl is also expected to remain "unpolluted," but the inscription gives no evidence as to what this entails. The pollution might be willing or unwilling, so it is difficult to suggest that sexuality is specifically what is at issue, especially considering the girl's virginal state. It is likely that two separate ideas are at play here: On the one hand, the girl must pay the penalty to Artemis before losing her virginity. However, she must also be in a state of ritual purity when she makes that offering. If, say, the girl lived in a house where a birth or death had recently occurred (both ritual *miasma*),[4] then she might be understood to be unwillingly polluted, and if she could not be ritually purified in time before the wedding to make her offering, then she is required to purify the sanctuary. If she willingly attended a funeral or other such pollution-inducing event, then she is willingly polluted, and must offer the sacrifice in addition to the purification.

Once she is married, the *nymphê* must go down to the second place, the *nympheion*. This can be taken either as "bride place" or as an actual shrine of the nymphs, although the former is the more likely. In an early publication of the site François Chamoux suggested that this *nympheion* consisted of a series of fountains and bathing units located next to the temenos of Apollo, where new brides could literally bathe in the baths of Artemis.[5] However, there is no evidence for the ritual use of this area next to the temenos, and thus the current hypothesis is that the *nympheion* may be a room within the temple of Artemis, located within Apollo's sanctuary.[6] The sanctuary being located on a lower level than the city of Cyrenê itself, the notion of "going down" refers literally to the physical location of the temenos. There is no evidence of what the new bride must do in the *nympheion* during the Artemitia. However, because the one who goes late must offer "what is customary [to sacrifice] at the Artemitia," it may indicate that she is offering late what brides normally offered in a more timely fashion. In addition, she must purify the sanctuary and offer an adult animal in recompense for her lack of alacrity.

Finally, the bride, about to become a new mother and thus, finally, a *gynê*, makes another dedication to the goddess. Animal sacrifice is implied, and the payment offered to the priestess, the Arkos, is clearly stipulated: head, feet, skin. Such specified payments to a priest or priestess for presiding over a ritual are commonplace in the ancient Greek epigraphy (see below), and is in no way a remarkable detail here, other than the specific title of the priestess. As ever, if the new mother does not manage to make the dedication before parturition, standard penalties are in place (and, let's face it, this one is going to be difficult to time well). It is uncertain what is meant by staying pure on the seventh through ninth days. These may refer to the days of the month, or to the days after parturition. If the latter, it is worth noting that according to the same inscription (face A, ll. 16–20), the parturient mother pollutes the household for three days after the birth. Her purity on days seven–nine may be part of her own re-attainment of ritual purity.

And so the bride still focuses her energies upon Artemis. She pays homage to the goddess before the loss of her virginity; and again once that virginity is lost. An animal is sacrificed before the birth of her first child, probably in the hopes that Artemis will not kill the new mother or child, and may even help with the birth.

MATERNITY

In the fifth and fourth centuries BCE the strangest thing happened: Artemis became a goddess of childbirth, to point of becoming an actual midwife. How strange is this? Well, first, Artemis is a perpetual virgin who mainly cavorts with other virgins and thus has no personal experience with pregnancy or childbirth. Second, Artemis is the goddess *who kills women* (*Il.* 21.483), and women are never so close to death as when giving birth. Pausanias was quite correct when he wrote (4.30.5):

> Just as in the *Iliad* he [Homer] made Athena and Enyo to have leadership of those making war, and Artemis to be a terror (*phoberan*) of women in labor, and to Aphrodite the works of marriage are a concern.

It is likely that it was this second aspect, at least in part, that led the virgin goddess to become the virgin *sage-femme*. As the goddess who kills women (in childbirth or otherwise), she is also the goddess one invokes *not* to kill women (especially in child-birth). All deities are capable of the positive and negative aspects of their powers. Thus Apollo, the god of healing (especially in his manifestation as Paian), is the god of plague in *Iliad* 1. Demeter, the goddess of food and fertility, brings famine in her *Homeric Hymn*. Aphrodite, the goddess of sex, makes the Lemnian women repugnant to their husbands as referenced in Aeschylus' *Libation Bearers* (ll. 631–634). And so it is possible for Artemis, the "lion to women," to refrain from killing them in their hour of greatest need.

The earliest evidence we have for Artemis as a goddess who watches over women in childbirth comes from Aeschylus' *Suppliants*, performed c. 465 BCE. Here, in line 675 speak the suppliant women:

> We pray always that other guardians of the land be born,
> And that Artemis-Hekatê watch over the women's travails.
>
> *Tiktesthai d'ephorous gâs allous eukhometh'aei,*
> *Artemin d'Hekatan gynaikôn lokhous ephoreuein.*

Before this verse, there is no extant evidence in the literary, epigraphic, or archaeological corpora that indicates that Artemis had any role in childbirth, no epithets such as *Lokhia* or *Lysizonos*, no dedications of votive uteri,[7] no prayers of thanksgiving for healthy children. It all begins here with Aeschylus.

Which, of course, begs the question of what the playwright himself was thinking. To this point Artemis is not a goddess of childbirth. Hekatê, although certainly a kouro-trophic goddess since Hesiod's *Theogony* (see Chapter 4), is also not a goddess of childbirth, and thus her syncretism with Artemis cannot serve as an explanation. It is possible, however, that Aeschylus summons Artemis as a goddess who inhabits and watches over the land itself (see Chapter 3). That is, her role here pertains more to the newly born guardians of that land than necessarily to the women bearing them. This focus is expressed/emphasized in the verse itself, where the birth of the newly reared guardians—*ephorous*—is watched over—*ephoreuein*—by Artemis-Hekatê. Hekatê then becomes a logical counterpoint, as it is she who tends to newborns as soon as "they see with their eyes the light of much-seeing Eos" (*Theogony* ll. 450–452). It is likely, then, that Aeschylus had in mind not the women in labor so much as the young guardians to whom they were giving birth. Aeschylus, himself a veteran of Marathon, was decidedly pro-military, and it is to be expected that he would invoke Artemis as a goddess associated with the victory at Marathon (see Chapter 3).[8]

It is not until the works of Euripides in the later fifth century that Artemis truly becomes a goddess of childbirth per se, specifically as Artemis *(Eu)Lokhia*—Artemis of (Good) Parturition. This epithet first appears in 428 BCE in Euripides' *Hippolytos*, ll. 161–168, when the chorus claims:

> "It is common for the awful, wretched impotence of
> Women to dwell with the intractable harmony
> Of birth pangs and folly.
> Through my own womb once shot this
> Stream. The heavenly Eulokhia,
> Queen of bows, I called on—
> Artemis, and she, always much-envied—visits
> Me with the gods' blessing."

Five years later Artemis receives the epithet of *Lokhia* in Euripides' *Suppliants* (ll. 955–960):

> "No longer blessed with children, no longer blessed
> With offspring, nor does good fortune abide
> With me amongst the son-bearing Argives;
> Nor does Artemis Lokheia
> Call to those who are childless."

Finally, in 415 with Eurpides' most famous drama *Iphigeneia Amongst the Tauroi*, the Chorus intones (ll. 1093–1102):

> Halcyon bird . . .
> I compare laments with yours,
> Unwinged bird,
> Yearning for the assemblies of the Greeks,
> Yearning for Artemis Lokheia,
> Who by the Kynthian hill dwells,
> And the delicate palm and
> The flourishing laurel and
> The sacred shoot of silvery olive—
> Dear travail of Leto.

It is perhaps not surprising that a new aspect of an old deity emerges in the works of Euripides. As is becoming increasingly evident in modern scholarship, an uncomfortable amount of ancient Greek religion and mythology seems to have been created by this exceptionally gifted playwright. As noted by Emma Griffiths and others, it was Euripides alone who invented the tradition that Medea murdered her children—a unique accusation in the Classical corpus.[9] Likewise, as discussed in Chapter 6, it was Euripides who single-handedly invented the idea that Iphigeneia was worshipped at Brauron and that Artemis' Brauronian cult statue came from the Crimea. All of these notions had far-reaching consequences in the later arts, obscuring their actual origins. It remains a possibility, then, that Euripides created something new in his references to Artemis Lokhia.

The next extant reference we have to Artemis as a goddess of childbirth—possibly even a midwife herself—appears in Plato's *Theaitetos*, written in 369 BCE. Here in §149b–c we read:

> SOCRATES: Consider then everything that pertains to midwifery (*maias*), and easily you will learn what I mean. For you know how not one of them while she is herself pregnant and child-bearing midwifes others, but those already incapable of childbearing.
>
> THEAITETOS: Of course.
>
> SOCRATES: They say the cause of this is Artemis, because being un-wed she has received childbirth as her lot. (*Artemin hoti alokhos ousa tên lokheian eilêkhe.*)

"Sokrates" was certainly less concerned here with matters of parturition than he was with the notion that a proper philosopher—in this instance: Sokrates—could draw philosophy out of a student rather than produce it himself.[10] Nevertheless, his analogy would not work if Artemis were not already commonly recognized as a virgin midwife. Thus we might argue that by the second quarter of the fourth century in Athens at least Artemis' role as goddess of childbirth and possibly as a midwife had become commonplace.

The contemporary epigraphic evidence supports the literary and philosophical. Indicative for Attika is an inscription from the sanctuary of Ekhelides in Phaleron dating to the beginning of the fourth century. *IG* II² 4547 reads:

Ἑστίαι, Κηφισ-	To Hestia, Kephis-
ῶι, Ἀπόλλωνι	os, Apollo
Πυθίωι, Λητοῖ,	Pythian, Leto,
Ἀρτέμιδι Λοχ–	Aretmis Lokh-
ίαι, Ἰλειθύαι, Ἀχ–	ia, Ileithya, Akh-
ελώωι, Καλλ–	eloös, Kall-
ιρόηι, Γεραισ–	iphoê, Gerais-
ταῖς Νύμφαι–	tes, Nymphs
ς γενεθλί–	Genethlian, Rhapsoi.
αις, Ῥαψοῖ.	

Here again we see Artemis' epithet Lokhia, indicating that the title moved out of the purely literary domain and into popular cult. Of particular interest is the fact that this Artemis of Childbirth is listed immediately before Ileithya, an alternate spelling of the birth goddess par excellence in Greek history (and prehistory)—Eileithyia.

Eileithyia is documented as early as the Late Bronze Age in Crete, where her cult at the cave of Amnisos is mentioned in tablet KN Gg 705 line 1:

a-mi-ni-so e-re-u-ti-ja ME+RI *209^{VAS} 1
Amnisos Eileithyia HONEY *209 1 VASE

Here the goddess receives a dedication of honey. Additional tablets from Knossos (KN Od. 714–716) record dedications of wool to the goddess. Such texts, of course, provide no evidence concerning the persona of the goddess or the nature of her cult (other than that she seems to like honey and wool). However, within her cave at Amnisos, about 10 feet from the entrance, is a smooth, rounded stone formation with a "belly-button" indentation. Farther in is a stalagmite that resembles a female body. The female imagery, especially the "pregnant belly," may already have suggested a birth goddess.

By the time of Homer either Eileithyia singular or a pair of Eileithyiai were decidedly goddesses of childbirth. Thus we read in *Iliad* 11.269–271 how:

Just as a sharp, piercing arrow grips a woman in labor,
Which the Eileithyiai, who help women in labor,
Daughters of Hera who send forth sharp pangs . . . (cf. *Il.* 19.119).

Likewise in *Iliad* 19.101–105 Zeus proclaims of the birth of Herakles:

"Hear me, all you gods and goddesses,
So that I might speak what the heart in my chest bids.
Today Eileithyia who helps women in labor brings to the light
A man who will reign over all his neighbors,
Those of the race of men who are of my blood."

Much later, in Theokritos' 17th *Idyll*, ll. 60–61:

For then the daughter of Antigonos, borne down by labor pangs
Cried out to Eileithyia Lysizonos ("Belt-Loosener").

While from the *Greek Anthology* we have a dedicatory epigram from Kallimakhos (6.146):

And back again, Eileithyia, come when Lykainis calls,
Eulokhos with skill in labor pangs.
Now this on behalf of a girl, Queen; later on behalf
Of a son instead something else may your sweet-smelling temple have.[11]

Evidence for Eileithyia's cult appears from Crete to Attika, according to the data accumulated in Semeli Pingiatoğlou's *Eileithyia* (1981). She did not, however, appear as an independent goddess north of Attika. Instead, the data from Boiotia and Thessaly indicate that there Eileithyia existed solely as an aspect of Artemis—Artemis-Eileithyia.[12]

Furthermore, the evidence for the worship of this Artemis-Eileithyia only dates back to the fourth century. It appears likely, then, that the Boiotians et al. received their birth goddess from their southern neighbors (i.e. Attika), once Artemis had acquired her birth-goddess aspects and thus not only became Lokhia, but also became syncretized in the north with Eileithyia.

From several cities throughout Boiotia come dedicatory inscriptions referring to Artemis Eileithyia (with variations in the spelling of both). Thus we have four fourth-century BCE dedications from the city of Thespiai:

Thebes Mus. 300:
To Artamis Eleithyia has Wastias, son of Pisis, Dioklia Orselaia, once a priestess, dedicated.

Thebes Mus. 301:
Saphpho from Phrygia to Artemis Eileithyia

Thebes Mus 304:
Akhelois, [wife or daughter] of Neon, priestess, to Artemis Eileithia

Thebes Mus. 1560:
Dedication of Xenokrateia to Artamis Eileithia[13]

From third-century Thespiai we have:

Thebes Mus. 302:
Ameinokrateia Poloukratida, once a priestess, has dedicated to Artemis Eileithia

Thebes Mus. 302bis:
Mnasis, [daughter] of Xeneas, a priestess, has dedicated to Artemis Eileithia[14]

From third-century Anthedon (*IG* 7.4174):

Matrôn Diônysios
Eiraida to Artemis
Eileithouiê

IG 7.4175:

]neis of Lousimakhos daughters Karaida and
Melanthida to Artemis Eileithouiê

An early third-century dedication from Orkhomenos—*IG* 7.3214—reads:

Antikrateis of Arkheiês Mita
To Artemis Eileithyiê

Most significant from the latter half of the third century comes a dedication from Gonnoi in Thessaly (Gonnoi II 175bis) which reads:

To Artemis Ilithyia Menepolis
[wife] of Epinos dedicated having finished giving birth (*pausotokeia*)

Other, undated dedications to Artemis Eileithyia come from Khaironeia and Tanagra in Boiotia (*IG* 7.3410, *IG* 7.3411, *IG* 7.555). In addition to these basic dedications are numerous manumission decrees from Boiotia wherein female slaves are freed under the auspices of Artemis Eileithyia. These can be found in Chapter 7.

This Artemis Eileithyia was occasionally linked to the Artemis Lokhia we met in Attika. Especially revealing is an undated inscription from Thespiai which reads (*BCH* 26, 292–292, #2):

> [Am]einokrateia [wife or daughter] of Poloukratides,
> Having been priestess, to Artemis
> Eilithiê and Lokhiê a prayer.

A damaged second-century marble inscription from Halmyros (*IG* 9,2 142) reads:]EMIDI /]KHEIAI, certainly Artemis Lokheia. A mid-fourth-century inscription from Delphi (*BCH* 80, 550, #2) dedicated in thanksgiving for the birth of a child addresses Kourotrophos, Lokhia, the Perfecting Fates, and Phoibos. Also from Delphi comes *SEG* 3.400.9, dating to the third century, which also mentions Artemis Lokhia.

Starting in the late fifth century, then, and most assuredly from the fourth, Artemis was recognized as a goddess of childbirth per her epithets Lokhia and Eileithyia, as well as the descriptions we get from Euripides and (to a lesser extent) Plato. The evidence from central Greece would indicate that Artemis had syncretized with the Bronze Age goddess of childbirth by the early fourth century at the latest.

Additional evidence for Artemis' new role comes from the votive deposits. As already noted in Chapter 4, marble reliefs depicting families (with babies) begin to appear in Artemis' sanctuaries in the late fifth century, such as the example discussed from Ekhinos or the numerous family reliefs dedicated at Brauron.[15] Also from Brauron come eight kourotrophic terracotta figurines (several from the same mold), all dating to the fifth century. No iconography would suggest a divine identity for the females, who appear to be mortal mothers with children.[16] The sanctuary of Artemis Lokhia on Mt. Kynthos on the island of Delos, dating to the fifth to third centuries, brought to light votive reliefs of families with small children bringing sacrificial animals to Artemis.[17] In his 1922 publication of the same sanctuary (although at the time attributed to Artemis-Eileithyia), Robert Demangel identified two bas-relief votives (both broken) which he believed depicted pregnant women bringing offerings to Artemis. The females wear loose-fitting khitons with no belts, and they are indeed looking a bit thick in the waist region.[18] In the Peloponnese at the site of Kamari, located between Argos and Nemea, was discovered a sixth to third-century sanctuary of Artemis identified by inscription as Artemis Oraia ("ripe," "in the bloom of youth," or "bringing to fruition"). As written by the excavator Markellos Mitsos, "It is interesting to note that among the terracottas found there is one representing a pregnant woman which thus gives further confirmation to the identity of the goddess."[19] Both Delos and the Peloponnese, then, have brought to light not only kourotrophic iconography, but also votives of pregnant women. To the east, the sanctuary of Artemis at Ephesos revealed no fewer than ten terracotta figurines depicting seated, veiled women holding infants, all dating to the first half of the fourth century.[20] To the north, the Artemiseion of Thasos revealed a group of votive kourotrophic statuettes, all apparently Hellenistic in date.[21] Once again, these are not depictions of Artemis, but of new mothers offering thanks.

Artemis' identity as a birth goddess and midwife remained an extremely important aspect of her cult well into Roman times, especially for women (not surprisingly). The *Greek Anthology* has numerous dedicatory epigrams recording prayers and thanks for the virgin huntress' aid in travail. *GA* 6.273, ascribed to either Nossis or Anytê, reads:

> Artemis, who possesses Delos and lovely Ortygia,
> Put away the holy bow into the bosom of the Graces,
> Bathe your pure skin in the Inopos, descend to Lokris,
> Releasing Alektis from harsh labor pangs.

While 6.59 reads:

> To the Paphian garlands, to Pallas the lock of hair,
> To Artemis a belt Kallirhoê dedicated;
> For she found the suitor she wanted, and had a temperate
> Youth, and having children bore boys.

Apollo

Perhaps no reference to Artemis' midwifery skills is as famous in modern times as that pertaining to her assistance at the birth of her own (twin) brother Apollo. It is thus rather surprising that there is only one such reference, and it is *Roman* in date. Artemis is *not* present at the birth of her brother in the Archaic *Homeric Hymn to Apollo*. Although by the time of Kallimakhos' *Hymn to Artemis* she is indeed a goddess of childbirth, there is no reference to her performing this role for her own mother, only that her own birth was easy (ll. 20–25):

> "I shall dwell in the mountains, and I shall concern myself with the cities of men
> Only when women distressed by sharp labor pangs
> Call to me for help; the Fates, when I was first born,
> Assigned me by lot to help them,
> Because my mother did not suffer bearing or birthing me,
> But untired she put me from her dear limbs."

It is not until the second century CE that Artemis assists in the birth of Apollo in Apollodoros' *Bibliothekê*, where, in Book 1.4.2–3:

> Leto having "been with" Zeus was driven all over earth by Hera, until coming to Delos she bore first Artemis, being midwifed by whom she bore Apollo after. Artemis then enjoyed hunting and remained a virgin.

While other texts refer to the twins as being born together, it is only Apollodoros who claims that Artemis played the midwife for Leto and Apollo. It is a small reference that acquired a giant following.

Maternity(?) wear

The vast majority of *pausotokeia* dedications mention offerings of clothing to Artemis in thanksgiving for successful parturition. Thus to Leonidas of Tarentum is attributed *GA* 6.202:

> A well-fringed belt together with this small dress
> Atthis placed above the virginal doors,
> O child of Leto, when her womb being weighed down in childbirth
> You released from her pangs a living child.

While *GA* 6.272 reads:

> This belt, child of Leto, and a flowery small dress,
> And the scarf tightly bound around her breasts
> Timaessa dedicated, when from the harsh pangs of childbirth
> In the tenth month she released her burden.

Even men could make dedications to Artemis to thank her for the birth of a healthy child to an intact wife (*GA* 6.271):

> Artemis, to you these slippers the son of Kikhsias dedicated,
> And Themistodikê some folds of her peplos,
> Because to her bed you gently came and both
> Hands, without a bow, held over her, Lady.
> Artemis, still more grant to see this infant child of Leon
> Grown in limbs.

The close connections between successful childbirth and the dedication of clothing to birth goddesses is shown in similar dedicatory epigrams to Eileithyia, who, outside of Boiotia, did not completely merge with Artemis. Thus from the *Greek Anthology* we have:

> 6.200: Eileithyia, fleeing the harsh pangs of childbirth
> Ambrosiê dedicated to you at your illustrious feet
> Her headband and peplos, when in the tenth month
> She brought forth twins from her swollen belt.

> 6.270: Amphareta's encircling veil and the watery veil,
> Eileithyia, are laid upon your head;
> These she vowed to you, bidding to cast away from her
> Painful death in her labor pangs.

> 6.274: Child-saving Mistress, this bridal brooch
> And crown from her head of shining hair
> Blessed Eileithyia received as an offering from
> Tisis who well remembers you guarded her in labor.

It is worth noting, though, that such dedications were not exclusive to (birth) goddesses, although the evidence does suggest that even in alternate circumstances the dedication of clothing was indicative of a change of life status. Thus we have in *GA* 6.282 the dedication of clothing and toys to Hermes, the god of boundaries, in thanksgiving for a well-spent youth:

> To you, Hermes, the felt hat of well-carded lamb's wool
> Kalliteles hung,
> And a double pin, and a strigil, and
> An unstrung bow, and a worn, greasy cloak,
> And arrows, and an ever tossed ball.
> But you receive, Friend of Boys,
> The gifts of well-ordered adolescence.

It is also worth noting that there is no *direct* correlation between clothing dedications to Artemis and her role as goddess of childbirth. As we saw in Chapter 4, adolescent girls who recovered from the "Illness of Maidens" were instructed to dedicate their finest garments to Artemis. We also saw how Timareta in *GA* 6.280 dedicated her snood and doll's dresses to Artemis before her marriage (perhaps a bit like Kalliteles here). As such, one source of data often invoked to show Artemis' role as birth goddess[22] is less reliable than it may perhaps at first appear—the dedication of clothing to Artemis Brauronia in Attika.

The epigraphic evidence for these dedications at Brauron dates back to the mid-fourth century. However, there is reason to suggest that the dedications themselves are earlier (although how much earlier is difficult to determine). That the practice was in place at least by the end of the fifth century might be surmised from Euripides' *Iphigeneia Amongst the Tauroi*. At the end of the play (ll. 1446–1466) Athena informs Iphigeneia that she will travel to Artemis' sanctuary at Brauron to be a priestess and the recipient of clothing of women who died in childbirth. Although it has been shown that no such cult of Iphigeneia existed at Brauron—it was purely a Euripidean invention (see Chapter 6)—this early reference to clothing dedications may indicate that the practice of living women dedicating clothing to Artemis (in a contexts of childbirth?) was already established.

The lack of documentation before the mid-fourth century might be ascribed to the fact that there was no need to record the dedications in the sanctuary until the Peloponnesian War, when the primary concern was to document the finer treasures that were moved from Brauron to the Athenian Acropolis. Gold and silver were recorded; dresses and belts were not. Nevertheless, in *IG* II² 1388, dated to 398/397 BCE, we already see some objects of finer apparel recorded from the Brauron Artemiseion, specifically a gold ring which Axiothea, wife of Sokles, dedicated (ll. 70–71).

By the mid-fourth century extensive records were kept of the dedications both at Brauron and the Brauronion temple in Athens proper. These record copious dedications of clothing offered to Brauronian Artemis. Thus one of the oldest records—*IG* II² 1514, dating to 349–343 BCE—documents (ll. 7–28):

> In the archonship of Kallimakhos a small, scalloped, multicolored khiton—Kallippê; it has letters woven in. Kharippê, Eukolinê, polka-dotted [garment] in a frame. Philomenê, a linen khiton. In the archonship of Theophilos, Pythias a polka-dotted, strigil-ornamented dress. In

the archonship of Themistokles, a small, multihued, purple khiton in frame—Thyainê and Malthakê dedicated it. A small, multihued, purple khiton in a frame . . . Eukolinê dedicated it. Philê a belt. Pheidylla a woman's white cloak in a frame. Mneso, a frog-green [garment]. Nausis a woman's cloak with a broad purple border with encircling wave pattern. Kleo a fine shawl. Philê a bordered [object]. Teisikrateia a multicolored Persian-style blouse. Melitta a white cloak and a small khiton, rags. Glykera, wife of Xanthippos, a small khiton bordered with washed-out purple and two worn-out [garments]. Nikoklea a linen khiton around the chair. Mirror having an ivory handle, on the wall—Aristodamea dedicated it. In [the archonship] of Arkhias Arkhestratê daughter of Mnesistratos of Paiania a khiton with tower patterns in frame. Mnesistratê [wife/daughter?] of Xenophilos a white cloak with purple border, which covers the deity's seated stone statue.

No reason is ever offered for why these dedications were made. Several women identify themselves as wives, but the fact that we have at least one specifically unmarried female—Arkhestratê daughter of Mnesistratos—indicates that not all the females named were necessarily wives and mothers. As such, we cannot *automatically* assume that all of the dedications at Brauron and the Athenian Braunonion were made as thanksgiving dedications by grateful mothers, even though the literary evidence does emphasize this correlation. Some may have been clothes dedicated by recovered "maidens," others girls on the threshold of marriage.

What is of interest considering the date of the inscriptions is the fact that we have any women's names at all. From the end of the fifth century and growing increasingly emphatic in fourth was the tendency in Athenian public culture to refrain from mentioning the name of any living woman.[23] Respectable women were not named in public, only the dead and the meretricious. And yet in the dedicatory inscriptions we see numerous females named, often with no reference to either father or husband. Artemis' cult, heavily focused as it could be on females, gave females an opportunity to express themselves and receive public recognition for their actions.

Why now?

The question remains as to why Artemis became a goddess of childbirth in the fifth century: Why in the Classical period did the goddess put down her bow and help women rather than hunt them? Although no definitive answer might be offered with the current evidence, four data might be offered as contributing to the development. One important contributor is no doubt Artemis' syncretism with Eileithyia in the fifth and fourth centuries. Although Eileithyia had a long-standing cult in Crete and southern Greece since the Bronze Age, there is little evidence for her cult north of the isthmus before the Classical age. The fourth-century inscription from Athens mentioned above is one of the earliest pieces of evidence for her cult in Athens, while two fifth-century inscriptions mentioning Eileithyia from the temenos of Athena Pronaia at Delphi offer slightly earlier evidence for her cult farther north.[24] It is likely that this goddess was partially syncretized with Artemis when her cult arrived in Attika, just as she was completely subsumed by Artemis in Boiotia in the fourth century.

The second datum is the writings of Euripides. It is possible, although perhaps not incredibly likely, that Euripides started the trend of seeing Artemis as a goddess of childbirth, just as he started the trends of seeing Medea as a paedocide and Iphigeneia as receiving clothing from women dead in childbirth. However, neither of these traditions "took" in ancient Greece: Pausanias (2.3) still preserves the standard tradition that Medea's children were stoned to death by the Corinthians, and there is no archaeological evidence at Brauron that Iphigeneia ever received a cult there. As such, although Euripides clearly had extraordinary influence over how later peoples (including us) understood early Greek religion, he did not have very much influence over cult practice. He may have helped to publicize the new understanding, but I doubt he invented it.

The male medical establishment

Also contributing to Artemis' new aspect was the rise of two new sources of medical expertise at this time: the cult of Asklepios and the earliest origins of the Hippokratic Corpus. The cult of Asklepios—god of medicine and healing—achieved panhellenic importance in the fifth century, spreading out from the cult's epicenter in Epidauros and establishing itself in Athens in 420 BCE, as well as having some 200 sanctuaries throughout Greece by the later fourth century.[25] From this point on, evidence votive and epigraphic indicate that he, more so than Artemis, was the deity invoked for problems with conception, pregnancy, and parturition. It was to his sanctuaries in Athens, Epidauros, and Kos that women made dedications of votive breasts, vulvae, and uteri. It is from his temple in Epidauros that we read tales of miraculous cures for infertility and "awkward" pregnancies:

> Kleo was pregnant for five years. Having been pregnant for five years she came as a suppliant to the god and slept in the abaton. As soon as she left the abaton and was outside the sanctuary, she bore a boy, who immediately upon being born washed himself in the fountain and walked around along with his mother. Experiencing these things she inscribed on the votive: "The size of the pinax [plaque] is not all that amazing, but the divinity is. For five years was Kleo pregnant in her belly, until she fell asleep and he made her healthy."

> Nikasibula the Messanian, sleeping for children saw a dream. It seemed that the god came to her bringing a snake slithering with him. She had sex with it. And from this two male children were born to her that year.[26]

More mundanely, the female body was increasingly coming under the hands of male physicians in the fifth and especially fourth centuries.[27] It was at this time that the various authors of the Hippokratic Corpus began practicing their *tekhnê*, which included the tending of girls and woman and their reproductive systems. Quite specifically, the extant texts indicate that these exclusively male practitioners were involved with the very same matters as was Artemis:

> A major concern of Hippocratic gynaecology is the transformation of immature girls into reproductive women: in Greek terms, making a *parthenos*, a girl who combines the features of being 'childless, unmarried, yet of the age for marriage' . . . into a *gynê*.[28]

In spite of the prevalence of "women's problems" in their repertoire, the evidence suggests that these exclusively male physicians received little or none of their data from actual women. Female anatomy was understood based on analogy and symbolism, usually involving passivity, sponginess, and hollowness, not to mention the first woman—Pandora. Females are mostly dismissed as sources of knowledge because, as is stated in *Diseases of Women* 1.62, women are prevented from knowing what is wrong with them—or from speaking about such things to a physician if they do—because of their youth, inexperience, and overall embarrassment.[29] Basically, women's understanding of their bodies is disregarded, often scorned, as is especially evident in the Hippokratic *Nature of the Child* 30, where we read:

> But those women who imagine that they have been pregnant longer than ten months—a thing I have heard them say more than once—are quite mistaken. This is how their mistake arises: It can happen that the womb becomes inflated and swells as the result of flatulence from the stomach, and the woman of course thinks that she is pregnant. And if besides her menses do not flow but collect in the womb . . . then she is especially likely to imagine that she is pregnant . . . Then sometimes it happens that the menses break forth . . . Now if they have intercourse with their husbands then, they conceive on the same day or a few days afterwards. Women who are inexperienced in these facts and their reasons then reckon their pregnancy to include the time when their menses did not flow and their wombs were swollen.[30]

Or, to put it another way, "You stupid woman, you aren't pregnant; you have gas!"

The authors of the Hippokratic Corpus rarely refer to having learned something from "knowledgeable" women (often understood as prostitutes or midwives); Ann Hanson lists only two related citations—*Nat. Puer* 13.1 and 55.8–15—for the Greek period.[31] However, even these may be suspect. As noted by Helen King, such references to "women's wisdom" may in fact be male invention, attributing aspects of their *gynaikeia* to women for the sake of lending authenticity.[32] "The ancient medical writers thus accept women's knowledge, but we should add the important provisos that it may be a knowledge which they have constructed *for* women, and that they reserve to themselves the right to judge exactly *whose* knowledge they will accept."[33]

Put simply, in the late fifth and early fourth centuries BCE, women's bodies were coming under male control like never before, in a way that was not merely legal or social, but medical and "scientific." Both Hippokratic and Asklepian medicine were in the hands of exclusively male physicians. And, as noted by Nancy Demand and Helen King, these physicians were paid by, and thus inclined to side with, the male relatives of female patients.[34]

It is possible, then, that the rise of Artemis as birth goddess in the fifth century emerged in part as a reaction against the appropriation of female reproductive processes by males both mortal and divine. Girls and women could psychologically engage in a more personal relationship with Artemis, and they could expect the virgin goddess to support the maiden and mother rather than the father and husband. Unlike the physician, girls and women *could* pay Artemis (with clothing), and they could sign their names to this effect. It is possible that the statistically significant fewer number of women recorded in both the Epidauran cure records (thirty-three males to thirteen females) and the Hippokratic Epidemics (two to one) came about because women were inclined to seek out Artemis rather than a male practitioner.[35] In this context it is worth noting that Asklepios' main sanctuary in Epidauros contained a temple of Artemis dating back to the late fifth century. Amongst the epithets listed in the inscriptions from this site is *Lysaia* (*IG* IV², 1: 162 and 275, both dating to the fourth century), "Releaser," probably relating to her function as goddess of childbirth.[36] The goddess was also present in other Asklepeia, notably at Pergamon and the Athenian Pireus.[37]

In the end it is difficult to determine why exactly virginal, huntress Artemis became a goddess of childbirth. At least part of the answer must derive from her role as goddess of transitions, as she helps women make the transition from pregnant woman to mother, and babies from pre-born to born. As the goddess who kills women, Artemis would naturally be invoked not to kill vulnerable women in childbirth. In central Greece especially, Artemis syncretized with the birth goddess extraordinaire—Eileithyia—which also contributed to this new aspect of her persona. In Attika, Corinthia, and beyond, Artemis offered an alternative—a sympathetic, feminine alternative—to the male medical establishment. Artemis was very much a woman's goddess.

PRIESTESSES (AND SOME PRIESTS)

As we saw in the previous chapter, Artemis frequently had girls serve as her cult functionaries, emphasizing her role as a goddess of the young. Nevertheless, she also had older priestesses who served her. In Chapter 1 was presented the story of Aristarkhê who traveled from Ephesos to Masalia to serve as priestess at the goddess's sanctuary which she herself founded and helped to design (Strabo 4.1.4). In the section above on the laws of Cyrenê was mentioned the Arkos (= Arktos, "Bear"), who served as the priestess of Artemis there (Hesykhios, "*arkos = hiereia tês Artemidos*") and whose title is preserved in other inscriptions from the city (*SEG* IX 13 and 17). In charge of the "little bears" in Attika was the priestess of Artemis Brauronia, whose authority over her sanctuary (*IG* II² 1524 and 1526) certainly implies an older, more mature age.

Artemis' priestesshoods, as for all the Greek deities, began at a variety of ages and continued for varying lengths of time. The children and older girls seen in Chapter 4 were typically active only for short periods of time, perhaps only a single day or ritual, or sometimes until marriage. Such is possibly the case for the priestess whose dedicatory epigram was recorded in the *Greek Anthology* (6.269):

> Children, though voiceless I speak clearly, if someone asks,
> Saying untiringly what is set down before my feet:
> "To Aithopia, daughter of Leto, Arista daughter of
> Hermokles, son of Saunaius dedicated me,
> Your servant, Mistress of Women. You enjoy it,
> Gladly glorifying our people."

The priestess's use of a patronymic instead of a husband's name suggests that she served the goddess before marriage.

However, some of Artemis' priestesshoods could continue into or during marriage, and might even be held for life. So much is indicated, for example, in a Hellenistic inscription from Halikarnassos on the south-western coast of Anatolia (home-town to Herodotos), which describes the procedure by which the priesthood of Artemis Pergaia was to be sold and the prerogatives of the priestess while in office (*Halikarnassos* 3, ll. 4–30):

> The sale of the priestesshood of Artemis Pergaia will be to a female citizen whose family has been citizens for three generations on both the father's and mother's sides. The purchaser will serve as priestess for life and will sacrifice the sacred offerings both public and private. She will receive from each of the public sacrifices one of the thigh bones and the things that go with it, and a quarter portion of the entrails and the skin. From the private sacrifices she will receive a thigh bone with dressings and a quarter of the entrails.

> The treasurers will give to the prytanes at the sacrifice to Artemis 300 drakhmas total. The wives of the prytanes will prepare the sacrifice having received what was given from the city in that prytanate in the month of Herakleion. Let the sacrifice take place on the 12th of that month. May the priestess have an equal portion to that of the wives of the prytanes of the things sacrificed for the populace. The priestess will offer a prayer of protection on behalf of the city every new moon, for which she will receive a drakhma from the city. In this month when the sacrifice takes place at public expense let the priestess make a collection before the sacrifice for three days— although she may not go to anyone's actual house; and let the collection belong to the priestess. The priestess furnishes the sanctuary as she wishes, and let her also furnish the treasury of the goddess.

As noted, the priestess will serve for life. This means the female in question will most likely marry (or already be married) and have children during her tenure. This high-lights the fact that Artemis' priestesses need not be wholly ritually pure throughout their careers, but that they lived their lives rather normally in addition to their "careers."

It is also to be noted that this priestess would regularly go out and "collect" for three days before the festival/sacrifice. This appears to be a form of what might be called ritual begging, a practice that was well attested especially for goddess cults in ancient Greece. In addition to the *agermos* ("collection") for the priestess of Artemis Pergaia at Halikarnassos was a similar practice for Artemis Pergaia on the island of Kos.[38] On the island of Delos, as Herodotos recounts of the Delian Maidens (4.35, 3–4):

> For the women collected for them, calling them by the names in the hymns that Olen the man of Lycia made for them; the islanders and Ionians having learned from these to hymn Opis and Argê, calling them by name and collecting for them . . . Also, when the thigh bones are burnt on the altar, they use up the ashes by tossing them onto the burial place of Opis and Argê. Their burial place is behind the Artemision.

Also on the island of Kos was an *agermos* in honor of Demeter, to be collected from women soon-to-be or recently married. This in itself recalls that most famous of collections, when the priestess of Athena Polias made the rounds in Athens, car-rying an aegis and begging at shrines and from newly wed women.[39] What all of these rites have in common is a focus on either women or goddesses (or both) with a concern for fertility and childbirth (even Herodotos recounts how the Delian maidens came to Delos to thank Eileithyia for successful births). It is possible, then, that one aspect of this ritual begging was as a good luck rite for women seeking successful childbirth.

In some instances it was required that specifically elderly women serve Artemis. Such is the case in one of the cults of Artemis Hymnia in Arkadia. Here according to Pausanias (8.5.11–12):

> There is a sanctuary of Artemis called Hymnia. This is on the borders of Orkhomenos, towards Mantineia. And from oldest times all the Arkadians indeed revered Artemis Hymnia. Back then a maiden girl held the goddess's priestesshood. But Aristokrates, when the maiden continued to resist his attempts to "be with" her, in the end dishonored her next to the statue of Artemis when she fled to the sanctuary. This is how the event was explained to everyone. The Arkadians stoned him to death, and from that time the custom changed; for instead of a maiden they give to Artemis as priestess a woman who has had enough of "being with" men.

This origin story appears to reflect two other etiologies in the Greek corpus on religious functionaries. On the one hand, we hear echoes of the story of Lokrian Ajax and Kassandra, when the former raped the latter while she clung to the cult statue of Athena in the goddess's temple during the fall of Troy.[40] On the other hand, the narrative wholly reflects the story of how Delphic Apollo came to be served by an elderly priestess—the Pythia. Thus recounted Diodorus Siculus in his *Library* (16.26.6):

> In the old days it is said that it was maidens who sang prophesies because of their undefiled nature and their similarity to Artemis. For they say the maidens were well-equipped to observe the secret sayings of the oracles. In more recent times they say that Ekhekrates the Thessalian having gone to an oracle shrine and having seen the oracle—an uttering maiden—fell in love with her because of her beauty and seized and violated her. And the residents of Delphi because of this experience henceforth stipulated that no longer would a maiden prophesy, but a woman over 50 years-old. She is dressed up in a maiden's garb, as a reminder of the prophet of old.

The evidence for the old age of the Pythia at least goes back to the fifth century (Aesch. *Eum.* 38), and thus it is clearly an old tradition. The etiologies appear to account for how youthful deities (Apollo, Artemis) came to be served by elderly officiates, and it is likely that one tale influenced the other.

Only in rare instances were Artemis' cult attendants required to remain ritually pure for life—an oddity in ancient Greece where marriage and childbearing were inevitably the norm. One of the few references we have to such a lifestyle also comes from Pausanias and pertains yet again to Arkadian Artemis Hymnia. As the perigete described it (8.13.1):

> In the territory of Orkhomenos, to the left of the road from Agkhision, on a slope of the mountain is a sanctuary of Artemis Hymnia—the Mantineians also claim it . . . and a priestess and a male priest. For them it is established that they be pure not only in terms of sexual intercourse but also in terms of daily living; theirs is not like that of the people. And they may not enter the house of a private man. Other such things I know the office-holding devotees of Artemis in Ephesos do, although not for more than one year. The citizens call them Essenes. They hold an annual festival for Artemis Hymnia.

Ephesian Artemis too was served by the ritually pure, especially her chief priest known by the title Megabyzos. This man was a eunuch as related by Strabo (14.1.23):

> They have eunuch priests whom they call Megabyzoi, and they always send out throughout the area for those worthy of such a position, and they lead them in in great honor. It was necessary for these men to serve together with maidens.

Just as the priests were literally unsexed, so too were their female assistants virgins, although there is no evidence that they served for life and thus remained as "pure" as both the megabyzoi and their fellow servitors in Mantineia.

Those priestesses who did not serve for life often offered dedications to the goddess in memory of their service. Such were the dedications seen in Chapter 4 for those girls who had served as fawns for Artemis. Many similar dedications came to light in Thespiai in Boiotia. Thus we read of:

> Xanthis
> (daughter? wife?) of Mnasaretos
> having been priestess (*hiareiaxasa*)
> To Artemis
> Eileithiê the
> brazier
> dedicated[41]

while:

> Mnasis (daughter? wife?) of Xeneas having been priestess (*hiareiaxasa*)
> To Artemis Eileithiê dedicated.[42]

And because sometimes once just is not enough, we read of:

> Theodota
> (daughter? wife?) of Amphikrates
> Having been priestess twice (*hiareiaxasa dis*)
> To Artemis Hagemonê.[43]

OVERVIEW

Perhaps more so than any other goddess Artemis was seen to be the goddess of women. It was she who received their offerings of toys and hair and baskets when they were ready to leave childhood and become brides and women. It was to her that expectant mothers made offerings in the hopes of an easy (relatively speaking), death-free parturition. Females of all ages dedicated the fruits of their looms to the goddess, showing off their artistic accomplishments while sharing elements of their most personal lives with her. Maid, mother, and crone all served as her priestesses, occasionally accompanied by a male who himself was barred from sexuality.

Nevertheless, there remained a dark side to Artemis' rapport with the female sex. Lurking behind the offerings of toys and baskets was the notion of ransom, the fear that the goddess would seek revenge against those virgins who abandoned her. Prayers to Artemis as midwife seem to have their origins in the fear that the "lion to women" would kill young mothers in childbed. Artemis who delighted in the young also killed them and those who bore them, and this aspect of her persona was never wholly absent even in her most beneficent moments.

NOTES

1 Leitao 2003: 112–129.
2 Deubner 1925: 210.
3 Graninger 2007: 157,
4 Parker 1983: ch. 2.
5 Chamoux 1953: 318–320.
6 Perlman 1989: 129–130.
7 Van Straten actually lists no dedications of votive uteri to Artemis at all. Of the three he lists, two were dedicated to Asklepios (Corinth and Kos), and one to the sanctuary of the Egyptian gods on Delos; Van Straten 1981: 99, no, 173.
8 Simultaneously, his tragedies reveal him to be anti-woman, and thus not inclined to be overly concerned about women's issues such as childbirth. See Zeitlin 1996: *passim*.
9 Griffiths 2006: ch. 6.
10 King 1998: 177.
11 On *all* references to Eileithyia, see Pingiatoğlou 1981: *passim*.
12 Parker 2005: 223; on Artemis in Boiotian cult, see Schachter 1981: 94–106.
13 Pingiatoğlou 1981: 166–167.
14 Ibid.: 167.
15 Kondis 1967: 188 sqq.
16 Mitsopoulos Leon 2009: 181–185.
17 Hadzistellou-Price 1978: 151–152.
18 Demangel 1922: 78–79, figs. 11 & 12.
19 Mitsos 1949: 75.
20 Hadzistellou-Price 1978: 157.
21 Ibid.: 164.
22 E.g. Pingiatoğlou 1981: 98; Van Straten 1981: 99.
23 Schaps 1977: *passim*.
24 Pingiatoğlou 1981: 160.
25 King 1998: 100.
26 Entries #1 and #42, Edelstein and Edelstein 1998.
27 King 1998: 76 and 101; Demand 1994: ch. 8; Hanson 1990: 311.
28 King 1998: 23.
29 King 1998: 47; Hanson 1990: 310.
30 Demand 1994: 94.
31 Hanson 1990: 309, #6.

32   King 1998: 136.

33   Ibid.: 138. Italics in original.

34   King 1998: 156; Demand 1994: ch. 8.

35   See King 1998: 109 for the statistics and related hypotheses.

36   Morizot 1994: 211 and note 33 with copious citations; Fossey 1987: 75–76.

37   Morizot 1994: 211.

38   Dillon 1999: 76.

39   Dillon 2002: 95–96 (on Demeter and Athena).

40   See Redfield 2003: 85–98 on this myth and subsequent ritual.

41   Plassart 1926: 413, #25.

42   Ibid.: #26.

43   Ibid.: 409, #24

6

ARTEMIS AS GODDESS OF PLAGUE AND CRUELTY

Artemis could be vicious. Like all the Greek deities, she had a degree of anger, called *mênis* in Greek, that was beyond the pale of mortal ken. Like all deities, she demanded her honors from mortals, demanded proper behavior, and was swift with punishment when her human subjects did not live up to her expectations.

TALES OF PLAGUE (AND REDEMPTION)

Like her brother Apollo, Artemis is a goddess of plague. Typically these plagues manifest as assaults on the processes of fertility: Crops do not grow, and women have miscarriages. However, the earliest reference to a plague sent by Artemis appears in the *Iliad*, where the angry goddess sent destruction and despair in the form of a great big boar (9.533–546.):

> For gold-throned Artemis set this evil in motion against them,
> Angry at them because Oineus offered her no first-
> Fruits from his orchard; the other deities feasted on hekatombs,
> But they offered nothing to the daughter of great Zeus.
> Either he forgot or was unaware; but she was greatly hurt at heart.
> In her anger at the godly race the arrow-pourer
> Roused a wild, white-tusked boar
> Which wrought many evils continuously on Oineus' orchard,
> And he tossed to the earth great trees, roots and all!
> By their roots and their flowering fruits.
> Him Meleager, the son of Oineus, killed,
> Having gathered hunting men from many cities,
> As well as dogs. For it was not subdued by a few mortal men,
> Such as it was, but sent many to the toilsome pyre.

In this instance Artemis uses her role as mistress of animals to punish humanity, sending a porcine "plague" that kills crops and men, just as a more standard plague would.

As noted by M.L. West in his *East Face of Helicon*, there is a strong possibility that this incident derives from Near Eastern prototype.[1] Specifically, it bears numerous similarities to the tale of Ištar's attempt to destroy the city of Uruk and its king in the

Epic of Gilgameš. Here, in Tablet Six, after Gilgameš and Enkidu had killed Humbaba, the guardian of the cedar forest, Ištar approaches Gilgameš in his bath and proposes to him. He rejects her (not politely), and in a rage the goddess flies off to heaven to demand the Bull of Heaven from Anu, the king of the gods, so that she might use it to ravage Uruk. Anu advises Ištar to make sure that the populace has enough to eat before the Bull begins his depredations, and Ištar assures him that the city is well stocked. Then she lets loose the Bull (Tablet Six, §4):

> Ishar [took hold] and directed it [the Bull].
> When it arrived in the land of Uruk
> . . . .
> It went down to the river, and seven [ ]
> At the snorting of the Bull of Heaven a chasm opened up, and one hundred young men of Uruk
> fell into it,
> Two hundred young men, three hundred young men.
> At its second snorting another chasm opened up,
> And another hundred young men of Uruk fell into it
> Two hundred young men, three hundred young men fell into it.
> At its third snorting a chasm opened up,
> And Enkidu fell into it.[2]

In the end, Gilgameš and Enkidu together kill the Bull, insult Ištar yet again, and thus set in motion a series of events that results in the death of Enkidu. In the *Iliad*, the slaughter of the boar sets in motion a war between the Kouretes and the Aitolians, leading to the burning of Meleager's city.

Cultic etiologies

A more common form of Artemis' wrath involved the sending of a plague to punish a community in which a sub-section of that community had acted badly. We have already seen several such narratives in this study. In Chapter 2 appeared the story of the children of Kondylea in Arkadia who once called Artemis "hanged" (Pausanias 8.23.6–7). Upon their execution the city was plagued until setting up a hero cult for the children at the behest of Artemis and the Pythia. In Chapters 2 and 4 was presented the story of Komaitho of Patrai (Pausanias 7.19.2), who brought plague onto her people for having had sex in Artemis' temple and who was sacrificed as a consequence. The human sacrifices only ended when a cult of Dionysos was introduced into the polis. In Chapter 4 appeared the story of the Athenian *arkteía*, and how Artemis sent a plague upon Attika when some men killed her bear. The plague only ended when a goat was sacrificed (instead of the little girl originally demanded), and little girls learned to "play the bear" for Artemis. According to the *Etymologicum Magnum*, a group of young Ephesians led by one Klymena once brought the statue of Artemis down to the seashore where they provided her with a picnic of wild celery and salt as well as a dance performance. Apparently the goddess thoroughly enjoyed herself, and when the practice was not repeated she sent a plague to Ephesos. Since then, the "Daitis" ("Feast") festival is held by Ephesian adolescents, who bring salt, wild celery, cloth, and adornments to the goddess.[3]

Such narratives fall into a standard pattern noted by A. Brelich in the 1960s. This pattern consists of: Transgression, Catastrophe brought on a by a divinity, Oracular Consultation, and the Foundation of a Rite.[4] Thus in the case of the children of Kondylea, the people stone their children (Transgression); Artemis sends a plague (Catastrophe); they send to Delphi (Oracle); who tells them to establish the children's hero cult (Rite). However, it is significant to note that in many instances two *additional* elements are necessary in these narratives pertaining to Artemis' cults. As seen in both Patrai and Attika, the initial remedial ritual is unduly harsh, requiring the sacrifice of a small child (Attika), or the initial sacrifice of two young people (Komaitho and Melanippos) followed by the annual human sacrifice of an adolescent girl and boy (Patrai). Thus a second Foundation of Rite is added, whereby the human sacrifice is swapped out for an alternate ritual, such as the goat sacrifice and "playing the bear" in Attika, or the night-time bathing ritual in Patrai. A sign of Artemis' mythic cruelty, then, might be noted in the fact that even her cultic corrections need corrections.

Be that as it may, all of these tales pertain to the *origins* of various rituals practiced in honor of Artemis throughout the Greek world. Many, such as the story of Komaitho, are set in the mythic past, which in Greek terms means before the Trojan War. It is thus quite unlikely that any of the "origin" details are factual—that a girl named Komaitho was offered as human sacrifice, that a bear was slaughtered, that a group of people stoned their own children for hanging an image of Artemis, etc. Instead, these narratives highlight the persona of Artemis while explaining the origins of some of her cults. Thus, as noted in Chapter 2, the story of the children of Kondylea emphasizes Artemis' virginity while explaining the children's hero cult. The story of Klymena of Ephesos not only explains the origins of the Feast festival, but also casts into high relief Artemis' fondness for liminal spaces—her picnic on the beach.

Not just Artemis, but even the goddess's cult statues could cause plague and madness. The xoanon of Artemis Ortheia in Sparta was clearly shown to be foreign by Pausanias (3.16.9):

> And here is my proof that Lakedaimonian Orthia is a xoanon from barbarian lands: For Astrabakos and Alopekos, sons of Irbos, son of Amphisthenes, son of Amphikles, son of Agis, having found the statue immediately went mad. Additionally, the Spartan Limnatians and the Kynosoures and those from Mesoa and Pitanê, when sacrificing to Artemis, had a dispute, from which they became murderously angry, and while many were killed at the altar a plague destroyed the rest.

Farther north, in Pellenê, Plutarch noted in his *Aratus* that (32.2.2):

> The Pellenians themselves say that the image (*bretas*) of the goddess is stored generally someplace off-limits, but whenever it is moved by the priestess, taken out, no one looks at it, but everyone turns away. For it is not only a horrible and harsh sight for humans, but it also makes trees barren and cast off their fruit, wherever it is led.

Lion to women

Related to Artemis' role as plague goddess—a goddess who brings unexpected death—is her function as a killer of women. Women who die an unexpected death are said to have been brought down by Artemis' arrows, and for this reason Hera in the *Iliad* (21.490) refers to her as a "lioness who kills women." In the *Odyssey*, Odysseus asks his mother in Hades (ll. 170–172), "But tell me truly, how did you die? Was it a long illness, or did Artemis shoot you suddenly with her gentle arrows?"

The most famous female victims of Artemis' "gentle" arrows were, of course, the Niobids, the daughters of Niobê who bragged that her own offspring outshone those of Leto. Leto's daughter Artemis killed all the girls, just as her brother Apollo killed all of Niobê's sons. Ironically, the sixth-century poet Sappho once remarked that, "Before they were mothers, Leto and Niobê were the best of friends."

TALES AND RITES OF CRUELTY

In addition to plague, Artemis is also infamous in myth and cult for her cruelty to individuals. One famous example is the young Theban hunter Aktaion, whom Artemis killed with his own dogs. As with all Greek myths, there are variations as to why she did this. In the earliest renditions, those of Stesikhoros and the Pseudo-Hesiodic *Catalogue of Women*, Artemis kills Aktaion for having courted Semelê, mother of Dionysos. By the fifth century, as appearing in Euripides' *Bakkhai*, the youth was stupid enough to brag that he was a better hunter than Artemis. She proved him wrong. By the Hellenistic and Roman eras the now more famous version of the story came into being, as recorded by Ovid, that the goddess killed him because he saw her when she was naked in the bath (*Metamorphoses* 3.165–252).[5] This last version inevitably comes across as the most irrational, as the voyeurism was wholly accidental, but, as we shall see, Artemis grew more vicious in the Roman era.

This is immediately evident in her cult at Patrai. According to Pausanias (7.18.8–13):

> On the acropolis of Patrai is a sanctuary of Artemis Laphria. The goddess's title is foreign, having been brought from elsewhere along with the statue. For when Kalydon and the rest of Aitolia was devastated by King Augustus so as to have Aitolia merge with Nikopolis above Aktion, then the Patrians got the statue of Laphria. For just as many other statues from Aitolia and around Akarnania were brought to Nikopolis, Augustus gave both the statue of Laphria and other spoils from Kalydon to the Patrians, and even up to my day it stands in honor on the acropolis of Patrai. They say the goddess's epithet Laphria comes from a Phokian man, for Laphrion the son of Kastalios, son of Delphos dedicated the ancient statue of Artemis in Kalydon, for whom it was a sign of Artemis' wrath. Over time they say this wrath against Oineus [see above: Kalydonian Boar Hunt] lightened (*elaphroteron*), and they prefer this as the origin of the epithet. The appearance of the statue is of one hunting; it is made of ivory and gold. Menaikhmos and Soidas the Naupaktians made it; they reckon them to be not much later than the *floruit* of Kanakhos of Sikyon and Kallon of Aigina. The Patrians hold a Laphrian festival for Artemis every year, in which their manner of sacrifice is a local one. In a circle around the altar they heap green wood, and each log is 16 cubits. Within these upon the altar lie the driest

logs. At the time of the festival they contrive to make the road to the altar smoother, placing earth upon the altar steps. First then they proceed in a magnificent parade for Artemis, and the maiden priestess rides at the end of the parade on a chariot drawn by yoked deer. Then on the following day it is their custom to do the sacrifice thus, and both the city publicly and no less the individual citizens hold this festival in high esteem. For they throw living birds onto the altar and comestible animals and sacral victims equally altogether, even wild pigs and deer and gazelles, and some cast on the cubs of wolves and bears, and some full-grown wild animals. They also set upon the altar the fruit of cultivated trees. Then they cast fire onto the wood. And there I saw a bear or some other of the creatures being ravaged by the first onslaught of the fire try to get out, some fleeing at full strength. But those who cast them in bring them back again to the fire. They recall no one being harmed by the animals.[6]

Such a sacrifice is called a holocaust, literally "All-Burnt," and is utterly atypical of Greek sacrifice. As is commonly noted, the end result of animal sacrifice in Greek religion is the provision of meat for a post-ritual banquet on the part of the participants, a sacral bar-b-que, if you will. To have the animals/meat completely consumed by flame renders impossible this aspect of the rite, with its concomitant bonding ritual between the members of the community both with each other and with the deities. The Patrai holocaust is also atypical in the lack of acquiescence on the part of the sacrificial animals. In Greek ritual, care was taken to make it look as though the victims were willing, including a ritual pouring of water upon the head to make the animal nod at the altar. For the animal to resist sacrifice was seen as inauspicious.[7] Finally, it was rare to have wild animals sacrificed in Greek religion. Domesticated animals were the norm: oxen, sheep, goats, birds, occasionally pigs and horses.[8]

By contrast, it seems as though the entire point of the sacrifice at Patrai was to cause maximum suffering to wild animals by burning them alive. Obviously humans, including Pausanias, then watched the spectacle.

Rather than seeing this as an aspect of the Greek cult of Artemis, it is far more likely that it is a Roman creation. As Pausanias notes at the beginning of the passage, the cult of Artemis Laphria was transferred to Patrai after Augustus razed the polis of Kalydon (site of the famous boar hunt). The cult was thus recreated in the first century when Rome was firmly establishing itself on Greek soil and in Greek culture. The torture of wild animals for public entertainment was also a well-engrained aspect of Roman culture already by the first century BCE. As discussed by Jo-Ann Shelton in her "Beastly Spectacles in the Ancient Mediterranean World":

In 55 BCE, Pompey produced spectacles at which he exhibited about four hundred leopards, six hundred lions (far exceeding the previous record of one hundred set by Sulla), twenty elephants, and a rhinoceros, the first seen in Rome. And in 46 BCE, Julius Caesar sponsored shows at which four hundred lions and, for the first time in Rome, a giraffe were displayed . . . In 80 CE . . . to celebrate the dedication of the Flavian amphitheater in Rome (later known as the Colosseum), nine thousand animals were killed over a period of one hundred days.[9]

The holocaust at Patrai rather pales in comparison, really. But the point is, the rite at Patrai, while at odds with Greek religious praxis, is quite in line with Roman spectacle, especially at that time when Augustus transferred the cult of Artemis Laphria to Patrai from Kalydon. As such, rather than an aspect of Greek Artemis' cult, or a manifestation of the goddess's cruelty, the Patrai holocaust casts into high relief Roman cruelty and the changes that occurred in Greece in the Roman period. As we shall see below, this was not an atypical effect of the Romans on Greek Artemis. As we shall also see, the Romans themselves preferred to blame the Skythians.

IPHIGENEIA (AND HEKATÊ)

One of the most famous victims of Artemis' cruelty is Iphigeneia. According to the most basic version of her myth, dating back to the seventh century BCE, Artemis refused to let the Greek forces set sail for Troy from Aulis until Agamemnon sacrificed his daughter Iphigeneia to her. This the king did, under constraint, although at the last second Artemis replaced the girl with an animal—typically a deer—and whisked the maiden off to the Crimea where she was either turned into a goddess herself, or became Artemis' priestess. In the latter version, Iphigeneia's brother Orestes found her years later and returned her home to Greece, bringing with them Artemis' Tauric-Skythian[10] cult statue.

The earliest attestation of this story appears in Proklos' summary of Stasinos' *Kypria* (one of the fragmentary epics from the Epic Cycle). Here it is written that:

> Agamemnon, out hunting, shot a deer and asserted that he had outdone even Artemis. The goddess was angered and sent storms to prevent them from sailing. And when Kalkhas declared the anger of the goddess and said that Iphigeneia should be sacrificed to Artemis, they sent for her on the pretext that she was to be married to Akhilleus and attempted to sacrifice her. But Artemis snatched her away and took her to the Tauroi, making her immortal; and she set a deer at the altar in place of the girl.[11]

Roughly similar is the version preserved in the pseudo-Hesiodic *Catalogue of Women*, where the girl, now by the name Iphimedê, was replaced by an image (*eidolon*), while she herself was made immortal by Artemis, thus becoming a version of Artemis called Artemis Einodia ("Artemis in the Road"), syncretized with the goddess Hekatê.

> The well-greaved Akhaians sacrificed Iphimedê on the altar of clear-toned Artemis of the golden distaff on that day when they sailed with their ships to Ilion to exact vengeance for the beautiful-ankled Argive—her image, that is. She herself the arrow-showering deer hunter easily saved, and placed lovely ambrosia upon her head so that her skin might be everlasting. She made her immortal and ageless for all time. Now the tribes of men on earth call her Artemis Einodia, attendant of the glorious arrow-shooter.[12]

The earliest data, then, revolve around the apotheosis of Iphigeneia, and explain how this heroine-goddess became connected to the cult of Artemis, possibly as Hekatê.

In later versions of the tale, Iphigeneia remains mortal, with various reasons given for why the goddess demanded her sacrifice (if not actual death). The Athenian tragedian Sophokles in his play *Elektra* follows Stasinos and claims (ll. 556–576) that Agamemnon was hunting in the goddess's grove (*alsos*, often understood to be sacred) when he shot a stag and bragged about the killing, and thus provoked Artemis to anger. By contrast, Euripides in his *Iphigeneia Amongst the Tauroi* set in the mouth of the seer Kalkhas that (ll. 18–23):

> "O Agamemnon, ruler of this Greek army,
> The ship may not set out from land
> Before you should sacrifice your daughter
> Iphigeneia, and Artemis receive her. For that which
> Is most beautiful, born this year
> You promised to sacrifice to the light-bearing goddess.
> And so your wife Klytaimnestra bore a child in the house—
> 'The most beautiful thing to be brought to me.'—
> And so you must sacrifice her."

Both themes were followed by the Roman-era compiler Apollodoros in his *Epitome* (3.21). In addition to blaming Agamemnon's boast for Artemis' anger, he also noted that the king's father Atreus had once vowed to sacrifice the most beautiful thing born in his flocks that year (apparently he had enough sense to put a limit on the vow). It turned out to be a golden-fleeced lamb, which he killed but kept for himself. One way or another, then, Iphigeneia's life was forfeit to her father's stupidity and/ or grandfather's greed.

Artemis, however, is not unduly cruel, and most versions of the Iphigeneia tale have the girl replaced by an animal for sacrifice. Originally this was a deer, as presented in the *Kypria* and Euripides' *Iphigeneia at Aulis* (ll. 1584–1590), where the bleeding corpse was discovered upon the altar.[13] In the Hellenistic period and later, animals other than a deer were used as Iphigeneia's substitutes. Nikander (fr. 58) claimed that it was a bull (*tauros*) that was sacrificed, thus forming an etymological link between Iphigeneia, the Tauroi, and the cult of Artemis Tauropolos ("Bull-Herder" or "Bull-Tamer"). By contrast, the Attik historian Phanodemos said that a bear was substituted, thus providing a connection between Artemis' cult at Brauron in Attika and the Athenian *Arkteia* ritual (see Chapter 4).[14] However, in fifth-century Athenian drama, there were also instances where no substitution was offered at all: At no point in Aeschylus' *Oresteia* trilogy does the poet even suggest that Iphigeneia survived her ordeal. Sophokles' Elektra also knows of no fate but death for her sister.

By the end of the fifth century, the standard version of the Iphigeneia narrative was that the girl was rescued, transported north, and made a priestess of Artemis in the Crimea. Having survived the ordeal of nearly being stabbed to death by her own father, Iphigeneia had a new trauma to face, for the cult of Tauric Artemis included human sacrifice, specifically of foreigners washed ashore. As the maiden put it herself at the opening of Euripides' *Iphigenia Amongst the Tauroi* (ll. 26–41):

> Coming to Aulis and suffering above the pyre
> High up I was raised, bled out with a blade.
> But Artemis stole me away, giving a deer in exchange
> For me to the Akhaians; through the bright air
> She brought me here, and settled me in the land of the Tauroi,

Whose land barbarian Thoas rules for
The barbarians, whose swift foot is equal to wings—
He got his name for this swift-footedness.
In these temples she made me priestess,
Where the goddess Artemis enjoys the customs,
Festivals fair in name only—
But I keep silent on other matters, fearing the goddess.
For I sacrifice—it being the law—before the city,
The man who has come down from Greece.
I begin, but the slaughter is the concern of others,
Horrid things within the goddess's temple.

These "horrid things" are described in more detail by Herodotos in his Skythian narrative (*Histories* 4.103):

The Tauroi use the following customs: They sacrifice to the Maiden (*Parthenos*) in the following manner those sailors and those they seize of the Greeks at sea. To start the rite they bash the head with a club. Some say that they toss the body down a cliff (for the cliff stands by the sanctuary), then they impale the head. Others agree about the head-bashing, but they do not say that they toss the body from the cliff, but rather bury it in the ground. The same Tauroi say that the divinity to whom they sacrifice is Iphigeneia the daughter of Agamemnon.

There are thus three versions of Iphigeneia's fate: She dies at her father's hands; Artemis transforms her into a goddess, typically Hekatê; she becomes a priestess of Artemis in the Crimea. Pausanias provides a handy summary (1.43.1):

That say it's the heroön of Iphigeneia, for she died in Megara. Now I have heard a different story about Iphigeneia told by the Arkadians, and I know that Hesiod recounted in his *Catalogue of Women* that Iphigeneia did not die, but was Hekatê by the will of Artemis. And Herodotos agreeing with this wrote that the Taurians who live near Skythia sacrifice ship-wrecked sailors to a Parthenos, and that they themselves say that the Parthenos is Iphigeneia daughter of Agamemnon.

All these data suggest that at the core of the Iphigeneia narrative is the process by which a (semi-)divine female—Iphigeneia, or the related name Iphimedê—became connected to the cult of Artemis,[15] either as the attendant goddess Hekatê or, later, as Artemis' heroic priestess. What we may actually be seeing is the syncretism between Artemis, the local, Greek goddess Iphimedê, and Karian Hekatê, cast in the literature as attendant (*propolos*) both of Artemis and, in the *Homeric Hymn to Demeter*, ll. 438–440, of Persephonê, Queen of the Dead.

That Iphigeneia, or at least Iphimedê, was a goddess in early Greece is suggested by the Linear B evidence, which indicates that a goddess called *i-pe-me-(de)-ja*—Iphimedê—received offerings in Pylos (PY Tn 316, v6). Thus a goddess known as Iphimedê ("Strong (in) Counsel"), Iphigeneia ("Strong (in) Birth"), or even Iphianassa ("Strong Queen," *Iliad* 9.145) may have had an independent cult before being subsumed by Artemis and/or Hekatê.[16] Iphigeneia's cult appears to have been localized mainly in central Greece. The literary tradition places her sacrifice in Aulis, on the eastern coast of Boiotia. In Hermionê in the northern Peloponnese, Artemis had the cult epithet *Iphigeneia* (Pausanias 2.35.2), suggesting a syncretism between the two. As noted by Pausanias, her heroön is located in Megara, where the locals claim she died (and *not* at Aulis). More significant is Pausanias' observation of Artemis' cult in Aigeira in Akhaia (7.26.5):

> The temple and statue of Artemis is of a workmanship of our own times; a maiden serves as priestess until she becomes ripe for marriage. And an ancient statue also stood there— Iphigeneia daughter of Agamemnon, as the Aigeiretans say. If they speak correctly, it is clear that the temple was originally made for Iphigeneia.

For her own part, Hekatê was Anatolian in origin; her cult came from Karia in south-western Asia Minor. The earliest archaeological evidence for her cult there comes from sixth-century Miletos, where an altar in the sanctuary of Apollo Delphinios was inscribed with her name.[17] The earliest evidence for Hekatê's cult in Greece appears in Hesiod's seventh-century *Theogony*, where the poet dedicated a lengthy section of his poem to the goddess in the middle of his narrative (ll. 411–452). The fact that Hesiod's father originally came from Kymê in western Anatolia may have contributed to Hesiod's own particular fondness for the goddess. Hesiod himself was a resident of Askra in Boiotia, and one can easily suggest that the cult of his Hekatê, goddess of good fortune, was strong in the same areas of Greece where tales of Iphigeneia's sacrifice were situated. Hekatê continued to exist both as an independent goddess throughout ancient Greek history and as a being syncretized with Artemis. Fifth-century inscriptions from both Athens (*IG* I³ 383, l. 125–126) and Thasos (*SEG* 42 785) refer to "Artemis Hekatê,"[18] as well as the passage from Aeschylus' *Suppliants* which refers to Artemis-Hekatê (see Chapter 5). In Koroneia in Boiotia, Artemis has the cult epithet *Monogeneia* ("Only-Child"), which else-where belongs to the only child Hekatê.[19]

The Crimean cult

So, the meeting and blending of the cults of Artemis, Iphigeneia, and Hekatê make rather reasonable sense. What is utterly baffling is Herodotos' statement that the Crimean Tauroi say that they sacrifice to Iphigeneia, daughter of Agamemnon, *not* Artemis, as presented in Euripides—*Iphigeneia*. Four ideas must be kept in mind when considering this conundrum. The first is that Herodotos did travel to the Crimea per-sonally, and thus he was a first-hand observer of this aspect of Tauric religion. Second, the historian specifies that it is the Tauroi themselves who make this claim, not Greeks who attribute this identity to a foreign deity. Third, it is obvious that both the word "Parthenos" and the name Iphigeneia are Greek, meaning that the indigenous Tauroi were clearly sufficiently influenced by their Greek neighbors by the fifth century at the latest to have adopted a foreign identification for their own goddess. Fourth, we have virtually no indigenous evidence about Tauric religion, and thus we are unable to see the native divinity behind the Greek overlay.

Nevertheless, what evidence does exist indicates that the primary deity of the Crimea was an Artemis-like goddess, called Parthenos by the fifth century. In addition to the evidence from Herodotos we also have a reference in Strabo (7.4.2):

> In this city [Chersonesos] is a sanctuary of Parthenos, some divinity, whose title also gives its name to the heights some 100 stades before the city called Parthenion; it has a temple and xoanon of the divinity.

More recently, to quote Pia Guldager Bilde:

> The Chersonese goddess is well known from a number of different sources, local as well as extra-Pontic. Numerous epigraphical sources from Chersonesos call her *Parthenos*, *Thea Parthenos*, and *Basilissa* ["Queen"] *Parthenos*, and local iconographical sources such as coin images and reliefs show her in Artemisian attire (long or short chiton with a cloak, occasional bow, quiver and/or spear), but the iconographical content shows no resemblance with either Mediterranean or Anatolian Artemis'es, since she poses as Promachos and Deer-killer, and we likewise find her racing a *biga* [two-wheeled chariot]. The generic iconography shows that she could be connoted with Artemis, but the specific iconography points to a different deity. It is obvious to view her as the homonymous Taurian goddess, the original protectress of the land, who was taken over by the first Greek settlers.[20]

The Greeks would have come upon this deity beginning with their earliest forays into the Black Sea. The Pontic region was colonized by the Greeks as late as the second half of the seventh century BCE, with aspects of Greek material culture (such as pottery) appearing there from as early as the eighth century.[21] The primary, if not exclusive, colonizer of the region up until c. 560 was Miletos. The Milesians focused their colonizing efforts mostly to the sea's northern coast, thus in the general region of the Crimea.[22] The Crimea itself shows evidence of Greek contacts from the sixth century, having brought to light pottery from Ionia (Miletos?), Athens, Corinth, Thasos, Lesbos, and Khios.[23] Thus, from as early as the eighth century, and certainly by the early sixth, there were Greek contacts with the region where the later Greeks would find the Maiden worshipped by the Tauroi.

In the sixth century, other areas of Greece began to expand into the Pontic region, with one of the best-known colonies being Heraclea Pontica on the south coast of the Black Sea. This city was founded by a mixture of Megarians and Boiotians in c. 560 BCE,[24] and it was Heraclea Pontica which later went on to colonize the Tauric Chersonese on the Crimea. Thus peoples from the region where the cult of Iphigeneia was strong became well established in the precise area where native Tauroi worshipped the Maiden. The chronology thus works out for how a Greek identity could devolve onto a Crimean goddess by the fifth century.

The fact that Herodotos could report that the natives worshipped Iphigeneia also derives from the Greek understanding of foreign syncretisms prevalent in Herodotos' day (see *Introduction*). In the works of Homer and Hesiod, there is little evidence that these poets, or the Greeks in general, recognized different pantheons. The Trojans and Akhaians worshipped the same deities by the same names using the same rituals. There was functionally one religion. By the fifth century, the Greeks still held on to this notion of one large family of deities, but they did recognize that different peoples called them by different names, and used different rituals in their various cults. Thus, for example, we read in Herodotos 1.133 that the Assyrians call Aphrodite Mylitta; the Arabs call her Alilat, and the Persians Mitran. In Book 2.42 we see that the Egyptians depict Zeus, known locally as Amun, with the head of a ram; and Osiris is simply the local name for Dionysos. For Herodotos writing in the fifth century, then, the idea that the Tauroi worship a Greek divinity is no cause for wonder; everyone worships *the* deities.[25]

What is of greater surprise is the fact that it is Iphigeneia, not Artemis (or Hekatê, or any other of the goddesses who hold Olympos) who was syncretized with the indigenous Maiden. This may derive from another aspect of Greek religious sensibilities in the Archaic and Classical periods. Specifically, for the Greeks, the deities were by definition immortal—the ever-living gods. A divinity who could die was not a *theos* (deity), but a *heros*—a hero/ine, or a *daimon*—divinity. Thus, for example, were the "dying and rising" gods of the ancient Near East incorporated into the Greek religious world view. Tammuz and Baal were translated into Adonis and Melqart respectively, the latter of whom became both the infant hero Melikertes of the Isthmian Games and the panhellenic hero Herakles. All of these were identified as heroes in the Greek repertoire, receiving cults, possibly even becoming immortal after death in the case of Herakles. But they were not gods.[26]

If (and it is not possible to know this with the current evidence) the Tauric Maiden were deemed mortal somehow,[27] then it went against Greek religious sensibilities to identify her as a goddess, thus neither Artemis nor Hekatê. So much seems to be implied in Strabo's statement that this Parthenos is "*daimonos tinos*" "some divinity," but not a goddess per se. But as her persona and iconography were sufficiently similar to those of the Huntress, the syncretism went to the mortal heroine most closely associated with Artemis, thus Iphigeneia. This identity would only be strengthened by the religious proclivities of the Greeks who settled in the Crimea, who themselves came from regions where the Iphigeneia cult was strong. Thus could Mary B. Hollinshead suggest:

> I believe it more likely that Greek sailors and merchants in the Euxine [Black Sea] associated the Parthenos of the Tauri with Iphigeneia, the virginal figure of heroic legend who was herself sacrificed, or else disappeared at the moment of sacrifice and became immortal. Tauric Chersonesos was a colony of Heraclea Pontica, itself a joint colony of Megara and Boeotia, which includes Tanagra, close neighbor of Aulis . . . Boeotians from Heraclea or other Greeks exploring the Black Sea, upon hearing of the Taurian Parthenos, might have recalled the girl put to death at Aulis. In this case Iphigeneia's change of role from victim to slayer would have been seen as less significant than the parallel occurrence of three elements: virgin—navigation—human sacrifice.[28]

One final idea to keep in mind regarding the cult of Iphigenia-but-not-Artemis in the Crimea is the general dearth of evidence for the cult of Artemis in the north, especially before the Hellenistic age. Herodotos, as usual our main source of historiographic evidence, knows only of Parthenos in the Crimea, and no Artemis amongst the Skythians. As he notes in 4.59:

> They [the Skythians] worship only these deities—Hestia most of all, next Zeus and Earth, and they believe that Earth is the wife of Zeus. After these are Apollo and Aphrodite Ourania and Herakles and Ares. All the Skythians recognize these, but those called the Royal Skythians also sacrifice to Poseidon. They call Skythian Hestia Tabiti, and Zeus—quite rightly so in my opinion—is called Papaios, and Earth Api. Apollo is Goitosyros, Aphrodite Ourania Argimpasa, and Poseidon Thagimasdas. They do not make use of statues, altars, or temples except for Ares.

Likewise, as Pia Guldager Bilde has noted, there is exceptionally little archaeological evidence for Artemis-worship in the Black Sea region before the fourth century BCE. It is to this century that dates the earliest potential shrine of Artemis Agrotera in Phanagoreia, possibly identified by an inscription dedicated by one Xenokles, son of Posis.[29] It is also in the fourth century that the earliest inscription documents a priestess of Artemis in Hermonassa; the priestess's name is not preserved, but the inscription does mention an *agalma* (cult statue) dedicated to the goddess.[30] Only a handful of dedications to Artemis came from Pontic soil before the fourth century, and it is perhaps worthwhile to note that none came from the Crimea before the Roman period.[31] In short, it seems it would have been just as surprising to find the Tauroi worshipping Artemis as it is to find them worshipping Iphigeneia.

The matter of Brauron

Remarkably, what the tale of Iphigeneia is *not* is an etiology for her cult at Brauron, the site most commonly associated with Iphigeneia's narrative in the modern literature. The tendency to see Iphigeneia as a heroine worshipped side by side with Artemis at the Brauron sanctuary on the eastern outskirts of Attika derives from the ending of Euripides' drama *Iphigeneia Amongst the Tauroi*. Here, the owl-eyed goddess commands (ll. 1446–1466):

> Heed, Orestes, my commands—
> For you hear the goddess's voice though she is not present.
> Leave, taking the statue and your sister.
> When you should come to god-built Athens,
> There is a land upon the mountain borders of
> Attika, neighbor of the Karystian ridge,
> Sacred, my people call it Halai.
> There, having built a temple you will dedicate the statue (*bretas*)
> Named for the Tauric land . . .
> . . . The rest of mortal kind
> Will hymn the goddess as Artemis Tauropolos.
> And establish this law: whenever the people celebrate,
> In exchange for the sacrificial slaughter hold a sword
> To a man's throat and let blood flow,
> For the sake of sanctity, and so the goddess might have her honor.
> And upon the holy stairs of Brauron,
> Iphigeneia, you must be key-bearer[32] for the goddess.

> And you will be buried there when you die, and a statue
> Of peploi they will dedicate to you, fine-textured weavings,
> Which the women having given up the ghost in childbirth
> Will leave in their homes.

This description made a considerable impact on the Greek team that excavated Brauron in the mid-twentieth century, encouraging an interpretation of finds that matched the dramatist's narrative. Thus, the cave area to the south-east of Artemis' temple was taken to be the tomb of Iphigeneia, just as the so-called "Small Temple" was identified as the heroine's heroön.[33] The northern stoa was, presumably, where the dedications of the dead women's clothes were displayed.[34]

Nevertheless, as Gunnel Ekroth has explained in great detail, there is no evidence for any cult of Iphigeneia at Brauron before Euripides, and remarkably little after him either. As Ekroth notes, there are no inscribed dedications, votives, or inscriptions naming or mentioning Iphigeneia from the published corpus from the sanctuary.[35] Likewise, there are no depictions of the heroine from the site.[36] The remains from the cave (supposedly Iphigeneia's tomb) show complete correspondence with the votive remains from other parts of the sanctuary. Additionally, pottery appropriate for ritual feasting was there brought to light. As such, the cave might simply be understood as a kind of *thesauros* and site of sacral meals.[37] The display of clothing upon wooden boards set into marble bases, as was suggested for the northern stoa, runs contrary to the practice with clothing dedications at other sites, including those made to Artemis at Brauron, where the clothes were either placed upon the goddess's cult statues or set in boxes within the sanctuary. Furthermore, as noted by Susan G. Cole, "Iphigeneia's mission to receive gifts made by those who have died has no ritual model. Death in childbirth would constitute a ritual failure, an ominous occasion for making a gift in a sanctuary."[38] All in all, the practice, and the way it was understood to function at Brauron, makes very little sense in light of Greek precedent.

Put simply: Iphigeneia is archaeologically absent from Brauron. Before Euripides, she is also literarily absent, belonging instead to Mycenae, Aulis, and the Crimea. After Euripides the only Classical reference to the heroine's presence at Artemis' Attik sanctuary comes from third-century BCE Euphorion as preserved in a scholion to Aristophanes' *Lysistrata*, where the commentator writes:

> Some say that the story of Iphigeneia took place in Brauron, not Aulis. Euphorion: "Seaside Brauron, the cenotaph of Iphigeneia." And it seems that Agamemnon sacrificed her at Brauron, not Aulis, and that a bear not a deer was put in her place. For which reason they perform a secret rite for her.[39]

The reference to bears is clearly an attempt on the part of the scholiast to reconcile the story of Iphigeneia with the ritual of the *arkteia* performed at the sanctuary (see Chapter 4). But there is no reason to suppose that the tale of Iphigeneia has anything to do with the *arkteia*, other than the single common element of being associated with Artemis. Even the supposedly common denominator of Brauron has become untenably weak.

All the evidence indicates that the story of Iphigeneia as priestess of Artemis at Brauron was invented, whole cloth, by Euripides.[40] The play *Iphigeneia Amongst the Tauroi*, produced in 413/412 BCE, appeared during the harshest period of the Peloponnesian War for the Athenians, after the loss of the fleet in Sicily, and when the Spartans had set up a permanent settlement at Dekeleia from which to raid the Attik countryside continuously. At the time of the production of Euripides' play, the Athenians had lost access to the sanctuary at Brauron, replacing it with the Brauronion shrine in the city Acropolis. In revenge (one might say) the Athenian playwright stole Iphigeneia from the enemy. The daughter of Agamemnon, King of Mycenae, the Peloponnesian heroine, was literarily established in the Attik countryside as a local heroine. With her she brought the cult statue of Tauric Artemis, a source of violence and power, to be used against the Lakonian kin who brutally tried to slaughter her.

In the end, the story of Iphigeneia reveals less of Artemis' cruelty than one might expect. Although it is true that all versions of the tale have the goddess demand the sacrifice of the maiden, most versions show that the goddess saves the heroine's life and makes her a goddess (Hekatê) or priestess. Her fate as a Brauronian priestess and heroine is a Euripidean invention. Instead, the tale of Iphigeneia appears to relate to the syncretisms that occurred between three goddesses in central Greece—Artemis, Hekatê, and Iphigeneia/Iphimedê. Both Hekatê and Iphigeneia retain the dark aspects of the hunting goddess, those pertaining to death and the underworld.

Halai Araphenides

For what it's worth, there is, in fact, a cult of Artemis Tauropolos at Attik Halai Araphenides, just as Euripides claimed. However, once again, there is no evidence outside of Euripides for the blood cult supposedly practiced there. According to the dramatist, during the rites of this goddess a man had blood drawn from his neck with a sword, thus replacing the human sacrifice associated with Tauric Artemis with a more minor kind of bloodletting. Considering the remarkable nature of such a practice, it is notable that not a single other source refers to this rite, not even those who clearly took their data from Euripides. Thus Strabo (9.1.22) tells us simply that there is a temple of Artemis Tauropolos at Halai. Apollodoros in his *Epitome* (6.27–28) relates the entire narrative as presented in Euripides, claiming that the xoanon was transported to Athens and "is now called Tauropolos." He also presents an alternate version, that the xoanon was actually brought to the island of Rhodes when Orestes et al. got blown off course on their homeward journey. But no blood.

Instead, we have a mid-fourth century BCE inscription (*SEG* XXXIV 103) wherein the people of Halai pay all due honors to one Philoxenos, son of Phrasikles, for having discharged his *leitourgoi* well and honorably, especially serving as *choregos* for the Pyrrhic dances. His honors were to be proclaimed by the herald of the Tauropolian Games, and the decree erected in the sanctuary of Artemis. The Pyrrhic Dances were war dances, mock battles to music, performed by (young) men. Thus the cult of Artemis Tauropolos at Halai hosted military training exercises for young men and dramatic violence. But, yet again, the more vicious aspect of her cult proves to be more literary than real.

ARTEMIS' WHIPPING BOYS

One of the most famous, in fact notorious, cult practices relating to Artemis in the ancient world was the so-called "endurance contest" of ancient Sparta, where boys-to-young-men were flogged at the altar of Artemis Ortheia for hours, some even dying under the lash according to visitors' reports. The scenario is so extreme it would probably have been passed off as a mythic construction if it were not for the copious contemporary evidence and commentary provided by eye-witnesses in both Greek and Latin.

The earliest evidence for the flogging ritual comes from the early fourth-century BCE historian-philosopher Xenophon, a Lakonophile Athenian. In his *Constitution of the Lakedaimonians* (*Lak.Pol.*), in the midst of his discussion of how the semi-mythic Spartan law-giver Lykourgos trained boys to be warriors, he claims (2.9):

> [Lykourgos] established it as a noble thing to steal as many cheeses as possible from Ortheia,[41] while he arranged for others to flog them, wanting to show by this that in enduring pain for a short time one would derive happiness for a long time.

By the second century BCE,[42] the *Institutions of the Lakedaimonions* was written, which was later incorporated into first-century CE Plutarch's work of the same name (*Inst.Lak.*).[43] Here the biographer-moralist recounts how (40.239c–d):

> The boys (*paides*) then are flogged with whips the entire day at the altar of Artemis Orthia, often until death; they—joyful and exultant—endure it, striving with each other for victory, whoever of them endures being beaten the most and worst. And the one who prevails in these things is held in the highest repute. This contest is called the Flagellation, and it takes place each year.

In his *Life of Lykourgos* (18.1), Plutarch mentions that he had seen this ritual himself, and that some boys died under the lash. Even before this, the first-century BCE Roman philosopher Cicero mentioned the practice in his *Tusculanae Disputationes* (2.34) noting:

> In truth, in Sparta the boys are so received with whips at the altar "that much blood flows from their bodies." Not only that, but when I was there I used to hear: to the death. But out of all of them not only did no one ever cry out, no one even groaned.

The latest evidence for the ongoing practice comes from the fourth century CE in some of the early Christian authors, before the change in religion annulled the tradition. The general opinion is that the "Flagellation" rite mentioned in Cicero and Plutarch amongst others[44] evolved out of the cheese-stealing ritual mentioned by Xenophon,[45] and that all of it was part of a ritual in honor of Artemis Ortheia whereby she (and the law-giver of Sparta) turned boys into men by means of shed blood.

The situation is actually more complicated than this.[46] To begin, both the descriptions of the actions and their chronology indicate that there is no continuity between Xenophon's cheese-stealing practice and Plutarch's Flagellation. As the evidence will show, the cheese-stealing was a non-religious practice that was but one of several aspects of food-theft in ancient Sparta, with no specific links to Artemis or her cults. By contrast, the Flagellation ritual was a Hellenistic creation tacked onto the cult of Artemis, and only superficially that of Ortheia. The inability of later authors to account consistently for the origins of the rite betrays the artificiality of the "*nomos,*" while simultaneously speaking volumes about Sparta's political concerns in the late Hellenistic and Roman periods.

What does become apparent from a study of both practices and the thin thread that serves as a connection between them is that the idea of being whipped was a deeply engrained notion of self for the ancient Spartans, or at least the male citizens. Thus, rather than being a matter of religious continuity, the two flogging practices—the Classical cheese-stealing and the Hellenistic–Roman Flagellation—show a continuity of this "key aspect" of the Spartan mentality: the ability to endure a specific kind of physical torment.

Stealing cheese from Ortheia

There is no evidence either from the textual data or the excavations at the sanctuary of Artemis Ortheia that the cheese-stealing practice was specifically religious in nature. No cult functionaries are mentioned, in contrast to the later Flagellation. There is no reference to the goddess's altar in the original text, merely that the cheeses are stolen *para Ortheias*, and the genitive of the goddess's epithet may simply derive from the *para* ("from"). We have no information concerning how often the custom took place, other than speculation as to how often cheeses would have been left as offering to the goddess.[47] This could be once a year in a special rite, or once a season as first-fruit offerings, or simply daily, bloodless offerings to Artemis. Because the boys were forced to steal provender frequently from whatever source, it becomes easier to argue that Ortheia's sanctuary was simply one more locale ripe for plunder, rather than a locale chosen for ritual purpose. This coincides well with the description offered by Plutarch in his *Life of Lykourgos* pertaining to the upbringing of young boys. In section 17.3–4 he relates:

> He arranges for the men to carry wood, and the smaller boys herbs, having stolen them. Some make their way about the gardens, others creep into the men's mess-halls well sneakily and guardedly. If one is caught, he receives many blows (*plegas*) with the whip, seeming to steal lazily and without technique. They steal whatever food they can, learning cleverly to set upon those sleeping or off their guard. To the one caught the penalty is whipping and hunger. For their meals are sparse, so that in this way they might defend themselves from want, and of necessity be daring and inventive.

In short, boys steal food to eat, from both Artemis Ortheia and elsewhere. We have already seen another instance where starving boys are permitted to steal food from Artemis, in Chapter 4, in Herodotos' anecdote (3.48) about the Korkyrian boys saved from castration by seeking sanctuary in a temenos of Artemis on Samos. This suggests that the reference to Artemis in Sparta pertains to the acceptability of starving children stealing sustenance from this goddess of youth without involving ritual impiety. Nevertheless, older boys are stationed in the temenos (?) to defend it with whips, while the caught youths get whatever beating might be at hand here and elsewhere. It is not a religious ritual, but an aspect of the boys' education.

That the focus was on experiencing whipping, and thus pain, rather than on the cult of the goddess comes across in other contemporary sources. The closest we come to Classical-period confirmation of the practice Xenophon described is a passage in Plato's *Laws*. Here (633b) the Spartan Megillos mentions in his discussion of how courage and virtue (in short—*aretê*) were fostered in the Spartans that, "There is a lot of endurance of pains amongst us, both in the hand-to-hand fights and in the stealing of things for which there are many blows (*plêgôn*)." There is no reference to either cheese or Artemis, merely the statement that boys steal and, apparently if caught, get beaten.

The Flagellation

The ritual described by Cicero, Plutarch, Pausanias, and others of the Roman period is of a different cut altogether. It occurs annually, ritually. It specifically takes place at the altar of Artemis Ortheia, with the goddess's priestess and cult image in attendance. (Pausanias 3.16.10):

> The priestess holding the xoanon stands by them; the xoanon is otherwise light because of its small size, but if the floggers are ever sparing in striking a youth who is pretty or noble, then the xoanon becomes heavy for the woman and no longer amenable. And the priestess makes out the floggers as the cause and says that she is oppressed because of them.

There is no mention of cheese, food, or theft, merely the endurance that the boys must show. This steadfastness at the altar, under the lashes, stands in stark contradiction to the aims of Lykourgos, who thought that the flogging would train the boys to be deft and swift, and thus *avoid* the blows as much as possible.

Chronology

Not only are the details pertaining to both whipping practices completely different (other than the fact of being flogged), the history of Sparta precludes continuity between the training of young men in Classical Sparta and the customs practiced by the Roman period. The actions described by Xenophon must, perforce, have been relevant in the Classical period, and thus we might date the cheese-stealing practice to the fifth to fourth centuries at the latest. However, both the so-called *agogê* and the practice of eating in common messes (discussed by Aristotle, and thus also dating to the Classical period) seem to have gone into abeyance as early as the later fourth century BCE. Michael Flower argues that both customs may have come to an end c. 330 BCE after the Spartan defeat at Megalopolis, when losses in manpower—the Spartan *oliganthropia*—would have been too severe to maintain either tradition.[48]

It is generally accepted that the first (re)creation of the Lykourgan "traditions" came about in the third century BCE during the reigns of Kings Agis and Kleomenes, when the Spartans were desperate to restore their stock of Spartiates.[49] Reforms in economics and land-tenure were backdated to the legendary law-giver, and it was certainly under Kleomenes that the *agogê* got its new elaboration. However, as Flower has noted, this occurred approximately one hundred years after the demise of the original traditions, and no one was left alive who personally remembered the Classical customs.[50] While the works of Xenophon and his contemporaries (none of whom, for the record, were Spartans) as well as oral tradition in all its mutability could have contributed to the "recreation," the chronology strongly suggests that the so-called Lykourgan customs were created out of a mostly new and innovative cloth. The weaver of this new cloth was Kleomenes' tutor and mentor—the Stoic philosopher Sphairos. As such, one might easily expect a heavy dose of Stoic idealism to pervade what were supposedly Archaic innovations.

If the century-long gap between the end of the continued practice of the Lykourgan *rhetra* and their (re)establishment were not enough to cast doubts on any notions of continuity, there was another period of interruption in the second century BCE. In 188 BCE Sparta lost yet another confrontation with the Akhaian League under Philopoimen, who received permission from Rome to curb the power of Sparta. This he did by demolishing the city's walls, restoring exiles, and, most importantly here, annulling the Spartan constitution and replacing it with the Akhaian. Specifically, he forbade the institution of the *agogê*, to which the flogging practices were strongly attached in both versions.[51] It took another forty years for the Spartans to get sufficiently back on the good side of the Romans that they could reinstitute their "traditional" constitution in 146. Unlike the previous period of abeyance, the so-called Lykourgan traditions would still have been in living memory in the second half of the second century BCE. Even if innovations crept in during this second wave of returning to "normal" they would have been less severe than in the true revolutions under Kleomenes in the previous century.

At the least, then, it can be argued that the Flagellation ritual is separated in time from the cheese-stealing custom by no less than a full century, and that the institution Plutarch saw with his own eyes was divided from that which Xenophon saw by no fewer than two complete gaps in Sparta's traditional constitution.

Etiology

The divide between the cheese-stealing practice and the Flagellation is brought into even higher relief when one considers that the ancient Greeks and Romans themselves were rather hard pressed to explain the origin(s) of the latter rite. This stands in stark contrast to what we see in the above-quoted passage from Plutarch's *Life of Lykourgos* (17.3–4), where the moralist discusses the beatings that result from awkward theft of food, a clear link to the earlier practice, but quite distinct from the Flagellation.

The earliest origin story we have for the Flagellation comes from the first-century BCE author C. Julius Hyginus in his mythological compendium *Fabulae*. At passage 261 he reports that Orestes:

Upon obtaining an oracle because he had lost his sister, had sought out Colchis with his comrade Pylades and, after the killing of Thoas, absconded with the xoanon [of Artemis Tauropolos], hidden in a bundle of wood . . . and brought it to Aricia. But because the cult's cruelty subsequently displeased the Romans, even though it was slaves who were sacrificed, Diana was transferred to the Spartans, where the custom of sacrifice continued in the whipping of boys, called Bomonicae ("Altar Victors") because, having been placed above the altar, they contended to see who could endure the most blows.[52]

This version is fleshed out later by Lucius Flavius Philostratos, a second to third-century CE Roman philosopher who recorded in his dialogue *Vita Apollonii* (6.20):

However, the custom of flogging is carried out in honor of Artemis from Skythia, at the command, they say, of oracles, and I think it is madness to go against the gods . . . Not whipping, but sprinkling the altar with human blood, since even the Skythians thought it worthy of these things. The Spartans modified the essential element of the ceremony and progressed to the endurance contest, from which there is no loss of life, while the goddess receives an offering of their blood.[53]

A variation on this Skythian theme is offered by Pausanias. In his version of the origins of the Flagellation (3.16.7, 9–11):

The region is called Limnaion, and there is a sanctuary of Artemis Orthia. They say that that xoanon is the one Orestes and Iphigeneia once stole out of the Tauric land. The Lakedaimonians say that they brought it to their own land, because Orestes was also king there . . . And here is my proof that Lakedaimonian Orthia is a xoanon from barbarian lands: Astrabakos and Alopekos, sons of Irbos, son of Amphisthenes, son of Amphikles, son of Agis, having found the statue immediately went mad. Additionally, the Spartan Limnatians and the Kynosoures and those from Mesoa and Pitanê, when sacrificing in Artemis, had a dispute, from which they became murderously angry, and while many were killed at the altar a plague destroyed the rest. And upon this an oracle came to them to stain the altar with the blood of humans. The one sacrificed was chosen by lot, but Lykourgos changed it to whipping youths there, and thus the altar is filled with the blood of humans. [Here is the section dealing with the priestess and the *xoanon*, given above]. Thus for the statue there remains the enjoyment of human blood since the sacrifices in the Tauric lands.

For Pausanias, the Flagellation came about because of a ritual pollution (*miasma*) caused by a murder within Artemis' temenos, which, somewhat illogically, required more bloodshed in her temenos to purge. Eventually, as is often the case with human sacrifices offered to Artemis, the ritual changed into something somewhat less homicidal, in this case the endurance contest. It is evident that by the second century CE there was considerable confusion about the origins of the Flagellation and Artemis' role therein. Pausanias manages to implicate the Skythians and Ortheia as well as Lykourgos and the oracles in the origins of the ritual, thus awkwardly pulling many of the threads together into a sort of semi-logical etiology.

In contrast to the Skythian Artemis etiology, there is the narrative presented by Plutarch in his *Life of Aristides,* who finds the origin of the rite at the Battle of Plataia in 479 BCE. According to Plutarch (17.8):

> Some say that Pausanias was sacrificing a bit beyond the battle line and praying when some of the Lydians suddenly falling upon him seized and cast about the sacrificial implements. And Pausanias and those with him not having their weapons struck at them with canes and whips. And now because of this they enact reenactments of this attack at the altar in Sparta by striking the youths and after them the parade of the Lydians.

The goddess to whom the general would have been sacrificing was Artemis Agrotera, to whom the Spartans sacrificed a goat before entering into battle (see Chapter 3). Thus the ritual is tied not to Artemis Ortheia or Skythian Tauropolos, but Artemis Agrotera, and the ritual has nothing to do with stealing or upbringing, but is part of a war memorial.

Each of the proposed etiologies has complicating, even contradicting, elements that set into high relief the propagandistic roles they filled in early Roman Sparta. The earliest origin story is the Skythian narrative, wherein Orestes (and presumably Iphigeneia) absconded with the cult statue of Artemis Tauropolos and relocated to Aricia in Italy before finally settling down in Sparta with the *xoanon*. This first-century BCE narrative stands in direct contradiction to the fifth-century Athenian tradition as created by Euripides in his *Iphigeneia Amongst the Tauroi* (ll. 1446–1463) as quoted above in the section on Iphigeneia. This is the oldest evidence we have for the tradition of Artemis' Skythian *xoanon* in Greece. As such, *any* "Skythian" narrative pertaining to either Orestes or Lykourgos is automatically anachronistic. In Roman times, especially in the texts of Strabo and Pausanias, this statue winds up in many cities, including Hermionê, Italian Aricia, Susa, Cappadocia, Tyndaris in Sicily, and, of course, Sparta.[54] Considering the chronology of the evidence, there is a strong desire to suggest that the Spartans symbolically "stole" the *xoanon* from the Athenians.[55]

In the period when such narratives were being generated, these etiologies served numerous propagandistic purposes for the Spartans who were trying to get back in touch with their warrior origins. To begin, the stories of Orestes reconnect the Spartans with their heroic past, specifically with the Trojan War Cycle. By reaffirming their links with Orestes, son of Agamemnon, Sparta could reach through the numerous military defeats of the final centuries BCE to a period of reasonably untarnished glory. The reference to Orestes as king of Sparta (through his marriage to Hermionê, epikleric daughter of Menelaos and Helen) bypassed the rather awkward situation in Mycenae and bound the hero to both great cities of Homeric fame.

In Hyginus' version of the Tauric *xoanon*, the narrative also brings the Italian city of Aricia into the fray; in fact, it is the only narrative that delves so far west on this topic. For Kennell, this detail relates back to an ongoing debate prevalent in the second and first centuries BCE over the cultural influence that Sparta exerted over Rome. Beginning no later than the writings of Polybios in the second century BCE, various authors ancient and modern were intrigued by the similarities in the Spartan and Roman governments—duel kings/duel consuls, *gerousia* of thirty/senate of 300, five ephors and ten tribunes, etc.[56] For some Greek intellectuals, the dependence of Rome on Sparta was self-evident, as for Posidonios in his claim that the Romans "imitated the constitution of the Lakedaimonians in every way and maintained it better than they" (*FrGrHist* 87 F 59). Hyginus' *Fabulae* allowed the Romans to turn the tables on the Spartans and argue that at least some influence went west to east, with the

Flagellation being a departure from the Arician custom of ritualized regicide in the cult of Diana at Nemi (see Chapter 7).

Taking the Tauric origins from a different perspective, Pausanias claims that the ritualized bloodshed came not from the bloodthirsty Skythians, but from a Greek cultic *miasma*—bloodshed in the temenos—in the presence of the Tauric statue. This spilling of blood took place between the four presumably established *phylai* of Sparta: the Limnatians, the Kynosourians, the people of Mesoa and those of Pitanê. Once again the narrative serves to legitimate an ancient "tradition" that in fact only dates back to the Hellenistic period, setting the Hellenistic-era tribes back into the dark ages of early Spartan history.[57] Such a hypothesis is strengthened by the fact that the most recently created tribe—the *Neopolitai* or "New Citizens"—is distinctly absent from this list. This fifth estate was probably a creation of Kleomenes, not being attested before the Hellenistic period.[58] By removing the Neopolitai from the list of groups who fought at Artemis' altar, Pausanias emphasized the (faux) archaism of the tradition.

In contrast to the preceding etiologies which all pertain to one extent or another to an imported Artemis at the altar of torment, Plutarch gives a wholly distinct origin of the Flagellation ritual. In his *Life of Aristides*, he claims that the Flagellation was enacted annually in memoriam of a hand-to-hand fight between the Spartans and Lydians at the Battle of Plataia. Unfortunately for Plutarch, his description is directly contradicted by Herodotos' fifth-century account of that conflict. In his *Histories* Herodotos reports that that Lakedaimonians and their Tegean allies (9.61.3–9.62.2):

> had no auspicious sacrifices, and then at the time many fell upon them and many more were hurt considerably. For the Persians being fenced round with wicker shields fired off arrows in lush abundance, so much so that Pausanias—with the Spartans getting their butts kicked and his sacrifices as they were—looks to the Plataian Heraion, invoking the goddess, praying that she not give the lie to their hope. While Pausanias was still invoking these things the Tegeans roused up in front and headed towards the Barbarians, and immediately after his prayer the sacrifices became favorable for the Lakedaimonians. Thus at last they too made for the Persians, and the Persians opposite threw away their bows. The battle started by the wicker shields, and when these had fallen the fierce battle continued long and hard by the temple of Demeter itself, until it came to close fighting. For the Barbarians having taken hold of their spears snapped them short.

It is clear from Herodotos' account that the Persians did not engage the troops under Pausanias in hand-to-hand combat, but rather shot at them from a distance behind a shield fence. It was only after they received good omens and charged the enemy away from the altar that the two groups came into close quarters. As such, it is not possible that the Lakedaimonians et al. fought them around the altar with the whips they had at hand.

Plutarch's narrative is thus unduly awkward, especially as it is evident that the scholar had access to Herodotos amongst other ancient sources. It is only possible to suggest that there was an alternate version in circulation to which we no longer have access, and which accounted not only for the different style of combat, but also addressed the matter of the later Spartan Lydian procession, for which, to date, this passage in Plutarch is our only attestation.

Nevertheless, drawing the Battle of Plataia into the Flagellation narrative is consistent with Spartan propagandistic tendencies of the first centuries CE. As discussed by Paul Cartledge and Anthony Spawforth, Sparta in the Roman period was keen to highlight its role in the Persian Invasions, especially in those years when Rome was engaged in wars with the Parthians, their own, personal Persians. Even before this, from the late second century BCE Sparta took a prominent role in the quadrennial *Eleutheria* ("Freedom") festival celebrating Hellas' triumph over the barbarians. During the early centuries of the Common Era, Sparta and Athens became famous for the rhetorical dual they fought at this event for the right to lead the festival's ceremonial *pompê*.[59] It is possible that the location of Orestes' Taurian *xoanon* became relevant in these debates, as Pausanias (3.16.7) notes that whereas the Spartans maintained possession of the cult statue over the centuries, the Athenians, in the follow up to the narrative provided by Euripides, admit to having lost the image to the Persians during the assault under Xerxes.

For the authors of the Roman period, the endurance contest does have some-thing to do with Artemis, typically a foreign, barbarian, blood-thirsty Artemis, but also their war ally Agrotera. And yet this seldom seems to be overly relevant. The etiologies are inconsistent with each other and, once again, wholly inconsistent with the narratives received from the earlier authors. Instead, the Flagellation offered a series propagandistic purposes that tied Sparta to ancient traditions that were, for the most part, recent inventions. In his *Life of Aristides*, Plutarch at least summoned memories of the early fifth century, even if his account ran in stark contrast to what we know from Herodotos. But the authors both before and after Plutarch attempted to archaize "customs" that were, admittedly, relatively old by the Roman period, but were certainly not to be dated back to some Archaic Lykourgos. And yet these etiolo-gies not only harkened back to the Archaic Age, but also even back to the Bronze Age, recalling the glory days of King Orestes, son of Agamemnon *anax andrôn*.

Those boys are whipped!

Rather than thinking of either the cheese-stealing custom or the Flagellation as aspects of the cult of Artemis (of whatever identity or epithet), it is better to consider the idea of whipping itself as the important detail. Perhaps as an important symbol of their fortitude, stamina, and endurance, the Spartans chose to think of themselves as literally whipped. It is, as Flower expressed it, a "key symbol" of Spartan (male) identity,[60] a self-defining, unique practice, such as the worship of a pantheon depicted as armed (even Aphrodite![61]), or dancing the Gymnopaideia in the heat of summer (which provided a similar test of endurance; see Plato, *Laws* 633c), or honoring two kings who apotheosized at death.[62] Possibly resulting from the cheese-stealing practice, or perhaps the origin of it, the Spartans held the flagellation of their males to be an important aspect of Spartanhood.

Eschewing Artemis or ritual connotations, focus on the notion of the flagellation alone creates continuity in the Spartan custom. At the beginning of that continuity are the texts of Xenophon and Plato, one referring to the cheese-stealing custom and the other to the beating of young thieves generally. These data are complemented by an additional passage in Xenophon's *Lak.Pol.* (2.2), where once more referring to the training of boys Xenophon notes:

> Lykourgos, instead of imposing slave tutors over each one individually, appointed a man from the highest station to have power over them, and who is called the *Paidonomos*. He authorized this man to muster the boys and to watch over them, and if someone should perform insufficiently, to punish thoroughly. And he gave to this man from the young men whip-bearers, so that they might assist him whenever necessary. And so there was plenty of modesty together with obedience there.

It is again the case that the notion of being whipped, in this instance by *mastigophoroi*, has nothing to do with Artemis and everything to do with being well-brought up, well-educated Spartans.

By the late fourth century BCE, it appears that the notion of whipped Spartans was well enough known to be either recorded or lampooned by Klearkhos of Soli, a late fourth to early third-century peripatetic philosopher. As preserved in Athenaios' *Deipnosophistai* (13.555c–d), in his book *On Proverbs* Klearkhos claimed that:

> In Lakedaimon the women at some festival drag the unmarried men around the altar and cane them, so that fleeing this outrage of this act they might love truly and approach marriage in due season.

It is well known that Lykourgos, as part of his "eugenics" policy, strongly discouraged citizens from remaining single and, more importantly, not reproducing (Plutarch, *Lykourgos* 15.1–2; *Lysander* 30.5; *Moralia* 227f).[63] As reported by Plutarch, the penalties were a kind of low-level social ostracism, whereby the men were disdained in public, or forbidden to take part in certain festivals. It is not possible to determine if Klearkhos' narrative was accurate or not, as we have no other contemporary data, beyond the fact that Klearkhos was considered to be a bit of a sensationalist by scholars both ancient and modern. Furthermore, it is methodologically unsound to attempt to verify Klearkhos' fourth/third-century BCE account with Plutarch's first-century CE writings. Whether or not Klearkhos' account is "true," though, may perhaps take a back seat here to the fact that his narrative was deemed representative of Spartan culture, and that the two aspects present in it—punishment for bachelordom and whipping around an altar—were distinctly Lakedaimonian. Or, to put this another way, being whipped by an altar was already seen as part of the Spartan *geist* by the dawn of the third century BCE. Klearkhos gives no hint as to whose altar, and from this we might surmise that either it was already so well known that Spartan males were whipped by Ortheia's altar that there was no reason to add it, or that the practice was not associated with any specific deity that Klearkhos knew of and what was important was the flogging itself.

There are no more extant references to Spartan flogging until we get to the Latin texts of Cicero and Hyginus mentioned above, by which point the endurance contest as it was known in Roman times was already well entrenched.

As Artemis was the goddess who presided over the transition of children into adults, it is not surprising that she was implicated in the various traditions that involved the beating of boys in the process of their education and maturation into men. As the savage Skythian goddess who demanded human blood, Artemis was also an appropriate choice for the endurance contest.

Nevertheless, the evidence indicates that the role of Artemis in both traditions was perhaps more accidental than anything else. Apollo (primary deity in Sparta and god of youth) or even Hyakinthos would have been equally appropriate maturation deities. Artemis and her priestess presided over the Flagellation mainly because it was Artemis—or at least Ortheia (see Chapter 1)—who was associated with the earlier custom. Klearkhos could have been referring to the altar of Aphrodite or Hera—or even Aphrodite-Hera in Lakonia (Pausanias 3.13.9)—for the castigation of his bachelors.

What is consistent throughout the mottled history of the whipping tradition is the whipping itself. Be it by altar or not, for food or not, for Artemis or not, for close to a millennium the Spartans vaunted to the world that they were the men who could stand up to a good flogging. They were insane.

SKYTHIAN ARTEMIS

Thor: Loki is beyond reason, but he is of Asgard and he is my brother.
Natasha Romanoff: He killed eighty people in two days.
Thor: He's adopted.[64]

The cults of Artemis Tauropolos and Artemis Ortheia shared two important aspects in the literature: Both were deemed bloodthirsty, and both associated their Artemis with northern barbarians, the Tauroi to be exact. This is not an uncommon aspect of Greek religion. For one reason or another numerous deities made the Greeks uncomfortable, and, almost inevitably, the Greeks found a way to claim that these deities were foreigners, natives of some exotic place where such unseemly qualities were to be expected. Dionysos, the god of drunken madness, was surely from Anatolia, if not India. "Hateful" Ares, god of carnage and destruction, was, of course, Thracian. Aphrodite, who could bend even the mind of Zeus, not to mention cause inopportune erections, was Cypriote, or Syrian, or Assyrian—however far east the Greeks could find a cognate for her.

Chaste Artemis was rarely cast that far afield from Greece. Her epithets reveal no foreign designations, such as Kypris. She does not fly home to some foreign land, like Ares. As goddess of wild animals she is seldom depicted with exotic creatures, like Dionysos' leopard.

Nevertheless, when she demands human blood or human life, she suddenly becomes Skythian. This fact results from the merger of three trends in the Classical world. The first is, quite simply, the tendency noted above to make "uncomfortable" deities somehow foreign. Thus, man-killing Artemis is Taurian.

The second trend was the extreme popularity of Euripides' *Iphigeneia Amongst the Tauroi*. As studied extensively by Edith Hall, this play was one of the most popular throughout both Greece and Rome following its introduction in the late fifth century. Scenes from the story become common motifs on Greek vase paintings, Roman wall paintings, and even on Roman sarcophagi in the Common Era.[65] The tale served as one of the foundations myths for the cult of Arician Diana and the rite of the Rex Nemorensis in central Italy (see Chapter 7), which itself was important to the propaganda of Augustus Caesar. As the popularity of the Iphigeneia narrative grew, more cities farther afield laid claim to some aspect of the myth, either highlighting their own role in the narrative, or laying claim to the Tauric *agalma*. Thus Hall:

> The places which we know for certain linked themselves to the story told in the play . . . included Halai Araphenides, Brauron, Sparta, Mycenae, the Troad, Laodicea in Syria, Comana in Pontus, Golden Comana and Tyana in Cappadocia, Castabala in Cilicia, Philadelphia in Lydia, in addition to the great sanctuary of Diana in the Alban hills of Italy, Kyme, Rhegion and Tyndaris, making at least fifteen in all.[66]

The third trend was the spread of Romanization throughout the Greek world, and with it the Roman predilection for violence and cruelty. As discussed in the sections above on the holocaust of Patrai and the flogging ritual at Sparta, much of Artemis' real bloodiness only emerged in the Roman period, when one might say blood sports became more common and popular. As a result, the cults of Artemis became bloodier, and with this development a concomitant need to cast this savagery onto a Barbarian "Other."

All of these trends are clearly visible in Sparta. As noted in Chapter 1, the cult of Worthasia dates back to the ninth century, with the goddess's syncretism with Artemis probably occurring in the sixth. However, there are no mentions of the goddess's (or her cult image's) origins in Skythia until the Roman period, with the writing of Hygineus in the first century. By this point, *Iphigeneia Amongst the Tauroi* had become popular and important to Roman propaganda. Likewise, by the time of Hygineus the original cheese-stealing ritual of the *agogê* had metamorphosed into the endurance contest—the Flagellation—whereby Spartan youths were flogged for hours at Artemis Ortheia's altar. Artemis' Tauric origins went hand-in-hand with the increased savagery of her rites: When more and more blood was demanded of Spartan youths, Ortheia suddenly came from Skythia—by way of Italy! By contrast, Artemis Ortheia of Messenê, who is attended by young girls, is never Skythian. A bit Thracian, perhaps, but this merely brings her closer to her sister Artemis-Bendis in Athens, Messenê's enemy-of-my-enemy ally against Sparta.

In the end, Artemis is far more likely to be Skythian in Pausanias than she is in Herodotos. In the latter, Iphigeneia is the Maiden worshipped with human sacrifice. For Pausanias, Artemis and/or her cult statues are Skythian in numerous regions of ancient Greece and beyond, from Aricia in Italy to Susa. This tendency toward greater "barbarism" goes hand-in-hand with the tendency toward greater savagery in her cults, most notable at Sparta and Patrai.

The cults of Artemis do often become more brutal over time. But we should note that this is not because Artemis is more Skythian, but more Roman. It is in the Roman period that the holocausts of Patrai are attested, and it is in the Roman period that we have the greatest evidence for death during the Flagellation rite. Artemis in myth was always a "lion to women" since the days of Homer, but her savagery remained mainly in the realms of myth. It was not until the Romans that she became savage in real life, which probably had a lot more to do with the Romans than the goddess.

OVERVIEW

Artemis is famous in modern literature for being both tender and savage. Her savagery manifests in her apparent thirst for blood, as she strikes down humans by various plagues and women in particular with her "gentle" arrows. She is the goddess most likely to demand human sacrifice, often children, and sometimes even other deities have to mollify her rites of retribution. At her worst, the Greeks disown her, blaming the Tauric Skythians for their goddess's brutality.

In the end, though, it is not the Tauroi, or even the Greeks, who were to blame for the most vicious of Artemis' rites, but the Romans. It was only under the empire that hordes of animals were conflagrated in holocausts, while Spartan boys died under the bloody lash. As we shall see in the next chapter, it was also in Italy under the Romans that the cult of ritualized regicide was attached to the cult of Diana.

NOTES

1 West 1997: 373.
2 Trans. Dalley 1989: 81.
3 Lesser 2005–2006: 49.
4 Brelich 1969: 371–374.
5 Full citations in Lloyd-Jones 1983: 99.
6 Isn't that nice: None of the folks throwing living puppies onto a bonfire got hurt.
7 On animal sacrifice in general in Greek religion, see Burkert 1985: 2.1.
8 Although the original cult at Kalydon, site of the famous boar hunt, did bring to light remains of boars and deer, as well as horses, suggesting a tradition of sacrificing wild animals to Artemis Laphria. See Larson 2007: 102.
9 Shelton 2007: 116 and n. 74; 118 and nos. 80–82, excerpted.
10 Herodotos is careful to distinguish between the Tauroi of the Crimea and the Skythians to the north (4.102–103). Later authors seldom made such distinctions, and thus there is a tendency to conflate Tauroi and Skythians in the literature. See Hall 2013: 66.
11 Trans. Dowden 1989: 10. That the Tauric aspect of this narrative may derive from Euripides' *Iphigeneia Amongst the Tauroi,* later picked up by Proklos and added to Stasinos' account, see Hall 2013: xxii.
12 Trans. Hollinshead 1985: 421.
13 Edith Hall, however, suggests that these lines may be a later addition to the text, to keep the narrative more in line with the later *Iphigeneia Amongst the Tauroi.* Hall 2013: xxvi.
14 Dowden 1989: 17.
15 At Aulis specifically, see Schachter 1981: 96.
16 Assuming that these names are related by more than just coincidence. See Hollinshead 1985: 421.

17 Johnston 1999: 204, with references.

18 Parker 2005: 223.

19 Schachter 1981: 100.

20 Bilde 2009: 304–305, with references.

21 Graham 1982: 123. See also Graham 1958: *passim*.

22 Graham 1982: 124.

23 Hall 2013: 64–65.

24 Graham 1982: 123.

25 Rudhardt 1992: 224–227.

26 Mettinger 2001: 114.

27 As Edith Hall has noted, there is speculation that she was the bird goddess named Obida in the twelfth-century CE Russian epic *Armament of Igor*, who came to be known as the "Swan Maiden" of the Crimea in Tatar folklore. "Both of these stories, in turn, have been connected with the ancient traditions relating to the Parthenos of the western Tauric Chersonese, as first mentioned by Herodotus (4.103): the temple of the Maiden, 'some sort of *daimon*,' who gives her name to the cliff outside the city—Parthenion—where the temple of the goddess and her image are to be found." (Hall 2013: 65)

28 Hollinshead 1985: 423.

29 Bilde 2009: 310.

30 Ibid.: 311.

31 Ibid.: 312.

32 One of the duties of priestesses is to carry the temple keys, and this is their most common attribute in artistic depictions.

33 Ekroth 2003: 67 and 75.

34 Ibid.: 67 and 87–89.

35 Ibid.: 70. See also Hollinshead 1985: 425.

36 Ekroth 2003: 72.

37 Ibid.: 79 and 84–87.

38 Cole 2004: 199.

39 Faraone 2003: 52.

40 Nor would this be the first time the playwright "tampered" with myth. Before his *Medea* all references to the eponymous witch made it clear that either Hera or the Corinthians killed her children, not their mother. Since Euripides, it is commonly assumed that this is an integral aspect of her narrative. On this (anti-)heroine, see Griffiths 2006: *passim*.

41 Her altar is generally assumed and appears in most translations, but is not present in the Greek.

42 On the problems of dating this work, see Hodkinson 2000: 48–50.

43 Kennell 1995: 111; 136.

44 For the full corpus of references to the flagellation ritual, see Kennell 1995: Appendix I.

45 Cartledge and Spawforth 2002: 192.

46 It usually is.

47 Contra Kennell 1995: 123.

48 Flower 2002: 195.

49 Ibid.: 196–198; Kennell 1995: 111.

50 Flower 2002: 196.

51 Kennell 1995: 9.
52 Trans. Kennell 1995: 150.
53 Ibid.: 157, excerpted.
54 Cole 2004: 199. See also Hall 2013: 150.
55 Just as Euripides "stole" Iphigeneia from the Lakonians.
56 Kennell 1995: 81.
57 Ibid.: 40.
58 Cartledge 2002: 53.
59 Cartledge and Spawforth 2002: 191.
60 Flower 2009: 202.
61 Budin 2010: *passim.*
62 Flower 2009: 202–214.
63 See also Cartledge 2002: 265.
64 *The Avengers* (film) 2012. Director: Joss Whedon. Marvel Studios.
65 Hall 2013: chs. 4–7.
66 Ibid.: 150.

7

SOME UNDERAPPRECIATED ASPECTS OF ARTEMIS

Many of the characteristics of Artemis covered in the previous chapters of this book are well known to both academic and popular readers. Mention the name "Artemis" and people will think of the goddess of the hunt, the kourotrophos, the midwife, the woman-slayer, and probably the moon because people tend to confuse Artemis with Roman Diana.

But there are other aspects of this goddess that are less well known, and may in fact seem to be somewhat contradictory to her more popular persona. As discussed below, in addition to her sylvan characteristics, Artemis was also worshipped as a city goddess in ancient Greece, and she was a goddess instrumental in the liberation of slaves.

ARTEMIS THE CITY GODDESS

As discussed in Chapter 1, Artemis has strong precedents in the Aegean Bronze Age in characters such as the Aegean Goddess of Nature and the Potnia Therôn. However, as early as the Archaic Age evidence from the literature and archaeology indicate that the goddess had a village, if not full-scale urban, aspect as well. Furthermore, many of her cults incorporated the personae of foreign goddesses such as the Great Goddess of Anatolia (Ephesos) and Persian Anaïtis. As such, it should not be too surprising that in regions where the links between Artemis and these eastern goddesses remained strong, Artemis took on aspects of her predecessors' eastern cults. As syncretisms strengthened during the Hellenistic period, so too did Artemis take on more aspects of a city goddess, especially in the Greek east.[1]

The earliest literary evidence we have for Artemis as a city goddess comes from the *Homeric Hymn to Aphrodite*, where the poet claims that among the things that Artemis loves, such as archery and dancing, is (l. 20) "a city of just men" (*dikaiôn te ptolis andrôn*). In the sixth century the lyric poet Anakreon added a new datum in his poem to Artemis of Magnesia on the Maiander (fr. 348 Page):

I supplicate you, Elaphebolos ("Deer-Shooter"),
Shining-haired daughter of Zeus, mistress
Of wild animals, Artemis.
And now how upon the city

Of brave-hearted men by whirling Lethaios
You look rejoicing
For the citizens (you see) are not
Savage flocks.

Here we see a perfect melding of the Artemis of the wilds and an emergent city goddess. Anakreon addresses the goddess as a mistress of wild animals (*agriôn despoin'* . . . *thêrôn*) and even refers to the citizens of the city as "flocks." However, Artemis is specifically rejoicing to see that, although flocks, they are not *savage* (*anêmerous*) flocks, but, presumably, "just men."

Archaeological evidence from the Greek mainland also indicates that Artemis had an urban aspect in addition to her more liminal orientation. For example, Artemis Mesopolitis ("Center-City") had a sanctuary located within the city walls of Arkadian Orkhomenos, located on a terrace just south of the city's agora. The temple's exceptionally long, narrow proportions suggest a construction in the early Archaic period, later complemented by a new altar in the third century BCE.[2] In Attika, Artemis' sanctuary at Brauron received a "partner" Brauronion on the Athenian Acropolis as early as the sixth century under the Peisistratids, indicating that its erection had nothing to do with lack of access to the original during the Peloponnesian War.[3] The two successive temples of Artemis Phosphoros (also known as Ortheia) in Messenê discussed in Chapter 4 were located within the city itself, dating back into the fourth century BCE and enduring well into the Roman era. Eric Brulotte's survey of Artemis cults in the Peloponnese revealed that:

> In fact, a quick glance at the geographical position of Artemis sanctuaries shows . . . that 77 of the cults dedicated to Artemis were located in cities and villages or their immediate neighborhood, while their number in the countryside merely reaches only 45 . . . [I]t is probably fair to assume that quite early on cults dedicated to Artemis spread from the countryside into the villages and cities and that at one point their number was equal in urban and rural settings.[4]

Nevertheless, it is in the Hellenistic era that the cult of Artemis city-protector truly expanded in the Greek East. The cities where Artemis' persona had been strongly influenced by indigenous goddesses grew more prominent and economically significant, and they were able to spread their own city cults throughout the expanding kingdoms of Alexander's wake. By the third century, cults of an urban Artemis had become prominent especially in Anatolia, in Lydia, Karia, Ionia, Phrygia, Lykia, Pamphylia, and Cilicia.[5]

Heralding in this new role of Artemis as city goddess was Kallimakhos in his extensive *Hymn to Artemis*. When asking father Zeus for the honors she desires, she requests the usual items and prerogatives we have come to expect: quiver, nymphs, mountains, etc. Zeus grants them, but adds in as well (ll. 31–39):

> "Take, child, gladly as much
> As you ask, and Daddy will give even more.
> Thirty walled cities and not just one tower shall I give,
> Thirty walled cities, which won't go to enhance another deity,

> But which will be called only yours, Artemis.
> Many cities are held in common,
> Both on the mainland and in the islands, and in each will be
> Altars of Artemis, and sacred lands too. And you will be
> The guardian of highways and wetlands."

One city Kallimakhos mentioned in this account is, not surprisingly, Ephesos. In lines 237–257 the poet describes how the warrior Lygdamis threatened to attack and plunder the city with a host of Kimmerians. But Artemis herself held him off, as do her "arrows guard Ephesos forever!"

Artemis' syncretism with the Persian-Armenian goddess Anaïtis/Anahita made her city goddess of Hypaipa, not far from Ephesos.[6] As mentioned in Chapter 3, this goddess emerged through a Zororastrian adoption and adaptation of the Mesopotamian goddess Ištar, goddess of war and love. Having also absorbed the attributes of a local water goddess, she came to be known as *anahita*, the "Immaculate One."[7] While she was often associated with Aphrodite/Venus from her origins in Ištar, the Greek deity to whom she was most often compared was Artemis in the function of a "pure" fertility goddess.[8] So much is attested in Plutarch's *Lucullus* (§24), the *Annals* of Tacitus (3.63),[9] and the Anatolian epithets of Artemis as Artemis *Anaïtis* and possibly Artemis *Persikê*.[10] Like Ištar, Anahita also has her militaristic side, and a bit like Euripides' Crimean Artemis the goddess received at her temple in Staxr the severed heads of enemies killed in battle.[11] As such, she was an ideal deity to serve as the patron and protector of the city and citadel.

Several other eastern Greek cities venerated Artemis as their urban patroness.[12] In Anatolia, Pergê in Pamphylia came second only to Ephesos as Artemis' darling, and both of these cities were instrumental in spreading the cult of urban Artemis throughout the eastern Greek states. Returning to the Magnesia on the Maiander mentioned by Anakreon, Artemis Leukophrynê/Leukophrys ("Gleaming White") was this city's primary deity since her epiphany there in the third century BCE. The goddess was revered as the city goddess of Iasos in Karia under the epithets *Astias* ("Of the City") and *Prokathegemon* ("Leader and Guide"), an epithet she also bore in Ephesos (*Ephesos* 2, #1). She took on the epithet Kyria ("Sovereign") in Syrian Laodikeia and Milyas in Anatolian Lycia, where she was also worshipped as Artemis *Eleuthera* ("Freedom") in the city of Myra. In Kindyê in Karia she was recognized as Artemis *Kindyas*, literally the city goddess, just as she was revered as *Sardianê* in Lydian Sardis.

Artemis was never as prominent a city deity as Athena or Apollo. Nevertheless, in spite of her more sylvan tendencies, the role of city goddess was not wholly alien to Artemis. As the long-standing goddess of borders and boundaries, she had always been important as the goddess who helped to determine the polis' territory.

ARTEMIS WILL MAKE YOU FREE!

There is one area of transitions where Artemis is less well known than the others presented in this volume, and that is the transition between slavery and freedom.

Like many of the transitions presented here, this one is unidirectional: Just as Artemis helps the child to mature and the virgin to become a mother, Artemis is instrumental in the manumission of slaves rather than in the process of subjugation. Artemis' role in manumission is not exclusive to the goddess, and there are other deities who have a larger function in this process than she. Nevertheless, her role in the freeing of slaves, and especially female slaves, from their masters is a significant aspect of her cult, and one that extends well into the Roman period and the cult of Diana.

Divine purchase and sacral manumission

Beginning in the fourth century BCE, when our relevant epigraphic evidence first appears, there were two ways that a deity could function in the manumission of a slave. One way was for the deity to buy the slave from the former master. Prominent especially at Delphi where over 1,200 such sales have been recorded from the second century BCE through the first century CE, this practice allowed for a slave to purchase his or her own freedom by giving the sale money to the god, who then bought the slave from his/her owner. Although there were frequent *paramonê* clauses—whereby the slave must remain with the master for a certain number of years after this "fictitious" purchase—the slave was officially free after the dictates of the *paramonê* clause, with no one having authority over him/her save the deity. Thus in a manumission decree dating to 154–153 BCE we read:

> Krato, son of Mesateos . . . has sold to Pythian Apollo a female slave named Irenê, Armenian by race, for three minas of silver; and he has received the price in full. Guarantor: Nikarkhos, son of Erato, according as Irenê has entrusted the purchase to the god, to the end that she is free and not subject to seizure by anybody, doing whatever she may wish, and running off to whomever she may wish. Witnesses.[13]

The second way that a deity could be instrumental in the manumission of a slave was through a kind of sacral manumission whereby the slave was freed to and under the protection of a deity. In such an instance it would appear that the manumission was a gift freely given by the slave-owner, not a purchase of freedom by the slave (by way of a deity), although *paramonê* clauses could and did often still apply. Such freed slaves were called "*hieros/hiera*" (m./f.) "sacred" to the deity to whom they were released, and later the term *hierodule* became common as well, especially in the east.[14] Such manumissions began in the fourth century BCE and continued well into the late Roman period.

The two deities for whom we possess the largest number of such "*hieros*" manumission decrees are the Greco-Egyptian god Serapis and the Greek healing deity Asklepios.[15] Considering the fact that the concept of *hierodouleia*—the consecration of an individual to a deity with concomitant protection and guaranteed freedom—began in Egypt,[16] it is perhaps not surprising that a Greco-Egyptian deity would feature so prominently in these dedications. Other deities who appear as "receiving" manumitted slaves include Poseidon, Apollo, Athena, Zeus, Herakles, the Mother of the Gods, and Artemis.

Hiera têi Artemidi

Artemis' role in this practice of sacral manumission is significant. For one thing, she is one of the earliest deities to be mentioned in the context of sacral manumission. A manumission inscription from Mount Kotillion in Arkadia (*IG* V², 429) dating to c. 360 BCE relates:

> God. Fortune.
>
> Klenis releases Komaithos as free, and Ombria and Khoirothyon. If anyone should lay a hand on them, either Wistias or anyone else, all their goods are "sacred" [given] to Apollo Bassitas, Pan Sinoeis, Artemis of Kotillion, and Worthasia.[17]

Later, at the dawn of the third century BCE, a similar decree was set up in Messenê invoking the goddess Limnatis (an epithet of Artemis) to guarantee the liberty of one Petraia (*IG* V¹, 1470). It begins:

> releases Petraia as free. If someone should try to re-enslave Petraia, may he owe ten sacred minas of silver to Limnatis.[18]

As time went on, the bond between the freed slave and the "receiving" deity became stronger. The terms "*hiera*" and "hierodule" became more common, as well as variations in the *paramonê* clauses whereby the manumitted slaves owed service to the deity in question. Thus a second-century BCE inscription from the island of Kos relates that (*SEG* XIV, 529):

> Pythion dedicated the temenos [and] this sanctuary of Artemis . . . and Zeus Hikesios and the ancestral deities. Pythion son of Praxilas and the priestess dedicated . . . a slave named Makarinos free [and] sacred to the goddess (*hieron tês theou*), so that he might care for the sanctuary; and all the sacrificers, ministers, and servants, as many as are in the sanctuary may Makarinos care for them and for all the other matters both sacred and profane just as is written in the sacred register, and the other matters as given by Pythion and the priestess.

Inscription *SEG* II, 396 recounts that "Aurelia Philipparin Eurodikês releases the slave by name Ariagnê to the goddess Artemis Gazôria as a hierodule."[19] And, as recalled from Chapter 1, there is the first-century BCE inscription from Hyampolis in Phokis which reads (in part):

> If someone should seize Eukrateia and lead her into slavery . . . in any way or under any pretext, may he pay 30 minas of silver to Artemis and Apollo, and may it be permitted to whoever wishes to come forward and seize up to a half of this (sum from him). And may Eukrateia be free using the appellation sacred (*hiera*) to Artemis and Apollo, no longer belonging to anyone in any way.[20]

The most focused set of manumission decrees pertaining to Artemis comes from Khaironea in Boiotia, where numerous women were freed under the auspices of

Artemis Eilithyia.[21] All date to the late third to second century BCE, and all but one contain a *paramonê* clause obliging the slave to remain with the owner for a specified period of time (usually for the life of the owner). Thus in *IG* VII, 3386 we read:

> God.
>
> In the archonship of Aristonikos, Eudamos, son of Aristodamos, dedicated as sacred (*hiera*) his slave by name Sosikha to Artemis Eilithyia, on the condition that she remain with him while he lives. He makes this dedication conforming to the laws with the assent of Nikon and Apollo.

While a contemporary inscription reads:

> In the archonship of Aristion, the 30th of Thioos, Hagesias, son of Noneis, dedicates his servant Kallis to Artemis Eilithyia, so that she might be sacred (*hiera*) forever. He made the dedication through the council intermediary according to the law.[22]

A similar manumission was effected in Thisbe, likewise in Boiotia, and also dating to the second century BCE (*IG* VIII, 2228):

> In the archonship of Empedon, Euandrias and Pasikrita [dedicated] Dôpura to Artemis Eileitheia to be sacred (*hieran*), on the condition that she remain with them as long as Euandrias and Pasikrita live. It is not permitted for anyone to mistreat her.

It is almost always the case that the slaves freed to Artemis are female, although we might note the dedication of male Makarinos of Kos. It is probable, however, that Makarinos was a *child* when dedicated, and thus he may have been seen to come under the protection of the kourotrophic goddess. A similar scenario appears in a mid-second-century BCE manumission decree from Kalydon in Aitolia, where Agemakha "sold" to Laphrian Artemis for three minas a child slave (*paidarion*) named Philinos, providing his freedom although including a *paramonê* that he decorate with wreaths an image of Agemakha's son for fifteen days every year from when Philinos was 10 years old until his death (*IG* IX I² 1, 137a).[23] This would seem to indicate that the boy was 10 years old at the time of the "sale" and once again suggests that, even though male, he came under the auspices of Artemis at least in part because he was a child.[24]

This is not necessarily to insist that slaves were freed to a deity somehow associated with them. It would appear that slaves were freed to whatever deity simply happened to be prominent in the local cult, thus Apollo at Delphi and the Mother of the Gods in Macedonia, for example. However, it must also be noted that in Boiotia it was specifically Artemis Eileithyia (with variant spellings) who received the freed women. One possibility is that this particular aspect of the goddess was most closely associated with women, and especially accompanying women during periods of difficult labor. As such, she was an especially apt goddess to invoke when freeing women from servile labor. Another possibility is that Artemis Eileithyia presided over a kind of rebirth of the liberated slaves into a new period of freedom, the *paramonê* clauses notwithstanding. In this she may perhaps be likened to Asklepios, who "cured" the slavery of freedmen and freedwomen.

Artemis at Ephesos

Another cult in which Artemis was popularly understood to be instrumental in the release, if not necessarily the manumission, of slaves was at Ephesos. There can be no doubt that this aspect of the cult was tied to the long-standing tradition of asylum at the Ephesian sanctuary, for which there is evidence from as early as the fifth century BCE (Herodotos 1.26) and most assuredly in the Roman era (Strabo 14.1.23: "[B]ut the temple remains a place of refuge, the same as in earlier times").[25]

Evidence for the temenos serving as a site of asylum for slaves specifically comes exclusively from the Roman era, with the earliest evidence deriving from Cicero's *Against Verres* II. Here (2.1.85), the orator notes that:

> Recently M. Aurelio Scauro . . . said that as *quaestor* he was prohibited by force at Ephesos from carrying off his own slave from the sanctuary of Diana—in which the slave had sought refuge—and Pericles the Ephesian, a most noble man, was summoned to Rome because he was shown to be the author of that injustice.

Unfortunately, the text provides no details concerning the rights (respected or not) of the slave, nor the outcome of his quest for asylum. Nevertheless, the text does provide two helpful data. On the one hand, it shows that the populace of Ephesos itself held the right of asylum, even for slaves, in sufficiently high regard that even a Roman quaestor would be defied if he attempted to violate the sanctuary's *asylon*.

On the other hand, Cicero provides some factual backing for a more literary exemplum of slave asylum under Artemis of Ephesos—Achilles Tatius' second-century CE novella *Leukippê and Klitophon* (7.13). Here we read:

> Now then, there was by the country homes a sanctuary of Artemis, and she [Leukippê] ran off to that and seized its temple. From ancient times that shrine was forbidden to free women, but open to men and maidens. If any woman entered inside, death was the penalty, unless it was a slave bringing a charge against her master. For her it was permissible to supplicate the goddess, and the *arkhontes* judged between her and her master. And if it happened that the master did nothing wrong, he took back his servant, having vowed not to hold a grudge for her flight. But if it seemed that the servant was in the right, she remained there a slave to the goddess (*doulê têi thei*).

Achilles Tatius is our one source for the tradition presented here, that female slaves suffering abuse had the right to seek sanctuary at the temple of Artemis at Ephesos, and that they could potentially be removed from the ownership of their masters. The text is most explicit about non-virgin slaves and their specific rights and procedures at the temple. The passage from Cicero makes it evident that male slaves could also seek asylum at the sanctuary, and we must assume that female virgins could as well. However, in contrast to these latter two categories, non-virgin females were supposedly barred access to the temple according to Tatius, and thus the need for specific regulations regarding their asylum.

What is of particular importance in this text is the status of the woman who became a "slave to the goddess" (*doulê têi thei*). Specifically, was this woman liberated or not? One possibility is that ownership of the woman was transferred to the goddess, and the woman thus became the property of the temple. Another possibility is that by "slave of the goddess" Achilles Tatius meant a hierodule, a "sacred slave" who, as seen above, was manumitted under the auspices of the goddess and was thus no longer a slave per se. Achilles Tatius' lack of technical vocabulary makes this a difficult question, although one should perhaps not expect too much specificity in a romance.

Both the evidence given in the preceding section and additional epigraphic evidence from Roman Ephesos indicate that the female slave in question became a (partially) manumitted hierodule. To begin, the use of the word "*hierodoulos*" was far more common in the eastern reaches of the Hellenistic and Roman empires than in the west. As such, this notion of sacred "slavery" was more common in Anatolia and would have been understood as such.[26]

More important, such *hierodouloi* (or *hieroi*) can be contrasted with the public slaves who served in Ephesos. Such public slaves were called *dêmosioi*, literally "public ones," and they appear in texts pertaining to both secular and sacred works.[27] These *dêmosioi* are specifically contrasted with slaves owned by the temple priests, who, unlike the *dêmosioi*, are not permitted to enter the *abaton*.[28]

Ambiguity regarding the status of the *dêmosioi* vis-à-vis the *hieroi* has emerged because of a series of reforms originally enacted in the early Augustan period and reestablished in 44 CE by P. Fabius Persicus. According to the surviving inscription (*IEphesos* II, 21), the *dêmosioi* were no longer permitted to consecrate (*kathieroun*) infants (*brephê*) to Artemis so that the temple funds would be used for their feeding.[29] Debord reads this as a case where the public slaves consecrate children as *hieroi* to the goddess and thus assure them of both liberty and a rise in social status.[30] However, the term *hieros/a* does not appear in the inscription, leading both Beate Dignas and Noel Lenski to suggest, rather less charitably, that this was a scam on the part of the *dêmosioi* to buy infant slaves of their own, have the temple pay for their up-bringing, and then claim then back when they are old enough to work.[31] This would have to imply that there was a status between the consecrated *hieroi* and *douloi* where people could be temporarily consecrated to the goddess, but then reclaimed and re-enslaved at a later date. Such data do not appear in the evidence, and it must also be noted that such "reclamations" are not related in P. Fabius Persicus' decree. It is thus possible that the purpose of the reform was purely financial, keeping down the costs of the sanctuary by limiting the number of consecrated infants it had to care for.

Additional information about the status of the sacred slaves at Ephesos is revealed in a decree of 86 BCE (*Syll.*[3] 742) wherein it was decided to grant citizenship to all those who joined the Ephesians in their fight against Mithridates, including the *isoteleis* (high-ranking resident aliens), *paroikoi* (resident aliens), *hieroi* (as above), *exeleutheroi* (freedmen), and *xenoi* (foreigners). Furthermore, the Ephesians resolved to liberate the *dêmosioi* and change their status to *paroikoi*.[32] It is clear that the *dêmosioi* were slaves (before being manumitted), and their status is distinct from that of the *hieroi*. It is also evident that the *hieroi* themselves are not citizens (before being enfranchised), and they are conceptually distinguished from the *exeleutheroi*. However, as the inscription reveals, there was no need to manumit the *hieroi* before enfranchising them, yet again emphasizing their marginal status which was nevertheless distinct from actual slavery.

So, where does this leave our suppliant in the shrine of Artemis? The evidence suggests that the goddess did not own *chattel* slaves of her own. Her priests did; and additional work in the sanctuary could be performed by the public slaves—the *dêmosioi*—owned by the city proper. When Artemis was associated with "slaves," especially in the eastern reaches of the Hellenistic and Roman empires, these were hierodules, "sacred slaves" who were in all respects comparable to the *hieroi* and *hierai* of the manumission decrees—thus free, but still attached to the goddess and under her protection. In this they might be contrasted with freedmen and -women (*exeleutheroi*), who appear to have been civilly, rather than sacrally, manumitted. Just as the epigraphically attested *hierai* and *hierodouloi* often served at the manumitting deity's sanctuary, so too did the *doulai* in Tatius' account remain at the sanctuary of Ephesian Artemis. It is perhaps worthwhile to note that a particularly famous "slave of Artemis" was Demetrios, one of the architects of the fourth-century temple (Vitruvius 7.pr.16—*Demetrius ipsius Dianae servus*).

It might be argued, then, assuming that Achilles Tatius was recording an actual piece of cultic history in his novel,[33] that the sanctuary of Artemis at Ephesos had as one aspect of its more universally acknowledged asylum the protection of potentially wronged female slaves. It must be noted, though, that this asylum did not automatically translate into manumission: The *arkhontes* tried the case and could decide that there were no grounds for the slave's complaint. She was sent home, although accompanied by an oath on the part of her master not to hold the incident against her. As such, Artemis did not so much serve as a liberator in such cases, but as a protector of the women involved, both in the offer of asylum and in the demand for forgiveness on the part of the owner. Should the owner turn out to be a total bastard, the slave was freed from his control and placed under Artemis' direct protection.

Diana at Aricia[34]

An interesting twist to the theme of Artemis as freer of slaves occurs not in the cult of Greek Artemis, but in the cult of Arician Diana, whose sanctuary lies on the coast of Lake Nemi just a few miles from the city of Rome. Unlike in Greece and Ephesos where Artemis was primarily (although not exclusively) involved in the manumission of female slaves, at Aricia her cult was dominated by a priest, the *Rex Nemorensis* (Nemi King) who arrived at the sanctuary as a fugitive slave. Here he would break off a branch from a sacred tree, challenge the previous *Rex* to mortal combat, and if he won, replace him until the next fugitive slave arrived. All the evidence for this cult comes from the Roman period, and according to Pausanias continued to function well into the second century CE at least.

Strabo 5.3.12:

> After Albanum on the Appian Way is the city of Aricia . . . The Artemiseion, which they call "*nemos*/Nemi" ["grove, wood"], is to the left on the road for those heading up from Aricia. They say the sanctuary of Aricia is dedicated to the Tauropolan, and truly something barbaric and Skythian holds sway at the sanctuary. For it is established that a fugitive becomes priest after he murdered the previous priest with his own hand. Bearing a sword he is ever looking about for attackers, ready to defend himself. The sanctuary is in a grove lying beside a marsh.

Pausanias 2.27.4:

> Apart from the others is an ancient stele; it says that Hippolytos dedicated twenty horses to the god [Asklepios]. The Aricians agree with the inscription, and they say how Hippolytos having died through the curses of Theseus was revived by Asklepios, and that once he came back to life he refused to forgive his father for disregarding his entreaties. So he went to Aricia in Italy, and he ruled there and devoted a temenos to Artemis where up to my day there are single combats and the winner is priest of the goddess. The contest is open to no free men, only slaves who had run away from their masters.

Servius *Ad Aen.* 6.136:

> A golden bough lies hidden in a shady tree. Although, in the matter of this branch, those who are said to have written about the rites of Proserpina assert that it is something used in the mysteries, nevertheless the general view is as follows: Orestes, after the killing of King Thoas in the Tauric land, fled with his sister, and the image of Diana that he brought from there he set up not far from Aricia. In her precinct, after the sacrificial ritual was changed, there was a certain tree, from which it was not permitted to break off a branch. Moreover, the right was given to any fugitive slave who contrived to remove a branch from it to contend in single combat with the fugitive priest of the temple, for the priest there was [also] a fugitive, to symbolize the original flight. And indeed, this opportunity of fighting was given as though in renewal of the original sacrifice.[35]

In every instance the man who would be king is a fugitive: Hippolytos in the account given by Pausanias was banished by his father Theseus for the supposed ravishing of his mother-in-law Phaidra (see Chapter 3). By contrast, both Strabo and Servius follow the tradition that the cult was founded by Orestes and Iphigeneia upon their return from the Crimea. Orestes was in flight after having murdered his mother and, in the process of rescuing his sister, murdering King Thoas of the Tauroi.

Both Pausanias and Servius agree that the fugitive eligible to be the next *Rex Nemorensis* must be an escaped slave. Strabo does not provide this detail, nor does he contradict it. What is of particular interest, then, is the fact that, although fugitives, neither Hippolytos nor Orestes were slaves. Quite to the contrary, they were princes, sons of kings (even if Hippolytos was a bastard son). As such, the Greek foundation myths of the cult at Aricia provide no help when trying to understand why the priest-king of Nemi must be a fugitive slave.

What they *do* provide is a kind of etiology for why a form of human sacrifice takes place on good Italian soil. Both origin myths—Hippolytos and Orestes—draw the origins of the cult back to Skythia.[36] Hippolytos was the son of Antiopê, an Amazon, and thus linked with the savage, man-killing *oiorpater* of Skythia. Iphigeneia served as a priestess of Artemis for the Tauroi in a cult which specifically called for the sacrifice of Greek sailors (Herodotos 4.103). More importantly perhaps in this etiological context, Orestes himself was guilty of manslaughter in Severus' narrative, having murdered the Tauric king Thoas in the process of his escape with Iphigeneia, Pylades, and the cult xoanon of Artemis. Thus, as Edith Hall suggests in her work *Adventures With Iphigenia in Tauris* (2013):

Servius' Orestes only became responsible for the preservation of the image and thus of the cult because he had *killed* King Thoas. The violent method by which each successive priest of Diana, each "King of the Wood" (Rex Nemorensis) was replaced in the cult, when a runaway slave mounted a challenge and then defeated the incumbent priest in single combat, was thus provided with an ancient precedent in Orestes' execution of the Taurian king.[37]

The importance of a Tauric/Skythian Artemis/Diana in the rites at Nemi became particularly significant in the first century under Augustus. Although the connection between Tauric Artemis and Arician Diana probably dates back to the fourth century BCE, when scenes from Euripides' *Iphigeneia Amongst the Tauroi* became popular in Italian vase and wall paintings, it was Augustus who specifically promoted the cult at Nemi.[38] Augustus' mother was Arician (Cicero, *Phil.* 3.6.15–17), and Augustus emphasized a connection between himself and Orestes, having brought the bones of Orestes from Aricia to Rome after the Battle of Actium. It is possible, then, that the Tauric element of the etiologies emerged at this point, in the first century BCE, when Augustus was using the cult to further his own familial propaganda.

Nevertheless, it must be noted that an alternate tradition was prevalent, whereby the cult had nothing to do with Orestes and was rather founded by Hippolytos. More in line with this version is an alternate hypothesis as to the origin of the blood rites, as put forth by Carin Green in her work *Roman Religion and the Cult of Diana at Aricia* (2007) and heavily predicated upon J. Fontenrose's *Orion: The Myth of the Hunter and the Huntress* (1981). Green argues the ritual derives from a primordial fear intrinsic to hunting cultures that the hunter will violate the laws of the forest and its deity and pay the ultimate price by becoming prey himself. As Green expresses it in terms of Greek mythology:

[T]he fear of uncontrolled wildness is crystallized in the hunting myths of Orion, Meleager, Callisto, Atalanta, Actaeon, and Hippolytos. The hunter (whether male or female) sees or does something that violates the goddess. The punishment is personal death, often through transformation into a figure completely wild, either an animal or a tree. The hunter loses his humanity or his life—or both. In some cases, though, the goddess, having demonstrated her absolute power in the wild, then brings the hunter back to life (as with Hippolytos in the form of the myth so closely associated with Aricia) or gives him a kind of eternal life.[39]

In the case of Aricia, then, the ritual of the *Rex Nemorensis* is a reenactment of this enduring tale, whereby the young hunter embodied in the fugitive slave "violates" the goddess by breaking her tree branch and then killing her priest. He ritually descends to the underworld by burying his predecessor, and then finds reconciliation with the goddess through his continued service to her as her forest-dwelling priest-king.

The association with slaves specifically (rather than just fugitives) came about later, according to Green, when the semi-legendary sixth-century Etruscan king Servius ("slave") Tullius established a cult of Diana on the Aventine, a cult that was famous for the asylum it granted to slaves and the prominence of slaves in its feast day on the Ides of August, which Festus records as (460.33–36 L):

> The Ides of August is thought by the common people to be a festival day for slaves, because on that day Servius Tullius, who was born a slave, dedicated the temple of Diana on the Aventine; she is the particular guardian of deer; from whose speed fugitive slaves (*servi*) are called "deer" (*cervi*).[40]

The importance of slaves in a cult dedicated to Diana by a "slave" came to emphasize the roles of slaves in the goddess's cult more generally, and bound the notion not just to the Aventine, but to Aricia as well.

There are problems with Green's interpretation. First, it explains a Roman cult by way of Greek myth, and a very early Roman cult at that. The cult of Arician Diana dates back to the sixth century at least, even if the earliest temple was only constructed c. 300 BCE.[41]

More problematic is that Fontenrose's construct of the "myth of hunter and huntress" does not follow the mythology as recorded. Aktaion serves as the model for Fontenrose's hypothesis: He was a hunter who vaunted his hunting prowess, or tried to seduce Semelê, or, later, saw Artemis nude in the forest, and was thus turned into a deer and killed by his own hunting dogs. In this the paradigm is somewhat maintained. Some, but certainly not all, myths pertaining to Orion claim that he boasted that he was a better hunter than the goddess, or tried to rape her or one of the Hyperborean maidens and was thus shot by Artemis. Or, alternatively, he was abducted by the dawn goddess Eos and lived happily ever after (Apollodoros 1.4.5). Hippolytos, the hero most closely associated with Aricia in the Pausanias version, did not "violate" Artemis at all: He offended Aphrodite, was killed through a gift of Poseidon, and was resurrected by Asklepios. Kallisto was raped by Zeus, turned into a bear and banished by Artemis, and was given her apotheosis by Zeus. Meleager was killed by his mother and stayed dead.

An additional problem with Green's interpretation is that it does not follow the standard trend in Greek rituals, whereby what went *right* in myth is repeated in ritual, and what went wrong in myth is *corrected* in ritual.[42] Tales of events that were pleasing to the deities find (typically annual) repetition in ritual, such as at Ephesos where a little girl's seaside picnic of celery and salt with Artemis so pleased the goddess that she demanded its annual reenactment (Daïtis). Likewise with the Thesmophoria, where Greek women joined Demeter in mourning the loss of Persephonê and celebrating her return, thus annually reliving and sharing this event in the lives of the goddesses. By contrast, in Athens the Arrhephoroi girls annually refrained from looking into the box that was illicitly opened by the mythic daughters of King Kekrops, leading to their deaths, just as at Troizen girls cut off tresses to leave with Hippolytos on their way to marriage in the way that the dead hero refused to go.

The myth of the hunter and huntress is clearly a negative myth, leading to the anger of the goddess and the death of the hunter. The resurrection of the hunter into human form is the truly exceptional outlier, and most versions of these myths just end badly. In proper Greek tradition, then, one would expect the ritual to *correct* what went wrong in the myth, as with the girls of Troizen. Instead, what we find at Aricia is a *reenactment* of the same story, with the recurring death of the hunter-priest-king who is replaced by the next hunted priest-king. And, once again, nothing in these apparent foundation myths explains why the *Rex Nemorensis* must be a slave. Quite to the contrary, as hunting became increasingly an aristocratic sport, the role of the hunter diverged sharply from the status of the slave.

An alternate suggestion was put forth by Natale Spineto. For him, a fugitive slave served as priest at least in part because no one else would be willing to risk the life-time of looking over his shoulder in fear of the next rival; only a slave would think that this was an improvement.[43] He is probably correct in this. More meaningfully, though, Spineto notes a close affinity between (Arician) Diana and slaves in general: Both are outside the conceptual definition of the *urbs*; they do not belong properly to the notion of the citizen body. Furthermore, the use of a fugitive slave as a priest emphasized the innate "otherness" of Diana's cult at Aricia. The non-city goddess was served by a non-citizen priest who was currently in defiance of the city laws. Literally an outlaw, almost less than human in this respect, the fugitive slave could more closely be associated with the wild animals in Artemis/Diana's purview than the citizen priests of other cults.[44]

Such an ideology may then have merged with the Euripidean traditions of Hippolytos and Orestes. As such, the Roman cult of Nemi became Hellenized, pos-sibly as early as the fourth century BCE, and certainly by the first, when Augustus Caesar actively promoted the tale of Arician Orestes in his bid for legitimacy as the head of Rome.

If there is to be any suggestion of continuity of *persona*, if not cult, between Greek Artemis and Roman Diana, one might suggest that the Greek goddess's role in the protection and manumission of slaves could be at least one aspect of the important role of fugitive slaves who become free by serving Diana at Aricia. In this there is some similarity with what we saw at Ephesos. In both instances a wronged slave could flee, seek sanctuary, and, if victorious in the courts (Ephesos) or combat (Aricia) remain at the sanctuary to serve as a functionary (slave/priest) of the goddess.

OVERVIEW

Although primarily known for her associations with wild nature, hunting, women, and plague, Artemis also had some far more civilized aspects to her persona. As the author of the *Homeric Hymn to Aphrodite* noted, she loved a city of just men, and by the Hellenistic era she found herself to be a city goddess to several poleis in the Greek world. Although this was primarily due to her syncretism with more urbane goddesses such as Kybelê, it is clear that an association with liminal places and the borders of states had always been an aspect of Artemis' persona.

From the fourth century BCE onward Greek Artemis was instrumental (at least on a conceptual level) in manumitting slaves, especially female slaves, and her temple at Ephesos was a sanctuary for female slaves who were being mistreated by their (presumably male?) masters. No violence was required, and the goddess could accommodate as many slaves as necessary. By contrast, the cult on Nemi Lake in Italy was exclusively male-oriented, highly restrictive, and maintained an aura of human sacrifice in its rites. Nevertheless, in both societies Artemis/Diana had a notable function as the goddess who manumitted slaves, thus presiding over the transition from slavery to freedom.

NOTES

1 Petrovic 2007: 201.
2 Brulotte 2002: 180.
3 Hall 2013: xxix–xxx.
4 Brulotte 2002: 182.
5 Petrovic 2010: 221.
6 Ibid.: 202.
7 Boyce 1987: 61.
8 Brosius 2009: 140–143.
9 Garsoïan 1989: 347.
10 Brosius 1998: *passim*.
11 Chaumont 1965: 172.
12 All references with full citations to be found in Petrovic 2007: 201–202.
13 Westermann 1945: 216.
14 Budin 2009: *passim*.
15 Darmezin 1999: 184.
16 Budin 2009: 200.
17 Darmezin 1999: 22. This Worthasia will later be written Ortheia, and the goddess syncretized with Artemis. See Carter 1987: 375.
18 Darmezin 1999: 26.
19 Papazoglou 1981: 177, no. 22.
20 Darmezin 1999: 117–118.
21 Ibid.: 64–72. See also Schachter 1981: 98.
22 Darmezin 1999: 70–71. See also *IG* VII, 3412.
23 Zelnick-Abramovitz 2005: 160–161.
24 As noted in Chapter 4, Artemis' rapport with small children becomes apparent in later antiquity, in the Hellenistic and Roman periods, when these decrees were produced.
25 Rigsby 1996: 385–393. See also Thomas 1995: 98–106.
26 Budin 2009: *passim*.
27 Debord 1982: 88.
28 Ibid.
29 Lenski 2006: 352; Dignas 2002: 153; Beard et al. 1998, Vol. I: 343; Debord 1982: 88 and 358, n. 106.
30 Debord 1982: 88.
31 Lenski 2006: 352; Dignas 2002: 153.
32 Zelnick-Abramovitz 2005: 123.
33 In spite of the fictional character of genre, as Christine Thomas has noted, "the novels are a reliable index of 'popular' religious attitudes." Thomas 1995: 82.

34 This final section leaves the realm of Greek Artemis for that of Roman Diana, and thus is technically outside the scope of this volume. I present it here as a kind of bridge into the final chapter—"Artemis Afterwards"—and as a conclusion to several Artemisian themes that have been present throughout this book.

35 Trans. Green 2007: 298–299.

36 Sound familiar?

37 Hall 2013: 136. Emphasis in original.

38 Ibid.: 140.

39 Green 2007: 179.

40 Ibid.: 200.

41 Hall 2013: 139; Green 2007: 15–16.

42 On this notion, see Redfield 2003: 120.

43 Spineto 2000: 22.

44 Ibid.

8

ARTEMIS AFTERWARDS

When the Romans conquered the Greeks at the end of the Hellenistic Age, Greek Artemis was syncretized with, and subsumed into, Roman Diana in the European west. Henceforth most of Europe would know the Roman lunar goddess far better than the Greek huntress, and the two would never again really have separate identities. What follows is a *very* brief survey of what happened to Greek Artemis (and often Diana) after the heyday of Greek powers, including her interactions with that new religion—Christianity—in Ephesos, what the Renaissance thinkers thought of her, and how she came to influence the modern arts and literature. We begin with how Artemis first came into contact with the Romans by way of Etruscan Artumes and thus became Diana.

ARTUMES AND DIANA[1]

Artemis' presence in Italy can be attested as early as the seventh century BCE, when the Etruscan sanctuary of Portonaccio at Veii received dedications inscribed to the goddesses Artimiti (Artemis/Artumes), Turan (Aphrodite), and Menerva (Athena).[2] A decorated bronze mirror from Vulci dating to c. 470 shows the goddess (identified by inscription as Artumes) playing the lyre before a young, beardless god named "Aplu" (Etruscan Apollo).[3] Later, a mid-fifth-century cup discovered at the southern temple terrace at Roselle bore the inscription "Artmsl" ("To Artumes").[4] More evidence of the goddess's name comes from the fourth century. From the *Ara della Regina* sanctuary at the Etruscan site of Tarquinia came a bronze staff inscribed with the name *Artum[es]*, found in context with a bronze arrowhead coated with gold foil, clearly votive in nature. Likewise, a late fourth-century bronze mirror from Orvieto shows the goddess (identified by name) riding sidesaddle upon the backs of a pair of deer.[5] So the goddess showed a presence in Italy since at least the seventh century, at least in Etruscan form.

Either through a syncretism between an indigenous Roman goddess and Artemis, or between these two and Etruscan Artumes, Roman Diana came into being absolutely no later than the late fourth century,[6] and probably well before this. As noted in the previous chapter, according to legend it was the sixth king of Rome—Servius Tullius, an Etruscan—who established the great "federal" sanctuary of Diana on the Aventine hill in Rome.[7] In the first century BCE, Augustus was anxious to emphasize symbolic links between himself, his Arician mother, and tales of Orestes, and thus promoted the cult of Arician Diana.[8]

As we have already seen, the goddess Diana was similar in many respects to Greek Artemis, but had a few extra features. Most significant was the fact that Diana was a moon goddess, seen to personify the astral body as did Selenê in the Greek pantheon. This aspect was strengthened by syncretisms with other goddesses, such as with Nanaya as we saw in the opening chapter. Even when Artemis reemerges in Western literature in the modern age (see below), this attribute will frequently remain with her.

From the Roman conquest of Greece onward, it was Roman Diana, rather than Greek Artemis, who was prominent in the religion, arts, and culture of western Europe. With the fall of Rome in 476 CE, western Europe's connections with the eastern empire (now called Byzantine in the modern scholarship) were weakened, and the Greek language fell out of use in preference for an increasingly dying Latin. It would not be until the fall of Constantinople in 1453 and the flight of countless Byzantine refugees westwards that the Greek language would once again emerge in the West, when there was a glut of language tutors looking for accommodations. So for about a millennium Artemis falls out of the picture in the West. However, she still had a significant role to play in the East, especially as a new religion—Christianity— began to butt heads with the goddess.

EPHESOS AND THE COMING OF CHRISTIANITY

The prominence of the city of Ephesos in the cult of Artemis cannot be overestimated. As seen in Chapter 1, this was one of the most widespread cults of Artemis, stretching from the coast of Asia Minor to the coast of Iberia, with many tributary cults along the way. It should perhaps not be surprising, then, that when the new religion of Christianity started making its way out across the Levant and Roman Empire, Ephesos would prove problematic for the new cult. Already in the New Testament (*Acts* 19) we read how Paul of Tarsus found himself in the midst of a riot when the city silversmiths, amongst others, complained that the new religion was driving away their business of making souvenir temples for those who came to visit the temple of Artemis. As put into the mouth of the silversmith Demetrius (19: 27): "And there is danger not only that this trade of ours may come into disrepute but also that the temple of the great goddess Artemis will be scorned, and she will be deprived of her majesty that brought all Asia and the world to worship her." Remarkably, the riot was quelled when a city official pointed out that there was no way that anyone could take the glory away from their goddess, which the Ephesians found more than reasonable.

In spite of beliefs that Christianity had a strong hold in Asia Minor in its early centuries (especially because of the ministrations of Paul of Tarsus), the evidence indicates that Ephesos remained staunchly pagan for centuries after the birth of Christ, and even after the conversion of Constantine in the early fourth century. The clearest attestation of the goddess's glory and renown is expressed in an inscribed proclamation now in the British Museum dating to 162–164 CE and set on record by the proconsul Gaius Popillius Carus Pedo. Having (accidentally) conducted business on a day sacred to Artemis, the proconsul admitted his folly and went on to declare (*I.Eph.* Ia.24, B8 sqq.):

> Since the goddess Artemis, leader of our city, is honored not only in her own homeland, which she has made the most illustrious of all cities though her own divine nature, but also among Greeks and also barbarians, the result is that everywhere her shrines and sanctuaries have been established, and temples have been founded for her and altars dedicated to her because of the visible manifestations effected by her. And this is the greatest proof of the reverence surrounding her, the month named after her, called Artemision among us, and Artemisios among the Macedonians and among the other Greek nations, and among the cities within their borders. During this month festivals and sacrifices are performed, particularly in our city, the nurturer of its own Ephesian goddess. The Ephesian people regard it as appropriate that the entire month named after the divine name be sacred and dedicated to the goddess, and through this decree approved that the religious ritual for her be stipulated. Therefore, it is decreed that the entire month Artemision be sacred for all its days, and that on the same (days) of the month, and throughout the year, feasts and the festival and the sacrifices of the Artemisia are to be conducted, insomuch as the entire month is dedicated to the goddess. For in this way, with the improvement of the honoring of the goddess, our city will remain more illustrious and more blessed for all time.[9]

Such affirmations rather strongly give the lie to the late second to third-century[10] text known as the *Acts of John*, wherein the disciple claims that upon praying to the god of the Christians at the temple of Artemis (§42), "immediately the altar of Artemis was parted into many pieces, and all the things that were dedicated in the temple fell and [were] rent asunder, and likewise of the images of the gods more than seven. And half of the temple fell down, so that the priest was slain at one blow by the falling [roof]. The multitude of the Ephesians therefore cried out: 'One is the God of John, one is the God who has pity on us, for you only are God . . . !'"

By contrast, a contemporary dedicatory inscription from Ephesos only gives the slightest hint that maybe some aspects of the cult fell into abeyance toward the end of the second to early third century CE. This inscription was dedicated by a woman having completed her tenure as priestess of Ephesian Artemis (*I.Eph* 3059):

> [Aurelia (?) Priestess of Arte]mis, completed her term of priestess piously and with decorum, restored all the rites of the goddess and funded (them) in accord with ancient custom, daughter of M. Aur(elius) Hierokleos Apolinarius the emperor-honoring General, Market-Director, Council Chairman, father of the priestess.[11]

We do not know what the "rites of the goddess" were that Aurelia restored, but the woman was clearly anxious to advertise that she set the cult right at her own expense during her tenure. Thus, yet again, there is very little evidence that the cult of the Ephesian was in evanescence during the early years of Christianity, or that the goddess even felt the rivalry of the new god.

Even after the reign of Constantine, the cult of Artemis at Ephesos endured and remained a formidable force, even if the early Christian authors themselves were loath to admit to that fact:

Fourth or fifth century inscriptions suggest Artemis was still seen as a rival cult even if Christians were claiming victory . . . In 348 CE, Prudentius claims "the huntress maid resigned Ephesus to thee [Christ]" (II.495). Very early in the fifth century, Chrysostom claims to have removed the power of Diana (PG 65.832). In the same century, Paulinus of Nola claims victory for the Christians over Artemis: "Diana, too, has fled from Ephesus, for John has thrust her out." (Poem 19). But Isidore of Pelusium wrote to Hierax in the same century regarding certain relics which the pagans had exhumed in the temple of Artemis of Ephesus and worshipped (PG 78.217c Ep. I.55). Then even as late as the sixth century John of Ephesus claims he converted thousands and overcame the power of idols (Historiae 3.125) . . . The evidence is quite conclusive that for at least three centuries of the Christian era, Artemis remained a dominant feature of Ephesian life.[12]

It is not until the fifth century that the tide started to turn for the goddess, when *asebeia* against the pagan deities came to be seen as acceptable. This is especially evident in a dedicatory inscription from the fifth century offered by one Demeas in Ephesos:

Having destroyed a deceitful image of demonic Artemis, Demeas set up this sign of truth, honouring both God the driver-away of idols, and the cross, that victory-bringing, immortal symbol of Christ.[13]

As Troels Myrup Kristensen notes, it is impossible to determine if a statue of Artemis ever actually did stand upon the re-used base.[14] What is significant in this context, however, is the fact that by the fifth century it was deemed permissible, even laudatory, to claim to have defaced such "idols" in preference for images of the cross. Only now was Christianity truly ascendant.

STILL LIKING THOSE BREASTS, THOUGH

Between the fall of Rome, the rise of Islam, and the coming of the Ottoman Turks, western Europe had rather little access to the Hellenic east for several centuries. Artemis faded into a distant memory. It was not until the Renaissance, and more specifically the early sixteenth century in Italy, that Artemis, mainly Ephesian Artemis, once again appeared upon the scene. Still without considerable access to Turkey or the Ottoman realms, the Italians did have copious access to Rome, where numerous replicas of varying states of accuracy of the cult statue of Artemis of Ephesos were found (see Chapter 1 on this icon). Notions of "sacks of plenty" were long forgotten, since the Roman age in fact, and Renaissance Europe instead began a long-standing love affair with "Diana Efesia Multimammia"—the many-breasted Ephesian Diana.

This is not, of course, what the Renaissance artists claimed to be interested in. Instead, Raphael, the first Western artist to make use of the image, used a pair of these Ephesian statues as legs of a throne upon which sat the anthropomorphic manifestation of Philosophy, as she appeared on a roundel above the "School of Athens" in the Vatican.[15] According to Marjatta Nielsen, Ephesian Artemis/Diana, both here and throughout the Renaissance corpus, represented the concept of wild nature. For Raphael, the personification of Philosophy sitting upon such an Ephesian throne marked the rule of human intelligence over raw (if fertile and sensually appealing) nature.

The statue of many-breasted Ephesian Artemis became a common symbol for nature throughout the Renaissance. Sometimes the Artemisian character was highlighted, especially when the statue was portrayed flanked or accompanied by deer. Such is her depiction in Raphael's Logge in the Vatican, as well as Perino del Vaga's relief in the loggia of Villa Lante al Gianicolo, built for Baldassare Turini, a papal official in the service of Pope Leo X.

Regardless of the symbolic (and high-minded) meanings of the Ephesian icon, the Renaissance artists could not escape the draw and appeal of the supposedly multiple breasts borne by the goddess. As early as 1524 the architect and painter Giulio Roman had sketched drafts for a fountain featuring the statue of Ephesian Artemis with water spurting from her many nipples. Alas, the fountain never came to fruition, even when the project was later taken up by Cardinal Ippolito d'Este—whose own name rendered him one to be most interested in this particular goddess—and his personal architect in residence Pirro Ligorio. It was not until 1568 that Gillis van der Vliete succeeded in erecting such a fountain—the *Fontana della Dea Natura*—in Tivoli (Figure 8.1).

If that were not enough, the Jesuit scholar Athanasius Kircher invented a mechanized statue that had milk spurting from the many breasts of the Ephesian "Mother Nature." This would be fantastic to have for coffee breaks at art historical conferences.

Figure 8.1 *Fontana della Dea Natura*, Villa d'Este, Tivoli, Italy, by Gillis van der Vliete, 1568. Photograph by Marjatta Nielsen. Used with kind permission.

ARTEMIS IN BROOKLYN[16]

The multimammary Ephesian continued to appear in the arts of western Europe until modern times. Artemis herself, though, only really began to reemerge in the nineteenth century, and even then she was still heavily mixed with the more traditional Roman Diana. Perhaps the most famous example of this is August Saint-Gaudens's gilded bronze statue of "Diana of the Tower," dating to the end of the nineteenth century. This was a famous—scandalous, really—weathervane that was placed above the Madison Square Garden Tower in New York City from 1894 until the garden was demolished in 1925 and is now in the Philadelphia Museum of Art. What made the statue "scandalous" was that, quite contrary to traditional portrayals of the chaste goddess, this one depicted Artemis/Diana in the nude (see Figure 8.2 for a smaller version currently in the Brooklyn Museum).

There was, in traditional Victorian manner, grave concern that children might see the nude goddess high above the city, a fear somewhat assuaged by one reporter who allegedly claimed that the children do not notice a thing, but that, "the Square is now thronged with clubmen, armed with field glasses."

The contrast not only with the Greek aesthetic, but also the Greek ideology, could not be more profound. The only Olympian goddess to be shown in the nude

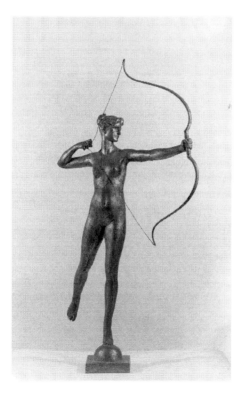

Figure 8.2 *Diana of the Tower*, by Augustus Saint-Gaudens, c. 1895, 23.255 Robert B. Woodward Memorial Fund. Published by kind permission of the Brooklyn Museum.

in Greek art was Aphrodite, the goddess of love and sex, and even this did not occur until the late fourth century, with Praxiteles' shocking Knidia. Artemis may reveal a breast when shooting, but otherwise the virgin goddess was modestly attired. To see her in the nude could bring grave punishment, as in one of the tales of Aktaion (see Chapter 6). Perhaps more relevant from a male perspective, what is the point in flaunting the unattainable? And additionally, is it a good thing to have a death-dealing goddess be so alluring, to draw in her prey? "Diana of the Tower" shows a remarkable ambivalence to the male gaze in this respect. She is nude, flying high above the city for all to see, sometimes with binoculars. But her celestial placement highlights her unattainability, while her dangerous nudity and drawn bow make her a threat to any man who gazes upon her, thus turning half of the population of New York into potential Aktaions.

Quite a different take on "Diana" was wrought by Paul Howard Manship in his bronze statue *Vivian St. George and Her Dog*, also in the Brooklyn Museum and dating to 1924 (Figure 8.3).

Here, instead of a nude in the violent act of hunting, we see a young girl, very much of the same age as the Greeks sometimes portrayed Artemis in the Hellenistic period. She carries an unstrung bow and a pair of arrows, while her left arm rests fondly

Figure 8.3 *Vivian St. George and Her Dog*, by Paul Howard Manship, 1924, 2008.68. Published by kind permission of the Brooklyn Museum.

around the neck of a dog that is almost as large as she is. She is quite chastely attired in a knee-length dress that covers shoulders and bosom, and so in many respects she appears even more demure than Artemis Phosphoros, with her shoulder and breast exposed. Violence may be implied in the presence of the weapons at rest in her right hand, but the little goddess's power is belied by her relaxed stance and diminutive stature vis-à-vis her own "hunting" hound.

MODERN LITERATURE: *EDITH WHARTON*

Just as Artemis/Diana began to reemerge in the Western plastic arts of the nineteenth century, so too did she come to influence the literature of the Victorian Age and after. A prime example appears in Edith Wharton's *The Age of Innocence*, where the hero—Newland Archer (!)—finds himself trapped between the Eastern, exotic Countess Ellen Olenska, and his own betrothed May Welland. The divorced countess summons images of sexual experience and Eastern abodes, and thus embodies a modern manifestation of Aphrodite; May is her innocent antithesis, the hopelessly virginal Artemis. As noted by Elizabeth Ammons in her essay "Cool Diana and the Blood-Red Muse: Edith Wharton on Innocence and Art":

> Unsoiled by life, May is always connected with white: her virginity, mentality and emotionality, cannot be touched. She is permanently pure. Likewise, Wharton implies, she is permanently juvenile. She has a fresh "boyish" quality that brings to mind the "invincible innocence" of her middle-aged mother, and suggests that May too will go through life sexually unaware and armed in innocence. To be sure, she is vigorously physical—she rides, rows, plays lawn tennis, wins archery competitions—but even this healthiness is deceptive, for the allusions Wharton surrounds May with are lifeless. She walks beside Archer and "her face wore the vacant serenity of a young marble athlete"; at another point her smile, we are told, is "Spartan." Elsewhere and most pointedly, Wharton says, the "faculty of unawareness was what gave her eyes their transparency, and her face the look of representing a type rather than a person; as if she might have been chosen to pose for a Civic Virtue or a Greek goddess."[17]

For Wharton, May is more Diana than Artemis, especially as the girl is often garbed in white and silver, reflecting Diana's moonlight. Nevertheless, Wharton was also influenced by Greek mythology, as is evidenced by her poem "Artemis to Actaeon," and thus one might argue that what we see with May Welland is a merging of both Roman and Greek archetypes.

The Artemis of "Artemis to Actaeon" is far more empowered than Wharton's fictional characters, insofar as she, as in the earlier myth, turns her voyeur into dog food. In this, Wharton creates a fascinating counterbalance to another of her tragic heroines—Lily Bart from *The House of Mirth*. As Jennie Kassanoff notes in her study of feminist experience in the works of Edith Wharton, these two heroines complement each other in their respective reactions to the male gaze. For Artemis, the empowered goddess, the unwelcomed glance of a male is punished with swift death. By contrast, Lily is wholly subject to the male, to the point that, in the words of her admittedly mercantile suitor, she is desirable because she is "a highly specialized product." Being mortal, and poor, Lily cannot escape the gaze to which she is subjected, in spite of her Artemisian rejection of marriage:

> Wharton not only restores Artemis's voice, but she also makes it possible for a woman to derive pleasure from the male gaze while not falling victim to its attendant objectification. Artemis serves as a powerful antidote to Lily Bart, her fictional predecessor. Because Lily cannot reconcile the various identities imputed to her by the novel's scrutinizing men, she commits suicide. By contrast, Wharton's goddess *herself* wields the potent gaze, transforming her mortal admirer into an eroticized male victim: indeed, like Lilly Bart who is "fashioned to adorn and delight," Actaeon is "fashioned for one hour's high use."[18]

ARTEMIS KATNISS

In the popular culture of twenty-first-century America, no literary character better embodies the character of ancient Artemis than Katniss Everdeen of Suzanne Collins's *The Hunger Games* trilogy. All of Artemis' attributes are present in this virginal, archer huntress who lives on the margins (literally the "Seam") of the civilized world of Panem.

Finding the Greek goddess in this work of young adult fiction is not random: Greek mythology was a contributing factor in Collins's creation of *The Hunger Games* mythos:

> Motivated by her father's Vietnam experience, Collins found the nucleus of a story in the unsettling conflation of a reality-TV competition and real war coverage. The embryonic story's details were soon enhanced by her interest in the Greek myth of Theseus versus the Minotaur and in the rebel subject of a favorite movie, *Spartacus* . . . From the first chapter of *The Hunger Games* through the epilogue in *Mockingjay*, Collins succeeds not only in updating classical mythology and common-era history through contemporary science fiction, but also in explicating her anxiety about the dangers inherent in the postmodern confusion of "acceptable" fantasy and "unacceptable" reality.[19]

In the initial description Collins provides of her heroine, the correspondences between Katniss and Artemis are explicit: "As soon as I'm in the trees, I retrieve a bow and sheath of arrows from a hollow log" (*HG* pg. 5); "I never smile except in the woods" (pg. 6); "I finally had to kill the lynx because he scared off game" (pg. 7). In the Games, Collins specifically describes Katniss's weapons (bow and arrows) as silver,[20] a reference to Roman Diana's lunar qualities, but still Artemisian.

Before the reaping which initiates the Games, Katniss's closest companion is Gale, a fellow hunter and Apollonian youth. Katniss herself claims that, "He could be my brother" (pg. 8). Rodney DeaVault notes that these two friends are virtually twins in appearance, "Katniss, with straight black hair, olive skin, and gray eyes, bears an uncanny resemblance to Gale, her male hunting partner."[21] They are not romantically involved, and yet they both seem to have several children to care for: "They're not our kids, of course. But they might as well be" (pg. 9); "I never want to have kids" (ibid.).

Thus we see the virginal huntress with her twin kourotrophos, caring for the young while refusing to have any herself.

As "Katniss, the girl who was on fire" (pg. 67), Katniss also embodies Artemis' aspects as Phosphoros. As the heroine notes, she and her partner Peeta "literally outshone them all" (pg. 72), creating a sense not only of light, but also of divinity in contrast to her more mortal (and eventually *very* mortal) contenders. Later, in *Catching Fire*, Katniss emphasizes her fiery qualities, discarding her "flickering flames and bejeweled gowns and soft candlelight frocks. She is as deadly as fire itself."[22]

The similarities do not stop with the initial description, however, nor with these basic aspects of Artemis' persona. A number of very specifically Artemisian narratives pertain to the heroine of *The Hunger Games*. Deeply symbolic is Katniss's history with the anonymous,[23] redheaded Avox (literally "voiceless"—her tongue had been cut out) who serves Katniss in the Capitol and her now dead male companion. As she describes the story to Peeta:

> For a moment I'm silent, as I remember how the sight of this strange pair, clearly not from District 12, fleeing through the woods immobilized us. Later, we wondered if we could have helped them escape. Perhaps we might have. Concealed them. If we'd moved quickly. Gale and I were taken by surprise, yes, but we're both hunters. We know how animals look at bay. We knew the pair was in trouble as soon as we saw them. But we only watched . . .
>
> A net dropped down on the girl and carried her up, fast . . . They shot some sort of spear through the boy. It was attached to a cable and they hauled him up as well. But I'm certain he was dead. We heard the girl scream once.
>
> (pg. 82)

These anonymous characters are reminiscent of Iphigeneia and Hippolytos. The boy in the woods, a political exile who has become prey, is killed in view of an unaiding Katniss, just as Artemis looked on literally helplessly as her favorite was banished by his kingly father (a patriarchal regime) and killed by the overwhelming power of Poseidon's bull. By contrast, the redheaded girl (calling to mind redheaded Menelaos and Agamemnon) is not killed. She is dead to her family, of course, but she survives to be brought to a hostile territory where she attends upon Katniss—just as Iphigeneia is spared her sacrifice and brought to the Crimea then Brauron to be priestess to Artemis. The primary difference is that in the *Hunger Games* scenario, Katniss is not (yet) sufficiently empowered to have saved the girl herself. Nevertheless, the pair achieves détente, just as the goddess and heroine in the older myth:

> "I should have tried to save you," I whisper.
>
> She shakes her head. Does this mean we were right to stand by? That she has forgiven me? . . .
>
> I spend the next hour helping the redheaded girl clean the room. When all the garbage has been dropped down a disposal and the food cleared away, she turns down my bed. I crawl in between the sheets like a five-year-old and let her tuck me in. Then she goes. I want her to stay until I fall asleep. To be there when I wake up. I want the protection of this girl, even though she never had mine.
>
> (pg. 119)

Katniss's close, protective, but ultimately doomed relationship with young Rue reflects Artemis' ambivalent relationship with adolescent girls. Although the myths often present Artemis as the goddess who demands the sacrifice of such girls, the evidence indicates that they are actually rarely slaughtered for the goddess, with the usual emphasis in the myths on the girls' salvation, as is the case with Iphigeneia, or the girls at Brauron. Rue is a fellow tribute, a competitor in the Games and thus one Katniss (or another contender) will be forced to kill. Actively defying her role as killer, Katniss instead chooses to take the girl under her wing. Likewise, Katniss's protective role vis-à-vis both her younger sister Prim and Rue emphasizes the heroine's kourotrophic aspects. As with the goddess (and Apollo), this kourotrophism is distinct from parenthood, and is even gender-ambiguous. This desire to nurture extends past even girls to encompass another group beholden to Artemis: mothers. As DeaVault notes, "Despite verbally eschewing motherhood, Katniss, nonetheless, becomes a surrogate mother to Mrs. Everdeen and Prim, who might as well be her children since they rely on her for sustenance."[24]

By contrast, Katniss's murder of the boy who killed Rue calls to mind Artemis as goddess of vengeance.

From early in the Games Katniss is not only saved by her hunting talents, but also by her ability to survive in the wilds, especially her ability to find water. In this we recall Artemis' own specially affinities with watery places (see Chapter 3). One scene in *The Hunger Games* is pointedly reminiscent of the tale of Lousoi, when Artemis cured the mad daughters of King Proitos. Instead of multiple raving daughters, though, Katniss bathes and heals the desperately wounded Peeta, using herbal remedies to tend to his wounds, cleaning him, and bringing down his fever (pg. 255 sqq.).

The cult of Artemis Elaphebolos in Hyampolis (and that of Apollo as well) is called to mind by Katniss's recollection of how she bought a goat (!) for her sister Prim. She recalls how she and Gale were out hunting one day when:

> We were resting a moment by a stream when we saw him. A young buck, probably a yearling by his size. His antlers were just growing in, still small and coated in velvet. Poised to run but unsure of us, unfamiliar with humans. Beautiful.
>
> Less beautiful perhaps when the two arrows caught him, one in the neck, the other in the chest. Gale and I had shot at the same time . . . Momentarily, I'd felt a pang at killing something so fresh and innocent.[25]

Here we see the standard ambivalence of the "Deer-Shooter." On the one hand, she revels in the act of hunting, of bringing down large prey especially. On the other, she is somewhat conflicted about bringing down an animal that is specifically described as young. Once again we recognize the Artemis who loves the young of wild creatures, then kills them.

When the Games are over and Katniss and Peeta have emerged victorious (what else do you expect from a goddess and her favorite?), Katniss muses on what her life will be like when affluent and (relatively) safe. Just as one would expect from the hunting goddess, the heroine notes:

No more fear of hunger. A new kind of freedom. But then . . . what? What would my life be like on a daily basis? Most of it has been consumed with the acquisition of food. Take that away and I'm not really sure who I am, what my identity is . . . I know I'll never marry, never risk bringing a child into the world.

(pg. 311)

The matter of survival becomes superfluous in the rendering of Katniss's character. Like Artemis, her hunting identity becomes detached from her need to eat. Just as the Greek goddess does not eat the flesh of her kills (Greek deities eat ambrosia), so too does Katniss realize that her hunting is not so much expedient as it is innate, part of what makes her who she is and how she relates to the world.

More significant to a twenty-first-century academy enthralled by Queer Theory, Katniss (like Artemis) the Virgin Huntress emphasizes gender-ambiguity. A small part of this, of course, is both maidens' lack of interest in romantic love, one of the few facts that draws attention to the parallels between the goddess and the heroine in popular scholarship, "Like the aloof, chaste huntress/goddess Diana, Katniss also chases away suitors as often as she hunts with her bow and arrows."[26] More compelling is Katniss who takes on the traditionally masculine pursuit of hunting. The extent to which Collins turns this archetype on its head appears during the Games when Katniss goes out to hunt, allowing Peeta to follow behind her, gathering edible roots and berries—completely confounding the male-hunter/female-gatherer paradigm.

The aspects of Katniss's persona that most upset standard gender paradigms are also those that most relate her to Artemis. As Jennifer Mitchell writes (with my emphases of Artemisian attributes):

Despite allusions to her long, dark braid—a seemingly feminine trait—Katniss's other gendered markers are primarily masculine. Her *hunting boots, hidden bow and arrow, and personal relationship with the woods* draw a significantly manlier portrait of Katniss. Indeed, all aspects of Katniss's life involve a blurring of gender boundaries. As a *hunter*, Katniss is a *predator in the woods*, following in her father's footsteps and adopting the traditionally masculine approach to the hunt . . . Katniss's *success in and enjoyment of the woods* defy conventional associations between women and the hearth. *Instead of cooking the food, Katniss stalks it, traps it, and kills it*; ultimately, *she thrives in the woods*, and subsequently in the arena, as a result of this power and prowess.[27]

A similar picture is painted by DeaVault:

Katniss forsakes the domestic space for the forest, assuming Mr. Everdeen's responsibility of breadwinner by hunting wild game as he once did. By her own admission, she is uncomfortable sitting at the hearth with her dainty mother and sister, preferring instead to be in the woods, where she is unencumbered by gender norms or the expectation to conform to them. *Forswearing both romantic love and motherhood*, Katniss remains content with the knowledge that she could at *any point flee into the woods*.[28]

Nevertheless, by the epilogue of the last book, *Mockingjay*, Katniss does become both wife and mother. While wholly non-Artemisian, this does display the liberties taken with the goddess in modern times, perhaps equivalent to showing her shooting in the nude far above the heads of voyeuristic Manhattanites. Even so, DeaVault notes how even in this apparent overthrow of her unengendered persona Katniss is empowered and, like a divinity, seizes control of her own destiny:

> The epilogue of *Mockingjay*, however, takes a curious turn by placing Katniss in the role of wife and mother. Given her violent bid for autonomy and independence throughout the trilogy, relegating Katniss to the domestic sphere seems to do her a grave disservice by destroying the power of her "other-ness." . . . [But] Katniss's ending affords her the luxury of creating and controlling her domestic space . . . For Katniss, who is battle-weary at the end of *Mockingjay*, motherhoods seems to be almost a reward for her hard work and sacrifice, a way for her to find peace. Disillusioned with humanity's cyclical capacity for self-destruction, Katniss chooses to walk away from an active role in government, deciding that people can make her beautiful and design weapons for her, "but they will never again brainwash me into the necessity of using them" (*M* 377). Instead, she plans to become her children's teacher, using her personal history to prepare them for what may lie ahead. In this way, she maintains her autonomy and identity long after the action of the trilogy has concluded.[29]

In modern times we mention, mutter, and grumble that such women who can seemingly "do it all" must be Superwomen. Perhaps they are goddesses.

OVERVIEW

Greek Artemis was eclipsed by lunar Diana when Rome conquered the various Hellenistic empires. This marked the evanescence of Artemis in the West, even as early Christians decried her presence in the Anatolian East. For years what remained of the virgin huntress was a stiff statue with a few too many breasts (not that anyone was complaining!). In the nineteenth century with the rise of philhellenism, Artemis began once again to appear in the arts of the West, although still very much tied to her Roman sister. Modern artists had their way with the goddess, showing her nude, as a helpless child, vapid, or even marrying her off. But for some artists, especially female artists, Artemis remains a symbol of gender alterity and empowerment, defying the male gaze by shooting it through the eye.

NOTES

1 For much more on Roman Diana, see Fay Glinister's book in this series.
2 Nielsen and Rathje 2009: 269.
3 Ibid.: 284.
4 Ibid.: 277.
5 Ibid.: 275–276.
6 Strelan 1996: 44, n. 45.
7 Green 2007: 200; Beard et al. 1998: 3.
8 Hall 2013: 140.

9 Trans. Horsley 1987: 75–76.

10 See Strelan 1996: 81 on the dating.

11 Trans. Baugh 1999: 455.

12 Strelan 1996: 81–82.

13 Trans. Kristensen 2013: 9, with full citations.

14 Ibid.: 12–13.

15 All references Nielsen 2009.

16 A tip of the nib to P.D.Q. Bach's *Iphigenia in Brooklyn*.

17 Ammons 2000: 396–397, slightly excerpted.

18   Kassanoff 2014: 459.

19 Pharr and Clark 2012: 11.

20 Collins 2008:199.

21 DeaVault 2012: 192.

22 Collins 2009: 207.

23 It is not until *Mockingjay* that we discover that her name was Lavinia.

24 DeaVault 2012: 193.

25 Collins 2008: 269.

26 King 2012: 111.

27 Mitchell 2012: 129–130.

28 DeaVault 2012: 192.

29 Ibid.: 197, excerpted.

BIBLIOGRAPHY

Ammons, E. (2000) "Cool Diana and the Blood-Red Muse: Edith Wharton on Innocence and Art." In C. Singley (ed.) *The Age of Innocence: Complete Text with Introduction, Historical Contexts, Critical Essays*. Houghton Mifflin Co. Houston, 393–403.

Athanassakis, A.N. (1977) *The Orphic Hymns: Text, Translation and Notes*. Scholars Press. Missoula.

Barclay, A.E. (2001) "The Potnia Theron: Adaptation of a Near Eastern Image." In R. Laffineur and R. Hägg (eds.) *Potnia: Deities and Religion in the Aegean Bronze Age*. Université de Liège. Liège, 373–386 plus plates.

Barnestone, W. (1988) *Sappho and the Greek Lyric Poets*. Schocken Books. New York.

Baugh, S.M. (1999) "Cult Prostitution in New Testament Ephesus: A Reappraisal." *Journal of the Evangelical Theological Society* 42.3, 443–460.

Beard, M., J. North, and S. Price (1998) *Religions of Rome, Vol. I: A History*. Cambridge University Press. Cambridge.

Beaumont, L. (2003) "The Changing Face of Childhood." In J. Neils and J.H. Oakley (eds.) *Coming of Age in Ancient Greece: Images of Childhood from the Classical Past*. Yale University Press. New Haven, 59–83.

——. (1998) "Born Old or Never Young? Femininity, childhood and the goddesses of ancient Greece." In S. Blundell and M. Williamson (eds.) *The Sacred and the Feminine in Ancient Greece*. Routledge Press. New York, 71–95.

Belayche, N. et al. (eds.) (2005) *Nommer les Dieux: Théonymes, epithets, épiclèses dans l'Antiquité*. Brepols, Presses Universitaires de Rennes. Turnhout.

Bevan, E. (1985) *Representations of Animals in Sanctuaries of Artemis and Other Olympian Deities*. Ph.D. Dissertation University of Edinburgh.

Bilde, P.G. (2009) "Quantifying Black Sea Artemis: Some Methodological Reflections." In T. Fischer-Hansen and B. Poulsen (eds.) *From Artemis to Diana: The Goddess of Man and Beast*. Museum Tusculanum Press. University of Copenhagen. Copenhagen, 303–332.

Boëlle, C. (2004) *PO-TI-NI-JA: L'élément féminin dans la religion mycénienne (d'après les archives en linéaire B)*. De Boccard. Nancy.

Bousquet, J. (1956) "Inscriptions de Delphes." *BCH* 80, 547–597.

Boyce, M. (1987) *Zororastrians: Their Religious Beliefs and Practices*. Routledge & Kegan Paul. London.

Brelich, A. (1969) *Paides e Parthenoi, I. Incunabula Graeca* 36. Rome.

Brosius, M. (2009) "Tempelprostitution im antiken Persien?" In T.S. Scheer and M. Linder (eds.) *Tempelprostitution im Altertum: Fakten und Fiktionen*. Verlag Antike, Oldenburg, 126–153.

——. (1998) "Artemis Persike and Artemis Anaitis." In M. Brosius and A. Kuhrt (eds.) *Studies in Persian History: Essays in Memory of David M. Lewis*. Nederlands Instituut voor het Nabije Oosten. Leiden, 227–238.

Brulé, P. (1998) "Le langage des épiclèses dans le polythéisme hellénique (l'example de quelques divinités féminines)." *Kernos* 11, 13-34.

Brulotte, E.L. (2002) "Artemis: Her Peloponnesian Abodes and Cults." In R. Hägg (ed.) *Peloponnesian Sanctuaries and Cults*. Paul Åströms Förlag, Stockholm, 180-182.

Bruneau, P. and J. Ducat. (2005) *Guide de Délos*. École Française d'Athènes. Athens.

Budin, S.L. (2010) "Aphrodite Enoplion." In A.C. Smith and S. Pickup (eds.) *Brill's Companion to Aphrodite*. E.J. Brill. Leiden, 79-112.

——. (2009) "Strabo's Hierodules: Corinth, Comana, and Eryx." In T. Scheer and M. Linder (eds.) *Tempelprostitution zwischen griechischer Antike und Vorderem Orient*. Verlag Antike. Berlin, 198-220.

——. (2004) "A Reconsideration of the Aphrodite-Ashtart Syncretism." *Numen* 51, 95-145.

Burkert, W. (1985) *Greek Religion*. Harvard University Press. Cambridge.

Calame, C. (2001) *Choruses of Young Women in Ancient Greece: Their Morphology, Religious Role, and Social Functions*. Rowman & Littlefield Publishers, Inc. New York.

Carter, J.B. (1987) "The Masks of Ortheia." *AJA* 91, 355-383.

Cartledge, P. (2002) *Sparta and Lakonia: A Regional History 1300 to 362 BC*. Second edition. Routledge. New York.

Cartledge, P. and A. Spawforth (2002) *Hellenistic and Roman Sparta: A Tale of Two Cities*. Second edition. Routledge. London.

Chamoux, F. (1953) *Cyrène sous la Monarchie des Battiades*. E. de Boccard. Paris.

Chapin, A.P. (2004) "Power, Privilege, and Landscape in Minoan Art." In A. Chapin (ed.) *ΧΑΡΙΣ: Essays in Honor of Sara A. Immerwahr*. ASCSA. Athens, 47-64.

——. (2002) "Maidenhood and Marriage: The Reproductive Lives of the Girls and Women of Xeste 3, Thera." *Aegean Archaeology* 4, 7-25.

Chaumont, M.-L. (1965) "Le Culte de la Déesse Anahita (Anahit) dans la Religion des Monarques d'Iran et d'Arménie au 1ᵉʳ Siècle de Notre Ère." *JA* 253, 167-181.

Coldstream, J.N. (1982) "Greeks and Phoenicians in the Aegean." In H.G. Niemeyer (ed.) *Phönizer im Westen*. Verlag Philipp von Zabern. Mainz am Rhein, 261-275.

Cole, S.G. (2004) *Landscapes, Gender, and Ritual Space: The Ancient Greek Experience*. University of California Press. Berkeley.

Collins, S. (2010) *Mockingjay*. Scholastic Inc. New York.

——. (2009) *Catching Fire*. Scholastic Inc. New York.

——. (2008) *The Hunger Games*. Scholastic Inc. New York.

Connelly, J.B. (2007) *Portrait of a Priestess: Women and Ritual in Ancient Greece*. Princeton University Press. Princeton.

Dakoronia, F. and L. Gounaropoulou (1992) "Artemiskult auf einem neuen Weihrelief aus Achinos bei Lamia." *AthMitt* 107, 217-227 and Taf. 57-60.

Dalley, S. (1989) *Myths from Mesopotamia: Creation, the Flood, Gilgamesh, and Others*. Oxford University Press. Oxford.

Darmezin, L. (1999) *Les affranchissements par consécration en Béotie et dans le monde grec hellénistique*. Études anciennes 22. De Boccard. Paris.

Davis, E.N. (1986) "Youth and Age in the Thera Frescoes." *AJA* 90, 399-406.

DeaVault, R.M. (2012) "The Masks of Femininity: Perceptions of the Feminine in *The Hunger Games* and *Podkayne of Mars*." In M.F Pharr and L.A. Clark (eds.) *Of Bread, Blood and The Hunger Games: Critical Essays on the Suzanne Collins Trilogy*. McFarland & Co, Inc. Publishers. Jefferson, 190-198.

Debord, P. (1982) *Aspects Sociaux et Économiques de la Vie Religieuse dans l'Antiquité Gréco-Romaine*. E. J. Brill. Leiden.

Demand, N. (1994) *Birth, Death, and Motherhood in Classical Greece*. Johns Hopkins University Press. Baltimore.

Demangel, R. (1922) "Fouilles de Délos: Un sanctuaire d'Artémis-Eileithyia à l'est du Cynthe." *BCH* 46, 58–93.

De Polignac, F. (1995) *Cults, Territory, and the Origins of the Greek City-State*. University of Chicago Press. Chicago.

Deubner, L. (1925) "Hochzeit und Opferkorb" *JDAI* 40, 210–223.

Dickinson, O. (2006) *The Aegean from Bronze Age to Iron Age: Continuity and Change Between the Twelfth and Eighth Centuries BC*. Routledge. New York.

Dignas, B. (2002) *Economy of the Sacred in Hellenistic and Roman Asia Minor*. Oxford University Press. Oxford.

Dillon, M. (2002) *Girls and Women in Classical Greek Religion*. Routledge. London.

——. (1999) "Post-Nuptial Sacrifices on Kos (Segre, *ED* 178) and Ancient Greek Marriage Rites." *ZPE* 124, 63–80.

Doumas, Ch. (1992) *The Wall-Paintings of Thera*. Kapon Editions. London.

Dowden, K. (1989) *Death and the Maiden*. Routledge. London.

Edelstein, E.J. and L. Edelstein (1998) *Asclepius: Collection and Interpretation of the Testimonies*. Johns Hopkins University Press. Baltimore.

Ekroth, G. (2003) "Inventing Iphigeneia? On Euripides and the Cultic Construction of Brauron." *Kernos* 16, 59–118.

Ellinger, P. (1984) "Les Ruses de Guerre d'Artémis." In L. Breglia Pulci Doria et al. (eds.) *Recherches sur les Cultes Grecs et l'Occident*, 2. Cahiers du Centre Jean Bérard, IX. Naples, 51–67.

Falb, D.Z.K. (2009) "Das Orthia-Heiligtum in Sparta im 7. und 6. Jh.v.Chr." In T. Fischer-Hansen and B. Poulsen (eds.) *From Artemis to Diana: The Goddess of Man and Beast*. Museum Tusculanum Press. University of Copenhagen. Copenhagen, 127–152.

Faraone, C.A. (2003) "Playing the Bear and Fawn for Artemis: Female Initiation or substitute sacrifice?" In D. Dodd and C.A. Faraone (eds.) *Initiation in Ancient Greek Rituals and Narratives: New critical perspectives*. Routledge. London, 43–68.

Felsch, R.C.S. (2007) *Kalapodi II: Ergebnisse der Ausgrabungen im Heiligtum der Artemis und des Apollon von Hyampolis in der anitken Phokis*. Verlag Philipp von Zabern. Mainz am Rhein.

Fischer-Hansen, T. (2009) "Artemis in Sicily and South Italy: A Picture of Diversity." In Fischer-Hansen and Poulsen (eds.) *From Artemis to Diana: The Goddess of Man and Beast*. Museum Tusculanum Press. University of Copenhagen. Copenhagen, 207–260.

Fischer-Hansen, T. and B. Poulsen (eds.) (2009) *From Artemis to Diana: The Goddess of Man and Beast*. Museum Tusculanum Press. University of Copenhagen. Copenhagen.

Flower, M. (2009) "Spartan 'Religion' and Greek 'Religion.'" In S. Hodkinson (ed.) *Sparta: Comparative Approaches*. The Classical Press of Wales. Swansea, 193–229.

——. (2002) "The Invention of Tradition in Classical and Hellenistic Sparta." In A. Powell and S. Hodkinson (eds.) *Sparta Beyond the Mirage*. Classical Press of Wales. Swansea, 191–217.

Fossey, J.M. (1987) "The Cults of Artemis in Argolis." *Euphrosyne* 15, 71–88.

Fostenpointer, G., M. Kerschner, and U. Muss (2008) "Das Artemision in der späten Bronzezeit und der frühen Eisenzeit." In U. Muss (ed.) *Die Archäologie der ephesischen Artemis: Gestalt und Ritual eines Heiligtums*. Phoibos Verlag. Vienna, 33–46.

Gallet de Santerre, H. (1975) "Notes déliennes." *BCH* 99.1, 247–265.

Garland, R. (1990) *The Greek Way of Life: From Conception to Old Age*. Cornell University Press. Ithaca.

Garsoïan, N.G. (1989) *The Epic Histories Attributed to P'awstos Buzand (Buzandaran Patmut'iwnk')*. Harvard University Press. Cambridge.

Graham, A.J. (1982) "The Colonial Expansion of Greece." *CAH*, Vol. III, 83–195.

——. (1958) "The Date of the Greek Penetration of the Black Sea." *BICS* 5, 25–42.

Graninger, D. (2007) "Studies in the Cult of Artemis Throsia." *ZPE* 162, 151–164.

Green, C.M.C. (2007) *Roman Religion and the Cult of Diana at Aricia.* Cambridge University Press. Cambridge.

Griffiths, E. (2006) *Medea.* Routledge. London.

Hadzisteliou Price, T. (1978) *Kourotrophos: Cults and Representations of the Greek Nursing Deities.* E.J. Brill. Leiden.

Hall, E. (2013) *Adventures with Iphigenia in Tauris: A Cultural History of Euripides' Black Sea Tragedy.* Oxford University Press, Oxford.

Hamilton, R. (1989) "Alkman and the Athenian Arkteia." *Hesperia* 58.4, 449–472.

Hanson, A.E. (1990) "The Medical Writers' Woman." In D.M. Halperin, J.J. Winkler, and F.I. Zeitlin (eds.) *Before Sexuality: The Construction of Erotic Experience in the Ancient Greek World.* Princeton University Press. Princeton, 309–337.

Hiller, S. (1983) "Mycenaean Traditions in Early Greek Cult Images." In R. Hägg (ed.) *The Greek Renaissance of the Eighth Century BC: Tradition and Innovation.* Swedish Institute in Athens. Stockholm, 91–99.

Hodkinson, S. (2000) *Property and Wealth in Classical Sparta.* Duckworth Press. London.

Hollinshead, M.B. (1985) "Against Iphigeneia's Adyton in Three Mainland Temples." *AJA* 89, 419–440.

Horsley, G.H.R. (1987) *New Documents Illustrating Early Christianity: Review of the Greek Inscriptions and Papyri Published in 1979* v. 4. Liverpool University Press. Liverpool.

Jamot, P. (1902) "Fouilles de Thespies: deux familles thespiennes pendant deux siècles." *BCH* 26, 291–321.

Johnston, S.I. (1999) *Restless Dead: Encounters Between the Living and the Dead in Ancient Greece.* University of California Press. Berkeley.

Kassanoff, J. (2014) "Edith Wharton." In E.L. Haralson (ed.) *Encyclopedia of American Poetry: The Nineteenth Century.* Routledge. New York, 455–460.

Kennell, N.M. (1995) *The Gymnasium of Virtue: Education and Culture in Ancient Sparta.* The University of North Carolina Press. Chapel Hill.

Kilian-Dirlmeier, I. (1985) "Fremde Weihungen in Griechischen Heiligtumern vom 8. bis zum Beginn des 7. Jahrhunderts v.Chr." *Jahrbuch des Römisch-Germanischen Zentralmuseums Mainz* 32, 215–254.

King, H. (1998) *Hippokrates' Woman: Reading the Female Body in Ancient Greece.* Routledge. London.

——. (1983) "Bound to Bleed: Artemis and Greek Women." In A. Cameron and A. Kuhrt (eds.) *Images of Women in Antiquity.* Wayne State University Press. Detroit, 109–127.

King, S.D. (2012) "(Im)Mutable Natures: Animal, Human and Hybrid Horror." In Pharr and Clarke (eds.) *Of Bread, Blood and* The Hunger Games: *Critical Essays on the Suzanne Collins Trilogy.* McFarland & Co, Inc. Publishers. Jefferson, 108–117.

Kondis, I.D. (1967) "Αρτεμις Βραυρωνια" *Arch. Delt.* 22, A1, 156–226.

Kontorli-Papadopoulos, L. (1996) *Aegean Frescoes of Religious Character.* Paul Åströms Förlag. Göteborg.

Kristensen, T.M. (2013) *Making and Breaking the Gods: Christian Responses to Pagan Sculpture in Late Antiquity.* Aarhus University Press. Aarhus.

Laffineur, R. and R. Hägg (eds.) (2001) *Potnia: Deities and Religion in the Aegean Bronze Age.* Université de Liège. Liège.

Larson, J. (2007) *Ancient Greek Cults: A Guide.* Routledge. London.

——. (2001) *Greek Nymphs: Myth, Cult, Lore.* Oxford University Press. Oxford.

Lefkowitz, M.R. and M.B. Fant (1992) *Women's Life in Greece & Rome: A Sourcebook in Translation.* Second edition. Johns Hopkins University Press. Baltimore.

Leitao, D.D. (2003) "Adolescent Hair-Growing and Hair-Cutting Rituals in Ancient Greece: A sociological approach." In D. Dodd and C.A. Faraone (eds.) *Initiation in Ancient Greek Rituals and Narratives: New Critical Perspectives.* Routledge. London, 109–129.

Lenski, N. (2006) "*Servi Publici* in Late Antiquity." In J.U. Kraus and C. Vitshel (eds.) *Die Stadt in der Spätantike: Niedergang oder Wandel?* Franz Steiner Verlag. Stuttgart, 335–358.

Lesser, R. (2005–2006) "The Nature of Artemis Ephesia." *Hirundo: The McGill Journal of Classical Studies* 4, 43–54.

Lloyd-Jones, H. (1983) "Artemis and Iphigeneia." *JHS* 103, 87–102.

Lundgreen, B. (2009) "Boys at Brauron: The Significance of a Votive Offering." In T. Fischer-Hansen and B. Poulsen (eds.), 117–126.

Maclean Rogers, G. (2012) *The Mysteries of Artemis of Ephesos: Cult, Polis, and Change in the Graeco-Roman World.* Yale University Press. New Haven.

McInerney, J. (1999) *The Folds of Parnassos: Land and Ethnicity in Ancient Phokis.* University of Texas Press. Austin.

Mettinger, T.N.D. (2001) *The Riddle of Resurrection: "Dying and Rising Gods" in the Ancient Near East.* Almqvist & Wiksell International. Stockholm.

Mitchell, J. (2012) "Of Queer Necessity: Panem's Hunger Games as Gender Games." In Pharr and Clarke (eds.), 128–137.

Mitsopoulos Leon, V. (2009) Βραυρον: *Die Tonstatuetten aus dem Heiligtum der Artemis, Die frühen Statuetten.* Bibliothetk der Archäologischen Gesellschaft zu Athen #263. Athens.

Mitsos, M.Th. (1949) "Inscriptions of the Eastern Peloponnesus." *Hesperia* 18, 73–77.

Morgan, C. (1999) *Isthmia VIII: The Late Bronze Age Settlement and Early Iron Age Sanctuary.* ASCSA. Princeton.

Morizot, Y. (1994) "Artémis, l'eau et la vie humaine." *BCH Supplément* XXVIII, 201–216.

Morris, S.P. (2008) "Zur Vorgeschicte der Artemis Ephesia." In U. Muss (ed.), 57–60.

——. (2001) "Potnia Asiwiya: Anatolian Contributions to Greek Religion." In R. Laffineur and R. Hägg (eds.), 423–434.

——. (1992) *Daidalos and the Origins of Greek Art.* Princeton University Press. Princeton.

Motte, A. and V. Pirenne-Delforge (1994) "Du « bon usage » de la notion de syncrétisme." *Kernos* 7, 11–27.

Muskett, G. (2007) "Images of Artemis in Mycenaean Greece?" *JPR* XXI, 53–68.

Muss, U. (2008) *Die Archäologie der ephesischen Artemis: Gestalt und Ritual eines Heiligtums.* Phoibos Verlag. Vienna.

Nielsen, M. (2009) "Diana Efesia Multimammia: The Metamorphoses of a Pagan Goddess from the Renaissance to the Age of Neo-Classicism." In T. Fischer-Hansen and B. Poulsen (eds.) *From Artemis to Diana: The Goddess of Man and Beast.* Museum Tusculanum Press. University of Copenhagen. Copenhagen, 455–496.

Nielsen, M. and A. Rathje (2009) "Artumes in Etruria: The Borrowed Goddess." In T. Fischer-Hansen and B. Poulsen (eds.) *From Artemis to Diana: The Goddess of Man and Beast.* Museum Tusculanum Press. University of Copenhagen. Copenhagen, 261–301.

Orsi, P. (1900) "Siracusa – Nuovo Artemision a Scala Graeca." *NSA* 1900, 353–387.

Osborne, R. (1985) *Demos: The Discovery of Classical Attika.* Cambridge University Press. Cambridge.

Pakkanen, P. (1996) *Interpreting Early Hellenistic Religion: A Study Based on the Mystery Cult of Demeter and the Cult of Isis.* Papers and Monographs of the Finnish Institute at Athens. Helsinki.

Papazoglou, F. (1981) "Affranchissement par Consécration et Hiérodulie." *ŽA* 31, 171–179.

Parker, R. (2005) "Artémis Ilithye et Autres: le probleme du nom divin utilisé comme épiclèse." In N. Belayche et al. (eds.) *Nommer les Dieux: Théonymes, epithets, épiclèses dans l'Antiquité.* Brepols, Presses Universitaires de Rennes. Turnhout, 219–226.

——. (1996) *Athenian Religion: A History*. Clarendon Press. Oxford.

——. (1983) *Miasma: Pollution and Purification in Early Greek Religion*. Oxford University Press. Oxford.

Perlman, P. (1989) "Acting the She-Bear for Artemis." *Arethusa* 22.2, 111-133.

Petrovic, I. (2010) "Transforming Artemis: From the Goddess of the Outdoors to City Goddess." In J.N. Bremmer and A. Erskine (eds.) *The Gods of Ancient Greece: Identities and Transformations*. Edinburgh University Press. Edinburgh, 209-227.

——. (2007) *Von den Toren des Hades zu den Hallen des Olymp: Artemiskult bei Theokrit und Kallimachos*. E. J. Brill Publishers. Leiden.

Pharr, M.F. and L.A. Clark (eds.) (2012) *Of Bread, Blood and* The Hunger Games*: Critical Essays on the Suzanne Collins Trilogy*. McFarland & Co, Inc. Publishers. Jefferson.

Pingiatoğlou, S. (1981) *Eileithyia*. Königshausen + Neumann. Wurzburg.

Pirenne-Delforge, V. (2004) "Qui est la Kourotrophos athénienne?" In V. Dasen (ed.) *Naissance et petite enfance dans l'Antiquité*. Academic Press Fribourg. Vandenhoeck & Ruprecht. Göttingen, 171-185.

Plassart A. (1926) "Fouilles de Thespies et de l'hiéron des muses de l'Hélicon. Inscriptions: Dédicaces de caractère religieux ou honorifique, bornes de domaines sacrés." *BCH* 50, 383-462.

Redfield, J.M. (2003) *The Locrian Maidens: Love and Death in Greek Italy*. Princeton University Press. Princeton.

——. (1990) "From Sex to Politics: The Rites of Artemis Triklaria and Dionysos Aisymnētēs at Patras." In D.M. Halperin, J.J. Winkler, and F.I. Zeitlin (eds.) *Before Sexuality: The Construction of Erotic Experience in the Ancient Greek World*. Princeton University Press. Princeton, 115-134.

Rehak, P. (2007) "Children's Work: Girls as Acolytes in Aegean Ritual and Cult." In A. Cohen and J.B. Rutter (eds.) *Constructions of Childhood in Ancient Greece and Italy*. ASCSA. Athens, 205-225.

——. (2004) "Crocus Costumes in Aegean Art." In A. Chapin (ed.) *XAPIΣ: Essays in Honor of Sara A. Immerwahr*. ASCSA. Athens, 85-100.

——. (1997) "The Role of Religious Painting in the Function of the Minoan Villa: The Case of Ayia Triadha." In R. Hägg (ed.) *The Function of the "Minoan Villa."* Paul Åströms Förlag. Stockholm, 163-175.

Rigsby, K.J. (1996) *Asylia: Territorial Inviolability in the Hellenistic World*. University of California Press. Berkeley.

Roller, L.E. (1999) *In Search of the God the Mother: The Cult of Anatolian Cybele*. University of California Press. Berkeley.

Rolley, C. (1983) "Les grands sanctuaires panhelléniques." In R. Hägg (ed.) *The Greek Renaissance of the Eighth Century B.C.: Tradition and Innovation*. Swedish Institute in Athens. Stockholm, 109-114.

Rougemont, F. (2005) "Les noms des dieux dans les tablettes inscrites en linéaire B." In N. Belayche et al. (eds.) *Nommer les Dieux: Théonymes, epithets, épiclèses dans l'Antiquité*. Brepols, Presses Universitaires de Rennes. Turnhout, 325-388.

Rudhardt, J. (1992) "De l'attitude des grecs à des religions étrangères." *Revue de l'Histoire des Religions*. CCIX-3, 219-238.

Sale, W. (1975) "The Temple-Legends of the Arkteia." *RhM* 118, 265-284.

Schachter, A. (1992) "Policy, Cult, and the Placing of Greek Sanctuaries." In A. Schachter and J. Bingen (eds.) *Le sanctuaire grec*. Fondation Hardt. Genève, 1-57.

——. (1981) *Cults of Boiotia, 1: Acheloos to Hera*. University of London Institute of Classical Studies. London.

Schaps, D. (1977) "The Woman Least Mentioned: Etiquette and Women's Names." *CQ* 27.2, 323–330.

Segal, R.A. (1991) "Adonis: A Greek Eternal Child." In D.C. Pozzi and J.M. Wickersham (eds.) *Myth and the Polis*. Cornell University Press. Ithaca, 64–85.

Shelton, J.-A. (2007) "Beastly Spectacles in the Ancient Mediterranean World." In L. Kalof (ed.) *A Cultural History of Animals in Antiquity*. Berg. Oxford, 97–126.

Spineto, N. (2000) "*The King of the Wood* oggi: una rilettura di James George Frazer ala luce dell'attuale problematica storia-religiosa." In J.R. Brandt, A.-M Leander Touati, and J. Zahle (eds.) *Nemi—Status Quo*. L'Erma di Bretschneider. Rome, 17–24.

Stampolides, N. Ch. (2003) "On the Phoenician Presence in the Aegean." In N. Ch. Stampolides and V. Karageorghis (eds.) Πλοες . . . *Sea Routes* . . . : *Interconnections in the Mediterranean 16th-6th c. BC*. University of Crete. Athens, 217–232.

Strelan, R. (1996) *Paul, Artemis, and the Jews in Ephesus*. Walter de Gruyter. New York.

Themelis, P. (1994) "Artemis Ortheia at Messene: The Epigraphical Evidence." In R. Hägg (ed.) *Ancient Greek Cult Practice from the Epigraphical Evidence*. Proceedings of the Second International Seminar on Ancient Greek Cult. Kernos Suppl. 1. Liège, 101–122.

Thomas, C.M. (1995) "At Home in the City of Artemis: Religion in Ephesos in the Literary Imagination of the Roman Period." In H. Koester (ed.) *Ephesos Metropolis of Asia: An Interdisciplinary Approach to its Archaeology, Religion, and Culture*. Trinity Press International. Valley Forge, 81–117.

Vallois, R. (1944) *L'Architecture Hellénique et Hellénistique à Délos. Première Partie: Les Monuments*. E. de Boccard. Paris.

Van Leuven, J.C. (1981) "Problems and Methods of Prehellenic Naology." In R. Hägg and N. Marinatos (eds.) *Sanctuaries and Cults in the Aegean Bronze Age*. Swedish Institute in Athens. Stockholm, 11–26.

Van Straten, F.T. (1981) "Gifts for the Gods." In H.S. Versnel (ed.), *Faith, Hope, and Worship: Aspects of Religious Mentality in the Ancient World*. E. J. Brill Publishers. Leiden, 65–151.

Vernant, J.-P. (1991) *Mortals and Immortals*. Princeton University Press. Princeton.

——. (1963) "Hestia-Hermès: Sur l'expression religieuse de l'espace et du mouvement chez les Grecs." *L'Homme* 3.3, 12–50.

Voyatzis, M.E. (1998) "From Athena to Zeus: An A–Z Guide to the Origins of Greek Goddesses." In L. Goodison and C. Morris (eds.) *Ancient Goddesses: The Myths and the Evidence*. University of Wisconsin Press. Madison, 133–147.

Wallensten, J. (2003) Αφροδιτη Ανεθηκεν Αρξας: *A Study of Dedications to Aphrodite from Greek Magistrates*. Lund University. Lund.

West, M.L. (1997) *The East Face of Helicon: West Asiatic Elements in Greek Poetry and Myth*. Clarendon Paperbacks. Oxford.

Westenholz, J.G. (1997) "Nanaya: Lady of Mystery." In I.L. Finkel and M.J. Geller (eds.) *Sumerian Gods and their Representations*. Styx Publications. Groningen, 57–84.

Westermann, W.L. (1945) "Between Slavery and Freedom." *AHR* 50.2, 213–227.

Younger, J.G. (1988) *The Iconography of Late Minoan and Mycenaean Sealstones and Finger Rings*. Bristol Classical Press. Bristol.

Zeitlin, F. (1996) "The Dynamics of Misogyny: Myth and Mythmaking in Aeschylus's *Oresteia*." In F. Zeitlin (ed.) *Playing the Other: Gender and Society in Classical Greek Literature*. University of Chicago Press. Chicago, 87–119.

Zelnick-Abramowitz, R. (2005) *Not Wholly Free: The Concept of Manumission and the Status of Manumitted Slaves in the Ancient Greek World*. E.J. Brill. Leiden.

INDEX

"Potnia Theron" - mistress
of wild animals - p. 14

Brandon - handicapped

Pfege

Made in the USA
San Bernardino, CA
18 July 2019